BRAZIL
ON THE
RISE

BRAZIL
ON THE
RISE

THE STORY
OF A COUNTRY
TRANSFORMED

LARRY ROHTER

palgrave
macmillan

BRAZIL ON THE RISE
Copyright © Larry Rohter, 2010, 2012.
All rights reserved.

First published in hardcover in 2011 by PALGRAVE MACMILLAN® in the US—a
division of St. Martin's Press LLC, 175 Fifth Avenue, New York, NY 10010.

Where this book is distributed in the UK, Europe and the rest of the world, this is by
Palgrave Macmillan, a division of Macmillan Publishers Limited, registered in
England, company number 785998, of Houndmills, Basingstoke, Hampshire RG21
6XS.

Palgrave Macmillan is the global academic imprint of the above companies and has
companies and representatives throughout the world.

Palgrave® and Macmillan® are registered trademarks in the United States, the
United Kingdom, Europe and other countries.

ISBN: 978-0-230-12073-0

The Library of Congress has catalogued the hardcover edition as follows:

Rohter, Larry, 1950–
    Brazil on the rise : the story of a country transformed / Larry Rohter.
        p.   cm.
    Includes index.
    ISBN 978-0-230-61887-9
    1. Brazil—Politics and government—2003–   2. Brazil—Social life and customs—
21st century.   3. Brazil—Social conditions—1985–   4. Social change—Brazil—
History—21st century.   5. Brazil—Economic conditions—1985–   6. Interviews—
Brazil.   I. Title.
F2538.3.R64   2010
981—dc22

                                                                              2010013063

A catalogue record of the book is available from the British Library.

Design by Letra Libre

First PALGRAVE MACMILLAN paperback edition: March 2012

10 9 8 7 6 5 4 3 2 1

Printed in the United States of America.

For Clo

CONTENTS

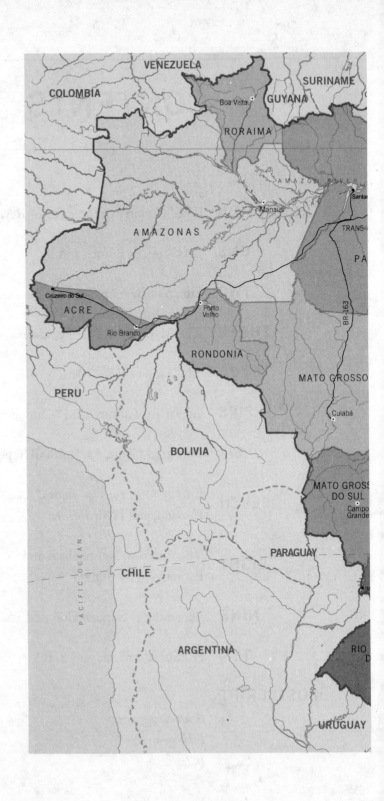

Map of Brazil (IBGE/Eric Amaral Rohter)

BRAZIL
ON THE
RISE

INTRODUCTION

THE "COUNTRY OF THE FUTURE" REVEALS ITSELF

I FIRST TRAVELED TO Brazil in September 1972, and like most new arrivals, I had very little idea of what to expect. In those days, I was a graduate student in modern Chinese history and politics and a part-time employee in the New York bureau of Brazil's largest media conglomerate, Rede Globo, so I was thrilled when I got an invitation to visit headquarters in Rio de Janeiro and work on a music festival there. At the New York office, I was surrounded by Brazilians who spoke yearningly and nostalgically of the soccer rivalries, samba, Carnival, delicious food, and beautiful beaches and women they had left behind; "saudade," I eventually learned, is the evocative Portuguese-language word for that kind of bittersweet longing. To hear them tell it, I was about to get a taste of something very close to paradise.

My strongest initial impressions, though, were of the repressive military dictatorship that ruled the country and the backwardness of the economy, then still dominated by agricultural products like coffee and sugar. At the airport, I could not help but notice the walls covered with "wanted" posters showing photographs of "terrorists" the government was hunting, many of them earnest-looking long-haired students not that different in appearance from me. The press was censored, as I discovered when I attended my first mid-afternoon editorial meeting to discuss the main nightly news broadcast and found a military officer at the table, telling editors which stories would be permitted and which would not. At night, heavily armed police stopped the cars in which I was riding with my Brazilian colleagues, brusquely demanding identity papers from all of us who were passengers.

The chic Zona Sul of Rio, where my hotel was located, felt less like a Third World country, repressive and underdeveloped, and much more like Fifth Avenue or Rodeo Drive. Walking past the fashionable boutiques that lined the streets of Ipanema and Copacabana, I saw the tanned beauties, on their way to the beach, who had been made famous by the lilting bossa nova songs I knew from the radio in the United States and noticed the striking locally produced jewelry and fashions in the windows. But I also could not avoid observing the knots of beggars sitting on the sidewalks in those chic neighborhoods, pleading for alms while keeping an eye out for the police whose duty it was to run them off, with beatings if necessary. Some of the mendicants were groups of street urchins, while others consisted of entire families who had obviously spent the previous night huddled together in the cardboard boxes on which they now clustered. Their ragged poverty offered a stark contrast to the gracefully designed sidewalk on which they sat, a work of art with a colorfully abstract, undulating stone mosaic that extended unbroken for the entire length of the beach. It was discomfiting to see these poor people, almost all of whom were black, in the midst of so much affluence and yet so removed from it, and to note the indifference of well-dressed passers-by to their plight.

And at a noisy, stiflingly hot Sunday fair outside a half-finished coliseum whose construction had been abandoned, I listened as migrants from the northeast of Brazil, a drought-ridden region that has traditionally been the country's poorest, sang songs that spoke of their suffering and frustrated hopes with a plaintiveness that reminded me of the blues I had heard growing up in Chicago. They sang of the arduous trip south, standing for 1,500 miles on the back of a truck, exposed to the tropical sun. They sang of the poverty of the sharecropper's existence and the abusive landlords who profited from their labors. They sang of the political bosses who made promises they never kept. They sang of the poor-paying jobs they found in factories or as maids and janitors when they arrived in the south, of the slums in which they had to settle because they were poor, of the prejudice against them because of their distinctive accent and "hillbilly" appearance.

But the city had an enormous energy, or exuberance even, that was both immensely attractive and contagious. Listening to jokes and gibes at the government's expense, watching Brazilians walk with the jaunty, rhythmic self-confidence that, I later learned, they call "ginga," it became clear that no matter how bad the situation, Brazilians refused to let it get them down or submit to a defeatist attitude. Always there seemed to be an internal space, a core, that poverty and somber political circumstances could not penetrate, and that was where optimism and the true Brazilian spirit resided. I was smitten, on both an emotional and intellectual level. It was as if there were two separate Brazils, one official but unreal, the other real but hidden behind subterfuge. How could a society function with such a sharp contrast between outer and inner realities? I hungered to know more, and that is what drove me to return to Brazil as a correspondent, first in 1977 for an assignment that lasted five years and then again in 1999 for a nine-year stint.

When I first visited Brazil, my acquaintances there called my attention to the national flag and what it represents. The green that dominates the banner, I was told, symbolizes the vast lushness of the Brazilian countryside and the fertility of its fields. The yellow diamond-shaped figure near the center stands for gold and, by extension, the country's great natural wealth. At the very center, written across a blue globe, is the national motto, "Order and Progress." The sarcastic joke I sometimes heard at the time was that because Brazil's rulers had never been able to impose the first, the country would never be able to achieve the second, and that a more appropriate and realistic slogan would be "Disorder and Backwardness." Brazilians were accustomed to seeing things through that kind of skeptical prism, and it was difficult for them, with the built-in cynicism acquired through a history of extravagant ambitions and dashed hopes, to imagine that circumstances could change.

Over the past four decades, I have watched a very different Brazil come into being. Vestiges of the bitter realities of the past still linger in the form of pockets of poverty and authoritarian behavior on the part of some public officials. But today's Brazil can also boast of being the world's fourth-largest democracy and sixth-largest economy. Of developing countries, only China receives more direct foreign investment. But unlike China or India, Brazil is a robust producer and exporter of both manufactured goods and foodstuffs and raw materials. That includes growing large amounts of energy, thanks to major discoveries of oil and gas beginning in 2007 and the coming to fruition of a 30-year effort to develop a renewable fuel industry based on ethanol made from sugar cane.

This book is an attempt to trace and explain that transformation. In its early chapters, it offers a glimpse of Brazil's history and examines the society that Brazilians have constructed during their nation's five-hundred-year history—both its positive and negative aspects. But the principal focus is the extraordinary changes that Brazil has undergone since I first came in contact with the country in 1972, back when the Cold War was still going on, the Beatles had just broken up, and a gallon of gasoline cost only 36 cents in the United States. In purely historical terms, 40 years is barely the blink of an eye. Yet over the last four decades, Brazil has arguably experienced deeper and more profound changes than it did during some of the centuries when it was a Portuguese colony.

Part of Brazil's rise is explained by sheer good fortune, such as being blessed with vast expanses of fertile land and abundant supplies of minerals, water, and other resources. Circumstances that it does not control, such as the emergence of China as the fastest-growing market for Brazilian exports, have also played a role. But Brazil's political leadership, both the current civilian regime and even the earlier military autocrats whose rule I still find repugnant, deserve some credit too, as do the business community and the people whose sweat and toil continue to be exploited. In a country where long-term planning has always been anathema, which loves to improvise and has traditionally expected eleventh-hour miracles to resolve its problems, those in charge have finally realized the advantages of trying to act with forethought, and the country is now reaping those benefits.

After all, the land and the resources were always there, and their potential was obvious to everyone from the moment the Portuguese first arrived in 1500. But it took more than 450 years for Brazil to begin to put all the pieces together, to develop both the discipline and the perspicacity required to make the country start to live up to its extraordinary promise. Having achieved at least a modicum of order, though it may not seem that way to someone stuck in a traffic jam in São Paulo or Rio de Janeiro, Brazilians can now focus on progress. Has that hard-learned lesson been fully absorbed? That is one of the central questions of the twenty-first century for Brazil, and if it can be answered in the affirmative, there is almost no limit to Brazil's continued growth and advancement.

Because of its great natural beauty and the warmth of its people, Brazil inevitably makes a powerful first impression. Those incredible sea- and landscapes, with their vivid hues of green, blue, and white! The beaches, the pulsing music, the year-round sunshine, the easygoing tropical vibe! Everything about Brazil seems designed to provoke wonderment at the presence of so much splendor and abundance. The fifth biggest country in the world, Brazil is larger than the continental United States, with some states that are bigger than any country in Europe, and it also ranks fifth in population, with nearly 200 million inhabitants. As a people, Brazilians blend European, African, Amerindian, and Asian backgrounds and values in a way found nowhere else on earth, and their vibrant culture also reflects that intermingling. Where is the largest population of Japanese descent outside Japan? In São Paulo, Brazil's most populous city and state. Where is the biggest concentration of people of Italian descent outside Italy? Also in São Paulo.

Brazil has always been a country of extremes of generosity and selfishness, compassion and cruelty, in which things tend to be, as a Brazilian expression puts it, "either eight or eighty," and attitudes oscillate from excitement to disappointment, with little middle ground. It remains so. Great wealth exists alongside misery, almost literally in the case of cities like Rio de Janeiro, where slumdwellers live and die in shacks on hillsides overlooking elegant seaside neighborhoods such as Ipanema and Copacabana. The annual bacchanal of Carnival, with its uncontrolled Dionysian outbursts, immediately gives way to the austerity of Lent. The parched severity of the northeast backlands, still the country's poorest and most backward region, abuts the lushness of the Amazon, driving peasants from desert to jungle in a doomed search for an El Dorado.

Yet for a nation that is so dynamic and occupies such a large piece of the earth's landmass, including the biggest chunk of the Amazon, the world's largest and most endangered rainforest, Brazil remains relatively unknown beyond its borders. What are the images that come to the minds of most foreigners when Brazil is mentioned? Soccer, samba, and beaches lead the list, the

Brazilian government has found, to its dismay, when it has commissioned polls abroad. A couple of other items round out the inventory: "The Girl from Ipanema" and perhaps some other bossa nova songs, and the Amazon jungle, of course. Those who consider themselves cognoscenti may also be aware of trendy novelties such as the Brazilian body wax, the Havaiana sandals that the Brazilian supermodel Gisele Bündchen has made popular, the caipirinha cocktail, and power drinks like açai and guaraná.

But the deep, authentic, and serious Brazil is much more than glitz, fashion, and sensuality, and so "Brazil on the Rise" aims to show the country in another, more substantive light. While the rest of the world has been distracted by images of soccer players with fancy footwork and beauties in skimpy bathing suits, Brazil has without much fanfare become an industrial and agricultural powerhouse. Its leading exports now include airplanes and automobiles, its farms and ranches now feed much of the world, and downtown São Paulo, shown on the cover of this book, is the center of the largest concentration of banks, wealth, trade, and industry in the Southern Hemisphere.

Recognizing this recent economic boom, Wall Street analysts and investors have designated Brazil as the initial letter in the so-called BRIC group of emerging economies, which also includes Russia, India, and China. For a Latin American country used to having to operate in the shadow of American economic and military might, that is heady company to be keeping. Membership in the BRIC group confers both prestige and responsibility, for it is the BRIC group that is seen as symbolizing the transformation of the global economy in the twenty-first century, with the torch of dominance passing from the hands of the United States, Europe, and Japan and having to be shared with these new powers.

The next few years offer Brazil an unusual opportunity to bask in the world's attention, remind the rest of us just how far it has come, and stake its claim to belonging to the first rank of nations. In 2014, the World Cup of soccer, which the Brazilian national team has won a record five times, will be held in Brazil for the first time since 1950 and will be played in a dozen cities. Two years later, Rio de Janeiro will become the first South American city to host the world's biggest sporting event, the Summer Olympics. Thanks to their experience each year at Carnival, Brazilians really know how to throw a party, and they conceive of the two coming events as a sort of giant coming-out celebration, announcing Brazil's arrival as a player, not just in athletic competition but also on the global stage.

Brazil, however, accedes to this new status with a special burden, a kind of curse, really. Seventy years ago, the Austrian writer Stefan Zweig, a refugee from the Nazis who had settled in the cool, tranquil mountains above Rio de Janeiro because they reminded him of the Alps in his native land, wrote a global best-seller called *Brazil: Country of the Future*. In his book, he praised Brazil for creating "quite a new kind of civilization" and forecast that the country was "destined undoubtedly to play one of the most important parts in the future development of our world."

Ever since, that slogan has been a cliché, impossible for Brazilians to live up to, inevitably brought up in any discussion of the country, and thus as much "a stigma as a prophecy," in the words of the Brazilian writer Alberto Dines. This will be the only mention of Zweig's phrase in this book, and I do so here only to indicate the unattainably high expectations that Brazil has had to confront and the inferiority complex that has resulted: No matter how much Brazil achieves, it always seems to have fallen short of fulfilling the destiny predicted for it. As first Japan and then China and India zoomed by on their way to global prominence, and even South Korea and the "tigers" of Southeast Asia won praise, attention, and investments, Brazilians have responded with a mordant counter-cliché of their own: "Brazil is the country of the future and always will be."

But maybe, just maybe, the future has finally arrived. The Brazilian national anthem has a verse describing the country as "an intrepid colossus, beautiful and strong," but one that is "eternally recumbent in a splendid cradle." That high-flown language evokes the image of a Brazil that is indolent, too contented and infantilized, too satisfied with its great good fortune, and too confident that it is favored by God and destiny to be bothered to work in any sustained or disciplined fashion to achieve greatness. In moments when their country seems to fall short of its outsize potential, Brazilians often throw up their hands in disgust and recite those lines.

Today's Brazil, however, has clearly awakened from that comfortable slumber and has left the cradle behind as it strides with vigor toward full maturity. It is not just Brazil's substantial material achievements over the last generation that are worthy of attention, it is also the manner in which the country got to its present state, so full of promise. Brazil has had unpleasant brushes with authoritarian rule during its nearly two-hundred-year history as an independent nation, some of them quite recent, but none of those episodes compares to the totalitarianism that both Russia and China have had to endure. Brazil has come a long way in a short time, with its people debating and approving every step and change in policy, ratifying their choices at the ballot box: Since a right-wing military dictatorship fell in 1985, the country has been transformed into a democracy that, though fractious at times, is exemplary, with peaceful transfers of power, at least a nominal respect for the rule of law, and a sense of chagrin when politics or conduct fall short of what is desired.

As Brazil becomes more prosperous, powerful, and capable of exercising leadership, its engagement with the rest of the world grows, and there are more reasons for the rest of us to care about how Brazilians think and what they do. Yet there are many aspects of Brazilian behavior that are baffling to outsiders. Why does Brazil permit the wholesale devastation of the Amazon, whose health as a functioning eco-system is vital to all of us if we are to avoid global warming? Why does it so strongly resent suggestions as to how to reduce that destruction, especially when they come from the United States? Why is there such violence in its large cities? Why does a society built on notions of cordiality appear to turn a blind eye to terrible inequities based on class and race? Why has it sought to thwart U.N. Security Council efforts to curb Iran's nuclear program?

For years, friends and relatives visiting me in Brazil have asked me these and other basic questions. Since that first trip of mine in 1972, I've been fortunate enough to live in Brazil for more than fourteen years, longer than I've lived in any other place as an adult. One of my favorite Brazilian artists, the Grammy Award-winning bossa nova composer and pianist Antônio Carlos Jobim, used to warn newcomers that "Brazil is not for beginners." Witty and sardonic, the expression made me wonder if it would ever be possible to feel confident that you know the country. I've had ample time to think about responses and to test my ideas on Brazilian friends and my Brazilian relatives by marriage. I don't claim to have all the answers, and at times my explanations may seem overly critical or even harsh. But I write with a deep and abiding affection and sense of admiration for Brazil and its people. Their society is one of the most richly humanized I have ever experienced, both in terms of its many flaws and its equally plentiful virtues.

ONE

A HISTORY OF BOOMS AND BUSTS

LONG BEFORE THERE WAS A country called Brazil, a tree with that name grew in abundance all along the northeastern coast of South America. When Portuguese explorers, blown off course on their way to Asia, landed there on April 22, 1500, they immediately saw value in trees they called brazilwood. Natives who came to meet them at the shoreline were daubed in bright red dye extracted from the timber. The Portuguese were entrepreneurial and quickly saw the potential for profit. They turned brazilwood into a crimson powder that back in Europe was used to manufacture luxury fabrics such as velvet for an emerging middle class.

To the Portuguese, Brazil's natural resources seemed limitless. A Jesuit priest who visited in the early 1500s wrote, "If there is a paradise here on earth, I would say it is in Brazil." As waves of Europeans arrived to this verdant corner of the new world, what they had in common was a voracious appetite for its bounty, and they each figured out different ways to exploit the resources. The substances driving exploration and development have varied over the centuries, from timber, precious metals, and gemstones to foodstuffs such as sugar, coffee, and soybeans. Today, with its newly discovered reserves of oil and gas, Brazil stands to achieve extraordinary wealth by mining its fossil fuels. The often well-founded belief that another bonanza is just around the corner has made Brazilians a people who are both optimistic and sometimes heedless: "God repairs at night the damage that man does by day," an old Brazilian proverb assures.

This notion would prove to be a constant in Brazilian history and is evident in Brazil's self-image even today. But that bounty of endless wealth waiting to be uncovered has also led to dark moments. Through the centuries, Brazil's powerful elite have enriched themselves on the backs of workers. On many occasions, the hunt for instant and boundless riches has encouraged Brazil's elite to value their country's natural resources above its own people and to pour their energy into developing the first even at the expense of the second. And it all began with that simple discovery of brazilwood flourishing in the rich red soil of the Bahia coastlands more than five hundred years ago.

The Portuguese would probably have preferred to have stumbled upon gold or silver, and it is clearly a sign of their ingenuity and open mindedness that they saw potential in a substance other than shiny metal. The Spanish, their rivals, had already begun their own explorations of lands farther north, in the Caribbean basin, and quickly filled their coffers with precious stones. But as a small, underpopulated nation on the edge of Europe noted for its maritime skills, Portugal had learned to make the most of whatever opportunities came its way.

The Portuguese tried trading with the native peoples they encountered. But their initial admiration for the apparent harmony and simplicity of the natives' way of life soon soured: Once those Tupi- and Ge-speaking tribes acquired the metal pots and other tools they wanted, they lost interest in further commerce, and so the Portuguese then turned to enslavement. Demographers estimate the native population of Brazil in 1500 at somewhere between three million and eight million people. Whatever the figure, it was larger than the population of Portugal, which was about one million at the time. But the Tupi and Ge groups were constantly at war among themselves, allowing the Portuguese to adopt a classic divide-and-conquer strategy, which compensated for their smaller numbers. Each people sold the enemies it had captured to the Portuguese, who encouraged and instigated conflicts to keep the tribes from uniting against the European intruder.

The Spanish were just as quick to subjugate the native peoples of the Americas and to exploit their labor, but Brazil offered Portugal different challenges. The Spanish conquistadors brutally destroyed three indigenous civilizations: the Aztecs in Mexico, the Incas in Peru, and the Mayas in Central

America. In all of those civilizations the emperor was considered divine, and once he was eliminated, resistance crumbled. That was not the case in Brazil. Not only were the native tribes there less centralized and organized, but resistance was more diffuse. That made it harder to both overcome the armed opposition and govern the tribes once they were subdued.

Portugal was small and less wealthy than its European rivals, and the crown had to turn to private capital to harvest brazilwood and otherwise develop the new dominion. The king retained title to lands that had been claimed in Portugal's name but granted monopoly licenses to favored investors or nobles who then formed partnerships with those financiers. Brazil became "one vast commercial enterprise," in the words of the Brazilian historian Caio Prado Jr., which the Portuguese operated from fortified trading posts along the humid coast, venturing only hesitantly into a trackless interior of dry scrub and stunted cactus that came to be called the *sertão*.

The new country evolved rapidly into a system of hereditary *capitanias*. These were essentially fiefdoms or private estates in which a single grantee was responsible for colonizing, at his own expense, the entirety of the territory. To attract settlers who would cultivate the new realms, the landowners had the authority to carve up their territory into huge estates, some of which were larger than entire provinces back in the motherland.

Nearly five hundred years later, the origins of two of the country's enormous problems—glaring social imbalance and reckless exploitation of natural resources—are still visible. The owners of the fiefs were in essence sovereigns of their own domains, above the law and responsible only to a crown that was far away and had little capacity to enforce its will or even monitor what was going on. The mentality that this situation created has persisted into modern times. Especially in the northeast of Brazil, local political bosses and landowners defy the state's authority with impunity in areas that they regard as their personal kingdoms. In addition, the captaincy system created a preference for large estates that has made land distribution in Brazil extremely inequitable. Even today, a relatively small landed gentry controls the bulk of the country's most productive terrain, while millions of peasants have no plots of their own and are forced to eke out a miserable living as sharecroppers or to migrate to the Amazon in search of a plot of land they can call their own.

Since the colonists arriving from Portugal could not exploit their oversized estates by themselves, they had to find a way to obtain additional labor. Indigenous slaves, the initial choice, were not only recalcitrant, and thus an unsatisfactory solution to that problem, but were also viewed by the Roman Catholic Church as souls to be Christianized rather than enslaved. So by the mid-sixteenth century, landowners were already turning to Africa as their preferred source of slave labor. The first recorded instance of a cargo of slaves arriving from Africa dates to 1538, and by 1552, a Jesuit priest in Pernambuco, a center of the brazilwood trade soon also to become a hub of sugar cultivation because of its abundance of fertile land hugging the coast and balmy breezes, noted that "there are in this captaincy a great number of slaves, both Indian and African."

African chattel slavery would prove over the centuries to be the worst kind of curse for Brazil. It endured until 1888, a quarter of a century after it was abolished in the United States, and left a legacy of racism, poverty, and social discrimination and marginalization that continues to afflict the country in the twenty-first century. At the time, though, it seemed the only way the elite could find enough bodies to work the land.

The colonists didn't own the land and sought to extract as much from their holdings as they could, and as rapidly as possible, in hopes of returning to Europe as rich men; and since the crown retained title to the land, they had little incentive to treat it with care. The get-rich-quick mentality encouraged destructive practices and distorted economic development, another set of problems that continues to plague Brazil in our own time. While some settlers focused on cultivating crops such as cotton, tobacco, beans, and manioc (a native tuber that rapidly became a staple of the European diet), the biggest profits came from brazilwood, which was therefore exploited ruthlessly. Rather than replant what they cut, the Portuguese stripped the coastal forests teeming with exotic birds and beasts that seemed like fugitives from Noah's ark and moved on. The Atlantic rainforest was quickly destroyed, and today the tree for which Brazil is named can scarcely be found outside of botanical gardens. In this attitude we can also see the origins of many of the destructive practices that afflict Brazil in the Amazon today.

This boom-and-bust pattern, in reality, has been a constant throughout Brazilian history. Time and time again, landowners, government officials, and private investors have succumbed to the desire for quick riches and poured all of their money and energy into exploiting a single product or crop. At first, the returns are enormous. But such profits, combined with the illusion of limitless abundance, attract many others also in pursuit of immediate wealth, and inevitably one of two things happens: The resource is either completely consumed, or so much of it is produced that international markets are flooded and prices collapse.

After brazilwood stocks were exhausted, there was a rush, later in the sixteenth century, to produce sugar to satisfy Europe's growing sweet tooth. That carried the economy for almost a century, until competition from the New World colonies of other European powers caused prices to crash. But in the eighteenth century, gold was discovered in a rugged region of winding valleys, rushing rivers, and roaring waterfalls in the interior, farther to the south, and for a while Brazil was the largest single producer of gold in the world. In the nineteenth century, after independence was achieved, coffee emerged as the backbone of the economy, to be succeeded after 1880 by rubber, which was grown in the Amazon and flourished until 1920. This pattern of "cycles," as Brazilians call them, really only came to an end in the closing decades of the twentieth century as the result of an effort to diversify the economy that continues today.

Many of the hereditary fiefs floundered. But two, Pernambuco in the north and São Vicente, site of the present-day state of São Paulo, much farther south, flourished. In large part this was because leaders of those settlements, where women colonists from Portugal were scarce and the sexual appeal of unabashedly naked native maidens was obvious, were canny enough to marry daughters of local chiefs. That helped seal the tribal alliances that guaranteed supplies, labor, and protection to the Portuguese newcomers. Racial mixing became a defining trait of Brazilian culture as we know it today. At first limited to indigenous South Americans, racial mixing was eventually extended to Africans as the slave trade back and forth across the South Atlantic expanded dramatically in the seventeenth through nineteenth centuries.

In contemporary times, Brazilians have come to embrace miscegenation as a defining national trait. "We have all the colors of the rainbow" was the phrase trumpeted in a government radio campaign during the military dictatorship of the 1970s. But that sense of pride in racial mixing certainly was not the case either in colonial times, when it was seen as shameful, or into the early decades of the twentieth century. Even now, Brazilians are reluctant to admit the sordid origins of the phenomenon and the elements of sexual and class exploitation it involved.

By the mid-sixteenth century, the shortcomings of the system of private fiefs were apparent, and in 1549, the crown ordered direct royal rule everywhere except Pernambuco and São Vicente. Tomé de Sousa was designated the first governor general of Brazil and ordered to build a capital in the northeast, at the Bahia de Todos os Santos, which led to the founding of Salvador, today Brazil's third-largest city and a leading center of black culture. Warfare against native tribes intensified as Portugal sought to solidify its control of the region, but the new governor general's longest-lasting contribution to the construction of Brazil lay elsewhere. He arrived with a retinue of clerks, scribes, inspectors, registrars, and other functionaries, who immediately made themselves busy erecting a bureaucracy, extracting bribes, playing favorites, and indulging in the practice of nepotism. Brazilian historians often point to this moment as the beginning of their country's historic problems with corruption and official inefficiency, which worsened as the colony's territory and population increased and still plague Brazil today.

But profits from the brazilwood trade and the promise of even more wealth from sugar aroused the envy and greed of other European states, who, sensing Portugal's weakness, sought to create their own beachheads along the coast. Though the Dutch were to provide the biggest and most sustained threat, in the seventeenth century, the first challenge came from France. In 1555, an expedition consisting of two ships, six hundred soldiers, and Huguenot colonists established an entrepot in Guanabara Bay, the extraordinary natural harbor in front of present-day Rio de Janeiro. It took the Portuguese a dozen years to drive out the French, and largely in response to fear of other encroachments, the throne in Lisbon decided to step up its colonization efforts farther down the coast. This led directly to the founding of both Rio de Janeiro and São Paulo, today the country's two most important cities.

That didn't deter others, however, from trying to grab a piece of Brazil. In 1494, Spain and Portugal had, with the Vatican's blessing, signed a treaty that established a dividing line about thirteen hundred miles west of the Cape Verde Islands. All newly discovered lands east of that line were to go to Portugal, while those to the west belonged to Spain. Portuguese explorers had consistently ignored that demarcation, venturing deep into the interior of the South American continent. But in 1580, the King of Spain also became King of Portugal, an arrangement that continued through 1640. That threatened the identity of Portugal as an independent nation and brought Brazil under nominal Spanish control.

As an enemy of Spain, Holland now felt free to advance into Brazil, first in Salvador and then Pernambuco, which soon became a prosperous Dutch colony. And with the 1494 dividing line no longer an impediment, explorers and slave raiders based in São Paulo and known as *bandeirantes*, or "flag-bearers," took advantage of unification with Spain to penetrate the unexplored trackless interior of the South American continent and incorporate vast new domains into Brazil, ranging from sweeping plains and marshy lowlands to the immense area that came to be known as the "Mato Grosso" or "thick forest." Only after Portugal managed to reestablish its independence did Brazilian forces then focus their attention on reclaiming Pernambuco. That process took another 14 years but helped instill a sense of identity and pride among colonists. Until then, colonists in Brazil had had little contact with each other and often considered the colonies inferior to the mother country.

Once the Spanish interregnum was over, the Dutch threat eliminated, and Portuguese authority restored, Brazil fell into a period of stagnation, especially in its northeast heartland. The Dutch and the English established sugar plantations in Suriname and the Caribbean, permanently undermining Brazil's market position. But around 1700, word began leaking out of huge gold finds in the interior, near the headwaters of the São Francisco River. This set off an enormous migration, mainly of slave owners from the northeast and freebooters from Portugal, and reawakened the crown's interest in asserting stricter control over its Brazilian domains. The discovery around

1730 of diamonds in the same area, which came to be known as Minas Gerais, or General Mines, only accelerated all of those processes.

One almost immediate result was a permanent shift of Brazil's center of gravity from the northeast to the south-central coast, a thousand miles away. In 1763, the capital was transferred from Salvador da Bahia to Rio de Janeiro, formally ratifying the northeast's political and economic decline, a problem that persists in our own era. At the same time, Minas Gerais was emerging as a new powerhouse, at its peak producing nearly half the world's supply of gold. In 1710, only thirty thousand people lived there, contemporary accounts estimate. By the 1780s, though, the population of Minas Gerais had increased more than tenfold, giving it more inhabitants than any province in Brazil.

Minas Gerais, a vast landlocked plateau ringed by mountain ranges, was initially a fractious and violent place where rival claimants to gold and diamond strikes fought violently for control of the region's riches. Over time, though, it evolved into a showcase for the wealth accumulating there. By law, much of that treasure had to be sent via overland trail back to the coast and on to Portugal to finance the motherland's taste for English linens and other fineries. But what remained was still enough to pay for the construction of lavishly rococo churches and palace-like private homes for mine owners and merchants, who also commissioned religious paintings and statuary to fill those buildings as well as elaborate outdoor fountains and bridges. Even today, the baroque splendor of towns such as Ouro Preto, São João del Rei, and Diamantina attracts tourists from the world over.

Eventually, though, Brazil's colonial status began to chafe, especially in Minas Gerais. During the last quarter of the eighteenth century, Portugal tried to crack down on the contraband trade of gold and diamonds with Spanish colonies in South America. It also sought to brake the gradual emergence of workshops to manufacture clothing, which reduced the colony's need to import goods from the mother country. The crown logically viewed this as a threat, fearing that a self-sufficient Brazil would eventually break away, as the United States had just done from England. "Portugal without Brazil is an insignificant power," the royal minister for overseas dominions argued shortly before ordering the textile plants closed and abolished in 1785.

In 1789, some of the leading figures of Minas Gerais organized a plot to throw off the crown, arguing that Portugal had become a parasite that was holding Brazil back. Their platform included the lifting of restrictions on mines and factories, founding a university so that students would no longer have to go to Lisbon, freeing slaves born in Brazil, and setting up a parliament and a united independent state that would include Rio de Janeiro and São Paulo, too. Much of this was very progressive for its time. But commercial considerations also motivated the conspiracy: All debts to the royal treasury were to be cancelled, which obviously benefited many of the mine owners, landowners, merchants, judges, and clergy involved.

The "Inconfidência Mineira," as the conspiracy came to be called, was soon discovered and quashed, and Portugal again resolved to be more attentive to its colony in the New World. In 1798, with the French Revolution in full swing and a slave revolt in Haiti underway, the crown reacted harshly to a mulatto-led plot in Bahia. Brazil seemed to be sliding in the same direction as many of Spain's colonies in Latin America, where a restive Creole population would soon take up arms against the crown to enforce demands for independence. But the spread of Napoleon's power in Europe and the threat he represented to monarchical rule there would soon put Brazil on a very different path, one that for most of the nineteenth century would make its history unique in the Western Hemisphere.

In 1808, the Portuguese royal family fled Lisbon just ahead of Napoleon's troops and installed itself in Rio de Janeiro. Moving the court was unpopular with the local elites in Rio, who were forced to cede their homes and some of their privileges and status to the new arrivals. But it transformed Brazil from a neglected colonial backwater into the center of an empire whose reach extended all the way to Asia. Brazilian ports were opened to international commerce, and both trade and investment expanded greatly.

The most important consequences of the court's transfer, however, emerged only after the defeat of Napoleon, when it came time for King João VI and his family to return to Portugal. The monarch's son and heir, Pedro, was determined to remain, and when parliament ordered him back to Lisbon early in 1822, he defied their decree with a one-word declaration of personal independence that today is known to every Brazilian schoolchild as the moment Brazil was born as a nation: "Fico," or "I am staying."

Pedro was crowned the Emperor of Brazil, sparing the country the long, bloody, and debilitating civil wars that characterized independence struggles elsewhere in Latin America. There was still sporadic violence, and several provinces in the northeast with large concentrations of slaves mounted an unsuccessful effort to secede and form an independent Confederation of the Equator. But all of this occurred largely without the destruction and internal quarrels that soon led Gran Colombia, just to the north, to splinter into three separate nations. Similar problems also sapped the economy of neighboring Argentina, to the south, leaving it weak and divided from birth. Brazil, in contrast, was a cohesive state, unified around the figure of the emperor.

Pedro I clearly intended to be a progressive and benevolent ruler. He was, for example, deeply opposed to slavery, which he described as "a cancer that is gnawing away at Brazil." But the liberal constitution that he authorized ended up creating a parliament dominated by slaveholders. They adopted the language and forms of democracy, though not its substance, purely as a means of enhancing their own power. And after João VI died, in 1826, Pedro's opponents spread a rumor that he was plotting to supplant the constitution so as to be able to become monarch of a newly reunited Brazil and Portugal. In the end, Pedro's situation proved untenable, and in 1831 he abdicated in favor of his five-year-old son, also named Pedro.

Pedro II ruled over more than 50 years of expansion and modernization, even as Brazil's politics remained elitist. Like his father, Pedro II had enlightened views on many subjects and was quick to embrace new technologies, such as the telegraph, telephone, and railways, which he saw as means to knit together his far-flung domain. Production first of coffee and then rubber also boomed during Pedro's long reign; that ironically worked against the emperor's more progressive ideas, since it enriched the conservative oligarchy and strengthened its political power.

This new wealth had the effect of intensifying some of the worst, most regressive aspects of Brazilian society. Winning a lucrative state contract—or any form of social or economic advancement, for that matter—depended less on ability than on being able to access power through informal networks of family relationships, friendships, or favors granted by a patron. Without a powerful sponsor, almost nothing was possible; with access to such a godfather, virtually everything was permitted or overlooked.

Throughout this time, the slavery question continued to fester. In 1850, pressure from Britain forced the Brazilian government to outlaw the trans-Atlantic slave trade. That led to sharp increases in the price of Brazilian-born chattel labor as the need for manpower grew along with agricultural production, especially of coffee for export. Over the next three decades, a home-grown abolition movement gradually gained strength, leading to both large-scale escapes by slaves and manumission. In 1887, an army commander declared that the military, which was already refusing to lead missions to capture escaped slaves, had "the obligation to be abolitionist." A year later, with divisions on the issue growing even sharper, a law ending slavery was finally promulgated by the emperor's daughter while her father was on a trip abroad.

But abolition did not have the immediate positive effect that progressives desired and anticipated: Instead of strengthening a liberal monarch, it benefited the rural oligarchies. Since they no longer had to invest their money in buying and maintaining slaves, they were able to avail themselves of the cheap immigrant labor that was already beginning to pour into Brazil. Frustration among young military officers with republican leanings had been growing throughout the 1870s and 1880s, and in November 1889, they rose up in rebellion. Initially, they may have meant just to force the cabinet to be replaced. But as the movement gained force, its objectives broadened, and the result was a coup d'etat that toppled Pedro II and sent him and his family into exile.

During the First Republic, as the period from 1889 to 1930 is known, economic growth continued to outpace political change. The largely military-led coup that overthrew the emperor did not have enough popular support to risk elections, nor could its leaders initially agree as to what form of government they wanted. In the 1890s, rebellions erupted on the rolling grasslands of the far south and in the arid hinterlands of Bahia. Local oligarchs, dubbed "colonels" even though they were not military officers, took maximum advantage of the central government's weakness to strengthen the autonomy of individual states. Local bosses picked state governors, who in turn chose presidents, the more undistinguished the better, with only a tiny percentage of the population allowed to ratify that decision, in rigged votes.

Two coffee-growing states dominated the politics of the First Republic, Minas Gerais and São Paulo. They passed the presidency back and forth between them, advancing the often parochial interests of their leading families while ignoring those of other regions and classes. Along with several other states, São Paulo and Minas Gerais also fortified their own police forces, which virtually became armies that checked the power of the national armed forces. Social inequalities grew: After abolition, little had been done to help freed slaves, and with urbanization, the numbers of the disenfranchised rose even further. Education was not emphasized because the oligarchic families saw it as a potential threat to their authority. Since voters were required to pass a literacy test, the elite feared that greater schooling for the masses would swell the size of the electorate to levels they regarded as uncontrollable.

Economically, however, Brazil was progressing. Once slavery was abolished, the government encouraged immigration from both Europe (mainly Italy, Portugal, Germany, and Spain) and Japan to supply the labor that the coffee plantations needed (and also to whiten the population). Especially in São Paulo, coffee planters invested part of their profits in factories, manufacturing textiles, and other items ranging from matches to pots and pans. When World War I restricted international trade, even more factories sprang up. The resulting industrial surge created a need for more immigrant labor, which in turn helped create a domestic market that allowed Brazil the luxury of not having to gear its economy to exports, as other nations in Latin America had to do. Between 1890 and 1930, Brazil's population grew more than 160 percent, to 34 million people.

In 1930, though, everything fell apart. The global depression had already devastated the coffee industry, and Brazil's finances with it, when President Washington Luis decided to ignore tradition and chose another paulista beholden to coffee planters as his successor. Minas Gerais responded by allying with other resentful states and backing Getúlio Vargas of Rio Grande do Sul, in the far south of the country, for president. This "Liberal Alliance" lost the balloting held in April, but political tensions continued high, and in October,

Alliance supporters took to the streets in protest. The armed forces then stepped in, tossing out Washington Luis and establishing a provisional junta, which promptly offered the presidency to Vargas. And so the First Republic ended exactly as it had begun: with a military uprising.

Vargas proved to be the dominant figure in Brazilian life for the next quarter century. From 1930 to 1945, he ruled as a dictator, shuttering Congress, censoring the press, and jailing and torturing his opponents or driving them into exile. He admired Mussolini and Hitler and flirted with fascism until the entry of the United States into World War II made it clear he was better off favoring the Allied side. Even so, Roosevelt had to buy his cooperation by financing a steel mill in Volta Redonda, near Rio, that helped form the domestic industry. In return, the Allies got use of bases on Brazilian soil, which were crucial to the roundabout air bridge across the Atlantic to Africa and up to Europe, and to the deployment of Brazilian troops to fight alongside Allied forces in Italy.

When the war ended, Vargas was forced to step down. But in 1950, he was the winner in a democratically conducted election, vanquishing three other candidates. He governed in a populist style, leading to tensions in relations with the United States and comparisons, only partially justifiable, with Juan Perón of Argentina. Mobilizing the masses with the slogan "the oil is ours," he also founded a state oil company, Petrobras, which is still in government hands today and is Brazil's biggest company. But his administration was also marked by corruption and the intimidation of political enemies, which led to a political crisis in which the military demanded he step down. Rather than resign in disgrace, Vargas killed himself on August 24, 1954, and was interred as a national hero.

Vargas remains one of the most complicated figures in Brazilian history, both beloved and reviled even today. He clearly had autocratic tendencies. But the Estado Novo, or New State, that he created also helped modernize Brazil. Strikes were outlawed, but a labor law quite progressive for its time, guaranteeing a minimum wage and providing other benefits to workers, was also implemented. As a result, Vargas was nicknamed the Father of the Poor, and the party he founded, the Brazilian Labor Party, became the favorite of the urban working classes and peasantry.

Confusion and tension followed Vargas's death, but in 1955, just when it seemed that Brazil might slide back into authoritarianism, a brilliant and charismatic leader emerged as the victor in the presidential election. Juscelino Kubitschek de Oliveira won the vote by a narrow margin, and it took a military uprising to guarantee that the results would be respected. Kubitschek, the first of Brazil's presidents to be born in the twentieth century, was a physician who had served as mayor of Belo Horizonte and governor of Minas Gerais, and he took office with the kind of extravagant, outsize ambitions that have always fired the Brazilian imagination. "Fifty years in five" was the slogan he used to inspire the nation, and during his administration, Brazil did make huge strides forward.

Ever since Brazil had become a republic, the constitution had called for moving the capital from Rio de Janeiro deep into the heartland. JK, as the president was popularly known, made that dream a reality in four short years, creating Brasília out of an empty stretch of savannah in the cattle state of Goiás. He spent hundreds of millions of dollars, not just on the soaring buildings that became symbols at home and abroad of a new, progressive Brazil, but also on a network of highways that linked the new capital to the main population centers. With that, Brazil's center of gravity, for the first time in its history, began to shift away from the coast, and the vast and backward interior was finally opened to modernization and development.

Those achievements alone would have guaranteed Kubitschek a hero's status in the history of Brazil. But, through a combination of credits and cajoling, he also pushed for installation of a domestic automobile industry. That, in turn, stimulated the expansion of steel mills and heavy industry and construction of the dams and power plants to supply electricity to that growing manufacturing base, which also included ship construction and the large-scale production of appliances. As a result, Kubitschek's five years in office saw industrial production grow 80 percent and profits to Brazilian companies rise 76 percent.

Looking back, Brazilians remember the Kubitschek era fondly, as a time of growth, prosperity, abundance, and optimism. But the full cost of that progress and expansion became evident only later, in that the seeds of future problems were also being planted. In May 1960, for example, one month after the inauguration of Brasília, JK turned to the International Monetary Fund for a $47.5 million loan meant mainly to fortify the auto industry in São Paulo. Over the next 40 years, the IMF was to become a major player in the Brazilian economy, often clashing with governments, both civilian and military, and the local population over the belt-tightening measures it demanded in return for its loans, which grew larger and larger, reaching $41.5 billion by 1998.

Even more ominously, Brazil's foreign debt rose by 67 percent during Kubitschek's time in office, to $3.8 billion. Those loans were sought for a simple reason: The domestic credit market was incapable of financing all the purchases of equipment needed for industrial expansion, much of which was imported and had to be paid for in dollars or other hard currencies. In addition, inflation began to surge and, with that, real incomes to erode. From an already worrisome rate of 25 percent in 1960, inflation rose to 43 percent in 1961, 55 percent a year later, and 81 percent in 1963. By 1990, inflation was so deeply embedded that prices could rise 80 percent in a single month. But the origins of that problem, which for years threatened to strangle the economy and wipe out growth, can clearly be traced back to Kubitschek's time in office.

To Kubitschek's great credit, his years in office had also witnessed a consolidation of democratic institutions. The military's early fears that he would prove to be a radical populist in the Vargas mold, which led to threats of intervention, proved unfounded, as the president showed himself adept at negotiating with his opponents and respectful of Congress's authority. But almost immediately after Kubitschek left office in 1961, the political situation began to unravel, and not until 1998 would an elected civilian president again manage to complete a full term in office.

In the post-Vargas era, Brazilians cast separate ballots for president and vice president. As successor to Kubitschek, they chose Jânio Quadros, the outgoing governor of São Paulo, and one of Quadros's rivals, João Goulart, as vice president. Goulart had also been Kubitschek's vice president and, before that, minister of labor under Getúlio Vargas, his mentor. Like Vargas, he was a native of Brazil's southernmost state, Rio Grande do Sul, and, after the strongman's suicide, had emerged as his political heir, serving as leader of the Brazilian Labor Party. The Brazilian armed forces regarded Goulart as a

Communist sympathizer intent on destroying democracy and politicizing the military and were openly opposed to his ever becoming president. So long as he remained vice president, however, military leaders were willing to stand aside and not intervene overtly in the political process.

But on August 25, 1961, less than eight months after taking office, Jânio Quadros unexpectedly resigned as president for reasons that to this day have never been explained clearly. In his resignation speech, he spoke of being pressured by what the Brazilian press characterized as "dark forces." But Quadros was a notoriously heavy drinker and may simply have acted impulsively in an inebriated rage. Another theory is that he was trying to strengthen his hand politically, hoping that the political parties blocking his program would beg him to return rather than run the risk of seeing Goulart in power. Instead, Goulart became president, and the stage was set for confrontation. The next two and a half years were to be perhaps the most turbulent in Brazil's modern history.

Goulart happened to be in China on an official visit when the resignation was announced, and sectors of the military immediately moved to block him from taking office. He had to wait in neighboring Uruguay until a compromise acceptable to the military and civilian opposition was hammered out: Though Goulart was allowed to return to Brasília to be sworn in, the country shifted from a presidential system to a parliamentary form of rule, in which control of the day-to-day affairs of government and some of the president's constitutional powers were transferred to a prime minister, Tancredo Neves, a canny politician from Minas Gerais. That solution, however, did not prove to be durable. Goulart continued maneuvering to regain his lost powers, while his opponents stepped up their efforts to weaken him. In hopes of increasing his popular support, Goulart moved further and further to the left. He announced a "Three-Year Plan" that envisaged a sweeping agrarian reform, restrictions on remittances of profits by foreign-owned companies, extension of the right to vote to illiterates, limits on residents of urban areas owning more than one piece of property, and various other populist measures that seemed to confirm his enemies' worst suspicions.

The United States was also becoming increasingly alarmed by these developments. Fidel Castro had come to power in Cuba in 1959, and the

Kennedy administration feared the spread of his revolutionary gospel elsewhere in Latin America. Washington worried that Brazil, with its huge gap between rich and poor and other social inequities, was especially vulnerable. When Jânio Quadros announced an independent foreign policy and decorated Che Guevara during a visit to Brazil, the United States reacted with nearly as much irritation as the Brazilian right. The situation only worsened after Goulart took power and followed policies seen as hostile to American companies that had invested in Brazil, including allowing the nationalization of a subsidiary of ITT.

By March 1964, the situation was becoming unsustainable. At mid-month, Goulart and his supporters on the left and in the labor movement mobilized an estimated 150,000 people for a rally in Rio de Janeiro, at which the president announced plans to nationalize privately owned oil companies and to convoke an assembly to write a new constitution. His opponents responded with an even larger mass protest of their own in São Paulo, called the March of the Family for God and Liberty. On the night of March 31, military units moved on Rio de Janeiro. Goulart returned to his home state, where his supporters urged armed resistance. But rather than risk civil war, he crossed over into Uruguay, beginning an exile that would last the remaining dozen years of his life. Congress declared the presidency vacant, leaving control of the country in the hands of the armed forces.

The Brazilian left has always claimed that the United States instigated and directed Goulart's overthrow. However, there is little in Lyndon Johnson's private papers at the University of Texas or in other official U.S. documents to substantiate that argument. Washington clearly welcomed and unreservedly supported the coup, and the U.S. military attaché in Brazil, Colonel Vernon Walters, who would later serve as deputy director of the Central Intelligence Agency and ambassador to the United Nations, had been in contact with the coup plotters before they acted. Their leader, who became the first head of the military regime that would rule Brazil for the next 21 years, was General Humberto Castelo Branco, a friend of Walters since the two men served together in Italy in World War II.

In retrospect, as at the time of the coup, it seems clear that the officers who overthrew Goulart had sufficient resources and support to seize power on their own. It is indisputable, however, that Washington's enthusiastic backing of the military coup established a pattern that would soon be repeated elsewhere in South America. Over the next dozen years, Chile, Bolivia, Uruguay, and Argentina would all fall into the hands of right-wing military dictatorships. So American support for the coup of 1964 provided a template for an era in which political liberties and efforts to reduce social inequality and economic exploitation would be snuffed out all over Latin America in the name of national security and combating the Communist threat.

Initially, most Brazilians supposed that the new military government would be merely a caretaker one and that presidential elections would go ahead as scheduled in 1965, with the wildly popular Kubitschek likely to return to office. That may well have been what General Castelo Branco also wanted. But there were strong divisions within the military on that subject (as well as others), and in the end the hardliners won out. The military leadership had begun stripping important civilian figures of their political rights from the moment the coup took place, including their nemesis, João Goulart. But when they did the same to Kubitschek, in 1965, it became clear that they had no intention of giving up power anytime soon.

Castelo Branco thus gave way in 1967 to General Artur da Costa e Silva, who tightened the armed forces' control of the country even further. On December 13, 1968, a notorious decree known as Institutional Act No. 5 granted him dictatorial powers, suspended the constitution, dissolved Congress and all of the state legislatures, and imposed censorship. When Costa e Silva died of a stroke less than a year later, he was succeeded by an even more hard-line general, Emílio Garrastazu Médici, who had virtually no popular support outside the armed forces and therefore felt he had to rule with an iron hand.

Médici's nearly five years in power were perhaps the bleakest in modern Brazilian history. Repression bred resistance, most notably in the form of left-wing guerrilla movements, in both the cities and the far-off Amazon, which the government promptly classified as terrorist. These groups, which cultivated ties to Cuba and China, undertook bombings and bank robberies in the country's major cities and also kidnapped foreign diplomats, including the U.S. ambassador. The Roman Catholic Church, perhaps the country's most influential institution, also opposed the regime's abuses of human rights and its focus on economic development at the cost of social justice. In response, the military regime created a large, intrusive, and repressive intelligence apparatus that not only spied on those it regarded as potential opponents, including priests and nuns, but regularly abducted and tortured dissidents.

Human rights abuses occurred on a large scale, especially during the late 1960s and early 1970s; yet overall, political repression in Brazil, bad as it was, was still milder than in either Argentina or Chile. With nearly five times Argentina's population, Brazil had around four hundred political dissenters forcibly disappeared by state security forces during the 21-year period of rule by the armed forces, compared with estimates of up to 30,000 in Argentina in less than a decade. And unlike the situation in Chile under General Augusto Pinochet, no single, all-powerful dictator dominated the military regime. Instead, one army general gave way to another at fairly regular intervals, for a total of five in all.

Also in contrast to later actions by its counterparts in Argentina and Chile, the Brazilian military tried to maintain the appearance of some sort of democratic normality. While individual politicians were banned from office, Congress itself was not permanently closed. Existing political parties were outlawed, but they were replaced by a pair of new groupings: the National Renewal Alliance for supporters of the March Revolution, as the regime took to calling itself, and the Brazilian Democratic Movement for its opponents. Eventually, the regime even allowed the process of selecting the president to be conducted in public by a carefully screened electoral college, rather than in the barracks by the military high command.

To dilute the influence of São Paulo and Minas Gerais, the country's two traditional centers of power, the military also created several new states and simultaneously increased the minimum size of the congressional delegations from each state. The main beneficiaries were smaller, poorer states where military control was easier to exercise. But the larger, more prosperous, and urbanized states that ended up being underrepresented could not protest. This perverse system remains in place even today and continues to distort the principle of "one man, one vote" and to force Brazilian presidents to horse-trade with political bosses from those more backward states in order to get legislation through Congress.

The military government also tried to instill Brazilians with a greater sense of national pride and purpose. Slogans such as "Forward Brazil" and "Brazil: Love It or Leave It" proliferated everywhere, and when Brazil won soccer's World Cup for the third time, in 1970, the regime tried to expropriate the victory and make it an occasion for nationalist and triumphalist propaganda. Voices that dissented or even questioned or mocked these pretensions to a Brasil Grande were not tolerated: Censorship was imposed not just on radio, television, newspapers, and magazines but also on popular music and books.

Categorizing economic policy during this time is difficult. Though the government described itself as resolutely anti-Communist, it was not averse to giving the state a prominent role in the economy in the name of enhancing national security. Domestic entrepreneurship was encouraged, and foreign investment, the object of hostility during the Goulart years, was welcomed back. But state-run companies such as Petrobras and the mining giant Companhia Vale do Rio Doce retained their favored role, and the government itself also invested or directly participated in enormous projects meant to either strengthen the country's basic infrastructure or thrust Brazil into new and strategic areas of industry.

Thus, a state aircraft manufacturing company, Embraer, was established in 1969, as was a similar company that produced tanks and armored cars for both domestic use and export to countries such as Iraq. Work also began on giant construction projects, such as a 3,000-mile highway cutting across the Amazon and a bridge across Guanabara Bay to link Rio de Janeiro and Niterói, its smaller and quieter sister city across the water. In the early 1970s, after negotiating an accord with the corrupt dictator of neighboring Paraguay, Alfredo Stroessner, the government started construction of what was then the world's biggest hydroelectric power project, the Itaipu dam on the Paraná River. Pro-Álcool, a state-financed program to produce ethanol from sugarcane, was launched in 1974. Not long after, an accord was signed with West Germany to build several nuclear reactors, and work quickly began on the first of them, at Angra dos Reis, on a spectacular stretch of coast dotted with islands and white sand beaches west of Rio de Janeiro.

All of this contributed to a spectacular burst of growth in the early 1970s, a period that came to be known as the Brazilian Miracle. For four consecutive years, the Brazilian economy expanded by 10 percent or more, and both exports and foreign investment boomed. Inflation, which had ebbed in the first years of the military dictatorship, returned as a problem, but the economic team, led by Minister of Finance Antônio Delfim Neto, found what appeared at the time to be a canny solution. The government established a system of indexation in which interest rates and, to a lesser extent, salaries and other assets were periodically increased in order to protect them against the impact of inflation on their buying power.

The economic miracle came to an end, however, with the global energy crisis of 1974, which happened to coincide with a succession struggle within the military. This time the hard-liners lost out, and when General Ernesto Geisel became president that year, he began an effort to slowly steer the country back toward democracy. He replaced the most abusive regional military commanders with officers loyal to him, restored habeas corpus, allowed some exiles to return, offered a relatively muted reaction when independent labor unions reorganized and carried out the first strikes in years, revoked most of Institutional Act No. 5, and was able to impose a protégé sympathetic to his objectives as his successor: General João Figueiredo, head of the intelligence service.

Under Figueiredo, who took office in March 1979, the dictatorship would finally sputter to an end. He signed an amnesty law and promised a policy of *abertura,* or opening, which the opposition was quick to test. In February 1980, labor leader Luiz Inácio Lula da Silva and an assortment of intellectuals, liberation theology advocates, and environmentalists founded the Workers Party in São Paulo. The press and the church also grew increasingly outspoken, and in the 1982 gubernatorial and congressional elections, the opposition made big gains. Because Figueiredo was in poor health (he had cardiac problems that required open-heart surgery), his hold on power gradually weakened, and as the end of his term neared and maneuvering to succeed him began, millions of Brazilians took to the streets to demand that the country's next president be chosen by popular vote, a step that was certain to guarantee a civilian in power.

That campaign failed, but Figueiredo's physical and political weakness made him unable to impose his own choice of a successor on the electoral college that the military had created. That created an opening that opponents of the regime were quick to exploit. On January 15, 1985, they were able to engineer the selection of Tancredo Neves, a 75-year-old conservative who had served as prime minister during the Goulart years. One last surprise remained, however: Neves had to be hospitalized the night before his mid-March inauguration and died five weeks later of peritonitis. By this time, though, the military was so weakened and discredited that there was no possibility of their stepping in to halt the transfer of power to civilians, and 21 years of military rule thus ended not with a bang but with a whimper. Democracy had finally been restored, and the political system under which Brazil operates today was born. But the unjust social structure and the inequalities that had bedeviled the country since the arrival of the Portuguese nearly five hundred years earlier remained unresolved.

TWO

SIN AND SALVATION SOUTH OF THE EQUATOR

"SIN DOESN'T EXIST BELOW the Equator" is one of the most celebrated hits of the singer and composer Chico Buarque, and nearly forty years after he wrote it, the song continues to get air play on radio stations all over Brazil and to be sung by revelers at Carnival balls. But the amusing title has taken on a life of its own: Often uttered with a resigned or even sympathetic shrug, it has become a shorthand phrase widely used to explain and ironically comment on—or sometimes also to excuse or justify—moral lapses ranging from political corruption to sexual promiscuity.

Brazilians are prone to complaining that theirs is a country without principles or ethics. It's customary for them even to sit around over a beer or a *cafezinho* and enumerate the failings of their society, part of a flair for the dramatic that can also be a feature of Brazilian life. But Brazil is a remarkably tolerant society, and that has both good and bad aspects. The ethos that prevails in Brazil, which can be traced to its unique mixture of European, African, and indigenous values and practices, recognizes that human beings are flawed and makes allowances for their imperfections. It allows for diversity of religious beliefs and, to a wider extent than in many other places, even sexual practices. It emphasizes forgiveness and redemption, generosity and seeking common ground. Above all, it is flexible, taking into account the circumstances that surround specific acts or patterns of behavior.

It is not by accident that Brazilians regard themselves as "the cordial people" and value cordiality as both a personal and national trait. There is often a warmth and friendliness in personal relationships, even casual ones, that newcomers find enchanting. And while the French may have invented the term joie de vivre, Brazilians have perfected that art. They live with both gusto and a kind of sunny optimism, able to appreciate the beauty in small things and convinced that the universe is essentially benign, not hostile. As a popular saying puts it: "Everything is going to be all right in the end, and if everything is not yet all right, that's only because we haven't reached the end."

That is the positive side of life in Brazil. But those characteristics co-exist with others that are less attractive and that have long generated conflict and complaints among Brazilians. For all the lip service paid to the concept of equality, for example, Brazilian society is highly stratified, with yawning gaps and differences based on class, race, and gender. Many of the rich and privileged act as if they are above the law and often get away with flouting rules that are supposed to apply to all. Often, they treat those they consider beneath them as if they were servants. For their part, the poor also have little faith in the law and institutions, which they see as stacked against the little guy, and they are on the lookout for ways to circumvent the forces discriminating against them.

In a country of 200 million people, there are obviously enormous variations of behavior and beliefs from one person to the next. Yet there are also prevailing norms that Brazilians absorb just from having grown up in the society. One of the basic organizing features of daily life is the *jeito*, perhaps even more commonly known by its diminutive, the *jeitinho*. In its most literal sense, to have a *jeito* is to be adroit at something or to have an aptitude, knack, or talent. It also can mean to fix things, but it's usually used figuratively to describe the skill required to maneuver around the laws or social conventions that prevent you from achieving an objective.

Two of the most common synonyms for *jeito* are derived from the world of soccer. One is *driblando*, as in "dribbling" a ball with such dexterity and spontaneous creativity that you outwit the opponent in your path. The other is *jogo de cintura*, which refers specifically to a player's ability to move hips and waist with sufficient nimbleness or agility that an adversary is duped or faked out, much like a basketball or hockey player who feigns a drive or pass in one direction and then moves in the other.

Some forms of the *jeito* are almost universal and are easily recognizable even to outsiders. If a policeman in a Brazilian city stops a car for exceeding the speed limit or making an illegal turn, the driver is likely to ask, "Officer, isn't there a way to find a jeitinho to resolve this?" Or if you want to be seated at a corner table at a chic restaurant at the peak of the dinner hour, some money slipped into the hand of the maitre d' may help get you what you want.

But because so many institutions in Brazil are corrupt or inefficient or both, citizens are forced to band together and help each other to a larger extent than in many other places. Bureaucracy pervades everything from enrolling in school to getting electrical service or buying a house. Sometimes getting around laws or situations that are inconvenient involves a cash payment of a bribe, tip, or "gratification." Or it can involve other illegal means. So Brazilians find a *jeito* and create informal, parallel institutions or mechanisms to work around that problem. The emphasis is on exchanging favors or building the kind of durable personal relationship with someone who allows for favors to be asked.

The *mutirão*, for example, is similar to the now-vanished practice of barn-raising in the United States, in which a community pools its labor and resources in order to build a house, school, silo, church, or clinic. This custom is still quite common in remote parts of the country beyond the reach of basic government services, such as the Amazon or the interior of the northeast, and is sometimes used for planting and harvesting crops in the absence of modern machinery. Then there is the widespread practice known as the *filho de criacão*, which has no precise translation to English. If a neighbor or an employee dies and leaves an orphaned child, or if the biological parents are unable to raise their offspring because of poverty or other difficulties, someone else steps in and raises that child as his own. No formal adoption needs to occur. Instead, the child simply joins another family. That's how the internationally known black pop singer Milton Nascimento came to be reared by the white family that employed his birth mother. In this way, society compensates for the absence of an effective social welfare system and avoids having the child sent to an orphanage, where food, clothing, and affection would be lacking.

A *jeito* can also arise in response to deficiencies in the way a business operates. Until the 1990s, when the government-owned telecommunications company was privatized and the country was flooded with cellular phones, Brazil suffered from a chronic shortage of working telephone lines, and there was a long waiting list, up to a decade, to obtain a line. The *jeito* devised to deal with the situation was a black market in telephones. When an elderly person with a telephone died, ownership of that line would pass to heirs of the deceased. If they had phones of their own, they would sell the line to the highest bidder, sometimes going so far as to put an ad in the newspaper announcing the availability of a line. Rather than wait years and years, a person or company in urgent need of a phone line would pay $1,000 or more to have the line transferred to their use. This was an arrangement that left everyone involved happy, except perhaps the phone company itself. But since the company was seen as the cause of the problem, the impediment that had to be dribbled around, no one really cared much.

Like everybody else, I have had occasion to employ the *jeito*. In 2008, I was invited to São Paulo for a speaking engagement to promote a book of mine that had just been published in Brazil. But when I got to the airport in Rio de Janeiro to pick up the airline ticket that the sponsors of the event had left for me, I found that it had been issued in the nickname I used professionally instead of my full official name as it appears on my American passport and Brazilian resident foreigner's identification card. Because of that slight difference, the airline did not want to issue me the ticket, and I ran the risk of missing my flight and speaking engagement. What to do?

"Isn't there a way to find a *jeito?*" I asked. The clerk said that wouldn't be possible unless I had some additional document that showed my nickname. I didn't. Out of desperation, I reached into my suitcase, pulled out my book, showed the clerk the cover photograph, and asked, "How about this?" She laughed and said, "Oh, that's a good one," but agreed to consult with her supervisor. A couple of minutes later, she returned, smiled, and said, "You're good to go." After giving my speech, I went to lunch with the sponsors of the event and told them what had happened. My story amused and delighted them: "Larry, you've got *jogo de cintura*," they told me. "You've become just like a Brazilian."

All of these examples of the *jeito* are essentially harmless and don't really erode the social contract. But other common cases fall into a morally ambiguous area. Public hospitals in Brazil, for example, are chronically overcrowded and underfinanced. So let's suppose your mother is ill and has been told that no bed is available for her. But you have a friend who is a doctor. The *jeito* is applied by asking the doctor to intervene on your behalf, with the understanding that in return for admitting and attending to your mother, the doctor deserves a favor to be collected at some unspecified time.

Or let's imagine that your car has been stolen or your house broken into. The police, as is often the case, don't seem the slightest bit interested in investigating the crime or helping you get your property back. But if you have a friend who is a police officer, you can apply a *jeito* by asking him to intercede and put in a good word with the detectives in charge of your case. Of course, if you don't have an intermediary you can turn to, you can always give the investigators money to make an effort on your behalf. Brazilian insurance companies do that all the time, reasoning that it is cheaper to pay a "tip" to the cops and recover stolen goods than to have to shell out large amounts to the insured for a replacement car or computer.

One of the ways in which the *jeitinho* has been formalized is through the institution of the *despachante*, or dispatcher, especially in dealings with government bureaucracies. Suppose you want to obtain a driver's license without having to go through the normal procedures. You may simply be in a hurry and not want to wait. Or perhaps you haven't studied for the written test or have failed it in the past. Or maybe you don't know how to drive at all. The solution is to hire a *despachante* who has cultivated a personal relationship of some sort with key employees at the driver's license bureau and can get you your license in record time.

Many who resort to the *jeitinho* know they are doing something that they really shouldn't. But they shrug their shoulders and justify their actions with the phrase *Não tem outro jeito*, "There's no other way." Since everyone at one time or another uses the *jeitinho* to resolve a problem, and many of those who have the ability to use the *jeitinho* do so all the time, odds are that no one will look askance at what you have done. The alternative is to play strictly by the rules and be classified as an *otário*, a dupe or sucker, an object of ridicule and derision, and no one wants to be in that category.

The opposite of the *otário* is the *malandro*, the street-smart con artist who lives by his wits, often deceiving others with no regrets or guilt. Once, at the end of a meal at a restaurant with a group of other foreigners, who by definition are almost always considered suckers, I asked for the bill and was surprised to find a charge for "6 C. Cola" at about a dollar apiece. Since nobody had ordered Coca Cola, I questioned the waiter about the item. He merely shrugged his shoulders and replied, "Se cola." That means "if it sticks" and is pronounced the same way as "C. Cola." With that phrase, he was acknowledging that he saw our party as dupes, to be cheated without our realizing what was going on, and was trying to take advantage of us as a *malandro* would. Unfortunately, I had caught him at his own game, and he was forced to remove the charge. Another example would be the unfaithful husband who sweet-talks his wife into believing he is faithful when at the same time he is cheating on her with her sister, which was the subject of a 2009 pop song: He is a *malandro* and she is an *otária*.

The *malandro* is a recurring figure in Brazilian popular lore and has an ambiguous status. Officially he is censured as a swindler and cheat, preying on the innocent, trusting, and gullible. But he—and the *malandro* is almost always a *he*—is also the subject of sneaking admiration in samba lyrics, folk tales, books, and films, admired for his guile and his ability to think on his feet and deftly dribble around barriers and obstacles. In some quarters, especially certain neighborhoods in Rio de Janeiro, which other Brazilians regard as the *malandro*'s natural habitat, *malandragem*, the name given to the battery of strategies that the *malandro* employs, is even regarded as a kind of art form.

The *malandro*'s creed is summed up by what has become known as Gerson's Law. In the late 1970s, a popular television commercial for a brand of cigarettes featured a soccer played named Gerson, who ended his pitch by proclaiming, "Gosto de levar vantagem em tudo, certo?" Loosely translated, that means, "I like to come out ahead in everything, you understand?" The slogan caught on immediately and was quickly understood, in a more generalized sense, to mean that Brazilians like to have the upper hand in every situation. Even though Gerson eventually expressed regret for allowing his name to be associated with the phrase, it remains a shorthand expression of the code of the *malandro* today, cited whenever someone acts unethically, cynically, and in his own interest, often as a criticism, but sometimes as a justification.

Another (and related) feature of Brazilian life is the gap between codes of conduct for "the house and the street," as the Brazilian anthropologist Roberto DaMatta puts it. Anglo-Saxon societies subscribe to an ideal of fairness, equal opportunity, and impartiality. The fallibility of human beings and the realities of daily life mean that personal conduct often falls short of that ideal. But deviance from that principle is frowned upon and, if too blatant, can be punished, by either public censure or the law. Just look at what happened in 2007 when Paris Hilton finagled her way out of a brief jail sentence; the resulting public outcry was so intense that she had to go back and serve her time.

But Brazilians don't automatically expect people to act with the same probity on the street as they do in the house. Life in the house, the realm of family and friends, rests on ties of blood, affection, shared sacrifice, and regard for the collective welfare, with roles that are defined according to sex and age, and mutual obligations. But much of public life in Brazil, rather than being a domain in which the principles of egalitarianism apply, is governed by partiality, nepotism, and discrimination. It's a world of *salve-se quem puder*, or every man for himself, in which it is common to act for your own benefit and that of those closest to you while ignoring the general welfare. A public office is often seen not as a public trust but as a source of private gain.

For many Brazilians, the notion of family is one that extends considerably beyond the immediate nuclear unit to include cousins and even cousins of cousins. Until recently, the birth rate in Brazil was quite high, so that an extended family, especially in the interior, where the birth rate was highest, could include siblings in the double digits and dozens of cousins. In some cases, it might even be more accurate to talk about clans than simply families, and that is the terminology sometimes used in places like the northeast, where feuds of the Hatfield-versus-McCoy variety have sometimes raged for generations.

This extended family structure has often turned out to be a sword that cuts both ways: It ensures an individual a web of protection and support to fall back on, but also, thanks to the *jeito* system, has meant the individual is entangled in a web of obligations that can stifle one's own autonomy. More than once during the years I lived in Brazil, I was approached by cousins of cousins of my wife who wanted me to put in a good word with the U.S. embassy in Brazil to ensure that their visa application was handled quickly and with a favorable outcome. When I explained that the system did not work that way, that no amount of *jeito* could guarantee them a visa, some of them had hurt feelings and were convinced that I didn't want to make an effort on their behalf.

A preference for large, close-knit families has also had consequences in both politics and business. Traditionally, many of Brazil's largest companies were family owned and run, though this has changed in recent years as the country has become more integrated into the larger world economy. But politics in many places remains a family affair even today, with dynasties that are particularly powerful in the northeast and the Amazon, where governorships, mayoralties, and congressional seats are still handed down from father to son or daughter as if they were heirlooms.

Former president José Sarney, who for more than 40 years has been the political boss of the northeastern state of Maranhão, may be the most prominent example of this phenomenon. His oldest son, Fernando, was put in charge of the family conglomerate of television and radio stations and made a vice president of the Brazilian Soccer Confederation, posts he continues to hold after he and his wife were indicted in 2009 for racketeering, money laundering, influence trafficking, making false statements under oath, and falsifying documents. His sister Roseana has served three terms as governor of the state and also has been elected twice to Congress, while his younger brother, José Sarney Jr., has been a cabinet minister and now, after changing party three times, serves in the lower house of Congress.

As the country modernizes, though, this tendency to favor those closest to you faces challenges, with a growing tension between the old, highly personal way of doing things and the new, which calls for impartiality. Nevertheless, it would be foolish to assume that those in positions of authority or power in the public realm operate according to the principle of equal treatment for all. Often there is favoritism, either open or disguised, in the way services or favors are distributed and penalties or punishments meted out. In Portuguese, there is a proverb that says, *Aos meus amigos, tudo, aos meus inimigos o rigor da lei:* "For my friends, everything; for my enemies, the rigor of the law." More often than Brazilians would like, that seems to be the principle guiding those in authority, from the president of the republic down to the policeman on the corner.

With a sufficient number of friends in high places and the possibility of employing the *jeito*, it is even possible to be exempted from obedience to the law. No matter what the statute books may say, an exception can always be arranged and a violation overlooked. Hence, the notion that the full force and vigor of the law is reserved only for the enemies of those who wield power or authority. If you're a friend or relative of the mayor or a city council member, for example, you may not need to comply with zoning laws. Want to erect a building with more floors than those permitted in the construction code? Feel free. Would you like to open a store in a neighborhood zoned exclusively as residential? Go right ahead. But if a political opponent or commercial rival attempts the same thing, then the attitude is, "A lei neles!" or "Sic the law on them!"

Many Brazilians thus see the law as an instrument of power and coercion, and not of justice. It therefore becomes a point of pride, even an obligation of sorts, to try to avoid obeying the law and to attempt to get away with as much as possible. This is especially true if a law interferes with one's personal goals or interests. But sometimes it is done simply for sport, as an affirmation of individual autonomy. There is a curious expression that one often hears in discussions about certain rules and regulations that are simply not observed. *Aquela lei não pegou*, Brazilians will say, which means, "That law didn't catch on." To a newcomer from an Anglo-Saxon society, that phrase may seem unfathomable. After all, the law is the law, so how can it possibly not "catch on"?

An atypical example from American history that comes to mind is that of Prohibition, which in the end was repealed in large part because continued mockery of the ban was undermining respect for the rule of law. But Brazilian life is full of instances large and small of laws that didn't "catch on" and still exist on the books. There are giant corporations that fail to turn over to the government the social security and health care contributions for their employees that are mandated by law, and there are also motorists who routinely run red lights after dark in large cities. Disobedience of that latter law is so widespread that some cities, such as Rio de Janeiro, have simply caved in and had to pass laws that make stopping at a red light after 10 P.M. optional rather than mandatory.

At times, this tendency to defy laws and rules imbues daily life in Brazil with what seems to be a streak of either selfishness or anarchism. In either case, the result is a lack of civic solidarity. Every motorist on the road seems to think he is the only one with a car and drives accordingly, without regard for his fellow citizens. At the bank, a theater box office, the bus stop, or the grocery store, there is usually someone (or several someones) who believes he or she is much too important or in too much of a hurry to have to stand in line and pushes to the front. At a concert on the beach, latecomers think nothing of standing up to block the view of earlier arrivals sitting on the sand. When a movie is showing, people quite calmly answer calls on their cell phones and sometimes even argue with people who criticize them for their inconsiderate behavior.

The law is seen not as a binding code of conduct but merely as an expression of ideals and good intentions. The Brazilian constitution, for example, is one of the most generous and progressive in the world, guaranteeing citizens all sorts of rights that do not exist elsewhere. But many of those rights, promising benefits to the poor and other groups suffering from discrimination, exist only on paper. Despite the mandates, Congress has never appropriated the money to enforce those constitutional guarantees. It is as if the declaration of an intention to perform an act is the same thing as actually doing it, an attitude that spills over into many other areas of Brazilian life. Everyone knows the pledges will never be fulfilled, so no one takes them seriously, which is what allows them to be made in the first place.

For all the talk of equality before the law, notions of hierarchy, of different types and levels of treatment for people of different social and economic backgrounds, are actually built in to the legal code. Until recently, any person with a university degree who was accused of a crime was automatically kept out of cells holding "ordinary criminals" and placed in more comfortable surroundings. So when the wealthy young scion of a prominent business family in Rio was accused of getting drunk and beating a woman waiting in the pre-dawn hours for the bus that would take her to her job as a maid, he was able to invoke the "special imprisonment" provision. So was a newspaper editor in São Paulo who, in a notorious case that began in 2000 and dragged on for years, murdered his girlfriend in a fit of rage.

Those in charge—whether in business, politics, law enforcement, educa-tion, religion, or sports—tend to take their position to the extreme and pull rank in ways that have a distinct air of arrogance and reveal a tendency to re-gard any challenge, reservation, or expression of doubt as a form of *lèse-majesté*. One term often used as a substitute for "the Brazilian nation" is the phrase "the big Brazilian family," with the understanding that the president plays the role of the father. The traditional model of education is one that emphasizes a teacher instructing and students listening and memorizing, so that Brazilians coming to the United States for graduate studies are often star-tled when they first encounter the Socratic method. Athletes aren't supposed to question the decisions of coaches and team owners, and when they do, they are labeled troublemakers and benched or traded. Employees complain that their input is rarely sought, and that they are merely expected to follow orders.

And on those occasions when someone in a position of power is not treated with the deference he believes he is due, when he is treated as just an-other citizen and held to the same standards as everyone else, the results are equally predictable. One of the most common phrases heard in those cir-cumstances is "Você sabe com quem está falando?" which means, "Do you know who you are talking to?" If a big-wig finds his actions challenged—for example, if he wants to jump ahead of those patiently waiting in line for serv-ice at a bank or to buy tickets at the box office, or if he is stopped for a speed-ing violation—his response is likely to be "Você sabe com quem está falando?" Or if an off-duty police officer gets in a traffic altercation with another driver over a parking space or a dented fender, he too is likely to resort to "Você sabe com quem está falando?" He may even draw a gun just to underline the point. It happens all the time, and more often than not, no punishment is handed down.

Another common retort when those at the top of the pyramid feel they are being challenged or treated with insufficient respect is "Quem manda aqui sou eu," which means essentially, "I'm the one who's in charge here." When Secretary of State Alexander Haig made a similar assertion to the American press after a 1981 assassination attempt against Ronald Reagan, "I'm in control here," he was ridiculed and his stature was diminished. But in Brazil, such a statement, especially when pronounced in an indignant or affronted tone, is meant to restore an awareness of the ordained pecking order and to force the subordinate to retreat.

The very manner in which Portuguese is spoken in Brazil reinforces the concepts of hierarchy and stratification. In English, we have simply one form of referring to someone in the second person: The word "you" is employed in all situations, whether one is talking to the president or a garbage collector. Other languages, such as Spanish and Chinese, have two separate words, one familiar and one formal. Brazilian Portuguese, in contrast, has four different forms of address. There are two words for "you," both of which are relatively informal: *tu*, which is used in intimate settings, and *você*, which is used in ordinary settings with those one regards as one's equals. Then there are two formal modes of address: the extremely formal *o senhor*, used when one wants to show deference or respect, and an intermediate level that involves the extensive use of honorifics such as *doutor* or *seu*, or its feminine equivalent *dona*, attached to the first name. *Doutor* literally means doctor, but it has become a title of respect that can be attached to the name of anyone who has a college degree—or looks prosperous enough to have one. I certainly don't have a medical degree, and it has always made me uncomfortable when tradesmen and others who consider themselves my social inferiors address me as *doutor*, or as *chefe*, which means "boss." With the elevator operators in the building where I worked for eight years, for example, I would always use *você*, by which I meant to imply that I regarded them as equals. But they would always call me "Doutor Larry," and I could never get them to be less formal.

Public officials can be sticklers for such formalities, which serve to reinforce their sense of their own authority and remind petitioners of their inferiority. In 2003, I interviewed a junior lawyer in the public prosecutor's office in Rio about a rather silly obscenity case that she was handling and that I intended to write about. She was perhaps 20 years younger than me, but she upbraided me when I addressed her as *você*, insisting that I address her either as *a senhora* or "Doutora Joana." I found her demand for deference absurd and pretentious and continued to address her as *você* until she abruptly stopped the interview because of what she perceived as my lack of respect.

Even religion and the act of worship turn out to be domains in which hierarchies are imposed and Brazilians struggle against them, which brings us back to the *jeito*. Officially, Brazil is the largest Roman Catholic country in the world. In the last census, held in 2010, a strong majority, two thirds of all Brazilians responded that they were Catholic. In daily life, the presence of Catholic beliefs is widely felt: Walk into a bar in any city or town, and statues of saints, usually St. George and St. Barbara, are likely to occupy niches in the wall, right next to bottles of *cachaça*. On religious feast days, such as the Círio in Belém and Our Lady of Aparecida in São Paulo, millions of pilgrims flock to cathedrals to honor the Virgin Mary. Everyday speech is peppered with expressions of faith: A common response to a friendly farewell like "See you tomorrow" is "Se Deus quiser," or "If God so wills it."

But as in so many other areas of Brazilian life, those manifestations of what seem to be conventional religious belief mask a deeper and more complicated reality. According to the Brazilian Conference of Bishops, only one in five of those declaring themselves to be Catholic actually attends mass. Women far outnumber men among this group: In small towns in the interior, where the local church is usually on the main square across from the mayor's office and restaurants and bars, it's not unusual for men to sit in the square playing dominoes or checkers or to be in a pool hall or tavern while their children and womenfolk are at religious services. But even among the churchgoing, attendance is often limited to the big events in life: baptisms, weddings, and funerals.

And many of those who nominally profess Catholicism are also adepts of other folk-based religions, an example of the mixing and matching that is one of the principal characteristics of Brazilian culture. The most important of these are the Afro-Brazilian faiths known as *macumba, candomblé*, or *umbanda*, which are spiritual cousins of Haitian voodoo or Cuban Santería, sharing the same West African origins and a similar pantheon. Others describe themselves as "spiritists" and follow the teachings of the nineteenth-century French thinker Allan Kardec, who believed in reincarnation and thought it possible for the living to communicate with the dead, directly or through mediums.

Many of these believers, and they number in the millions, count in the census as Catholics and participate in many of the main Catholic rituals and rites. But when followers of *candomblé* or *macumba* attend mass or participate in religious festivals such as the Feast of the Annunciation, they do not really pay tribute to the Virgin Mary or seek the intercession of St. George or St. Barbara. Instead, they are praying to Afro-Brazilian deities such as Ogun, the god of iron and warfare, or Iemanjá, the goddess of the sea. This practice is a carryover from the era of slavery, when Africans, in order to avoid the wrath of their masters or the local priest, had to disguise their beliefs and apply a *jeito* by giving Christian names to their divinities. Outwardly they may appear to accept a Christian worldview, but inside they adhere to a parallel cosmology with a very different belief system.

To believers in the various Afro-Brazilian faiths—for they are not cults, but fully fledged religions with their own clergy and places of worship, known as *terreiros*—the most secure way to venture through the world, which is full of spirits both malevolent and benevolent, is under the guidance and protection of an *orixá*, or deity, such as Oxum, the goddess of rivers, beauty, and art, or Xangô, the god of thunder, lightning, power, and justice. Each deity has a different personality and skill set, and every person is believed to be born with a patron deity, whose identity a priest usually determines in a divination ceremony by throwing shells. But one is expected to submit to that deity, who manifests his or her presence by "mounting" the protégé, who then falls into a trance state. To placate one's personal deity, or thank him or her for protection or a favor granted, it is advisable to leave a gift, such as liquor, fruit, flowers, or cigars; throughout Brazil, "power spots" such as waterfalls and crossroads are often festooned with such offerings.

This tends to encourage fatalism: One cannot truly be the master of one's own fate, since rivals or enemies can work magic or witchcraft against you through their own *orixá* or even force you to act against your own will. This can lead to the kind of passivity that has long frustrated social campaigners working among the poor in Brazil and an unwillingness to take responsibility for one's own actions. The result is a recognition and reinforcement of the hierarchical nature of other areas of Brazilian life. Believers not only submit to their *orixá* but also rely on a priest or priestess (who is known to adepts as the "father [or mother] of the saint" in an implicit assertion of paternalistic authority) as an intermediary with the spirits.

With this deeply imbued respect for authority, the Afro-Brazilian faiths, ironically, in view of their origins as a sublimated form of rebellion, end up sharing a common attitude with the Roman Catholic Church, which, with its spiritual chain of command from the parish priest to the pope in Rome, is even more hierarchical. In both religions, the believer is more acted upon than a participant whose volition must be taken into account.

But as Brazil modernizes, that role may not be enough to satisfy believers. Census figures indicate that in recent years both Catholicism and *candomblé* have been losing ground to evangelical Protestantism, which offers its faithful a more direct and active role in the worship service through reading of the gospel, personal testimonies, the singing of hymns, and speaking in tongues. There is a minister, but the emphasis is on a direct dialogue with God, and to compete with what the evangelicals offer, a charismatic movement has in recent years emerged in Brazilian Catholicism.

Like any other institution whose rules are deemed too strict to be followed, the Roman Catholic Church is given nominal obeisance by the population but often ignored in practice. For example, cardinals and bishops regularly rail against what they regard as the rampant immorality on display during Carnival. The same goes for the sexually blunt language, promiscuity, and nudity that have become staples of prime-time television, especially in telenovelas. Even more dire imprecations against such evils regularly come from the Pentecostal ministers who view the Roman Catholic Church as being lax in morality. But year after year, ordinary Brazilians simply pay no heed and go about their business as they please, dancing their way through Carnival and tuning into the telenovelas as their daily accompaniment to dinner.

Abortion, however, may provide the best example of the *jeito* at work in the religious sphere. Officially, separation of church and state is in place in Brazil. Government officials, though, are usually wary of doing anything to offend the Church, and so Brazil's laws against abortion are among the strictest in the world. Unless a pregnancy can be shown by a doctor to put the life of the woman in danger or can be proven to be the result of a rape, an abortion is illegal. The Church's standards are even more restrictive: In a notorious case in 2009, after a nine-year-old girl, raped by her stepfather and pregnant with twins, was taken by her mother to a clinic in Recife to undergo an abortion, the local archbishop responded by excommunicating both the mother and the doctors who had performed the abortion.

The general population, however, simply ignores both Church and state and has devised a way around their prohibitions. All across Brazil, women who are pregnant and do not want to carry their fetus to term resort to what are known in Brazilian slang as "angel factories." These are clandestine clinics, the locations of which are widely known, where abortions can be obtained cheaply and with no questions asked. Though the illegality of this process makes it difficult to calculate how widespread it is, the ministry of health has estimated that as many as two million abortions are performed annually in Brazil. In 1991, a time when sexual matters were treated with more discretion than they are today, a World Bank report even estimated that the average lifetime abortion rate is over two per woman. Yet in 2007, a poll taken by the *Folha de São Paulo* newspaper found that two-thirds of those surveyed felt that Brazil's current abortion laws "should not be modified."

Until the late 1970s, divorce was also illegal in Brazil, and generations of unhappy couples who had married in religious ceremonies had to resort to a subterfuge recognized by the law but not by the Church—a classic example of using the *jeito* to resolve a seemingly intractable situation. Since the Church's opposition prevented couples from divorcing, they instead obtained a legal document giving them the status of *desquitado*, or separated. The marriage was not formally dissolved, but both parties were released from the obligation to live together as husband and wife. While that meant they could not formally remarry, being *desquitado* left them free to find new partners with whom they could live in a de facto situation as husband and wife. The children of such a union were treated as legitimate offspring, though in a strictly formal sense, and certainly in the eyes of the Church they had no right to that status. This often led to complicated inheritance struggles when wills were challenged.

Because of the dominance of Catholicism and *macumba*, and the tendency of many people to move back and forth between them, Calvinism and the doctrines and values associated with it have almost no place in Brazilian life. The world is not seen as irreparably fallen and inherently evil, but as a place to be enjoyed and used. This belief perhaps goes back to the notion of the original Portuguese explorers that Brazil was a terrestrial paradise. Because of the anti-Calvinist streak, profit and wealth are still seen in many quarters as fruit of the twin sins of usury and selfishness, not as virtues or a reward for service or sacrifice. But sin of any sort can be forgiven through confession, either to a priest or to a *pai de santo*, and repentance, through prayer or an offering to a deity. This leads to a continuous cycle of sin and absolution, sin and absolution, which is one of the things Chico Buarque is talking about in "Sin Doesn't Exist Below the Equator."

The notions of pardon and forgiveness are closely associated with a trait that Brazilians regard as one of the most positive features of their national character: tolerance. This concept applies not just to the foibles and idiosyncrasies of others, but even to their major failings and transgressions against the law. F. Scott Fitzgerald's statement that "there are no second acts in American lives" makes absolutely no sense to Brazilians. A pop star or soccer player leaving a night club who runs over a street vendor or a group of teenagers in his speeding sports car is quickly forgiven and may not even go to jail. Politicians disgraced in corruption scandals fade away for a time, then return as if nothing happened, winning election to office.

All of the cases just mentioned are real, not hypothetical. Another is the case of Fernando Collor de Mello. After his 1974 impeachment, Richard Nixon virtually disappeared from public life. Fernando Collor de Mello also resigned as president of Brazil, in 1992, after being impeached. But he was back by 2006, elected to Congress, where he joined several other senators and deputies who had been similarly dishonored. If there is one adage that applies to such situations, it is that of the writer and wit Ivan Lessa, who maintains that "every 15 years Brazilians forget everything that happened in the past 15 years."

Continued recourse to the *jeito*, and the inability to stamp it out, reflect the fact that even today Brazilian society remains essentially hierarchical in structure. It is true that Luiz Inácio Lula da Silva's rise to the presidency, which will be discussed in the chapter on politics, would seem to contradict such an assertion. But the story of his emergence, like other recent success stories cited as examples of social mobility, is less the rule than the exception. Everyone knows which groups are privileged and take precedence over which others: rich over poor, whites over blacks, men over women. Race is such a thorny, nebulous, and complicated subject that it will be dealt with separately in the next chapter. But class and gender offer more clear-cut examples of how hierarchy and stratification work on a daily basis, both at home and on the street.

Historically, Brazil has been a society with a very small elite at the top of the pyramid, enjoying great wealth and privilege, and a vast mass at the bottom, often living in terrible poverty. This arrangement was formalized for 350 years by slavery, but even after abolition was decreed, in 1888, the attitudes and behaviors typical of this system of organization persisted. Despite the appearance of a modern middle class in recent decades, Brazil still depends on a servant class. It can even be argued that the rise of the middle class has intensified this phenomenon, for as more people prosper, they want to enjoy the perquisites of their higher status, and one of the main symbols of having arrived is to hire domestic help. Almost no one in the American middle class has servants, whereas nearly everyone in the Brazilian middle class does.

This class stratification leads to any number of distortions in both values and behavior, in part because the middle class, rather than sympathizing with those below them, tends to emulate the conduct of the elite they aspire to join. In a household with servants, for instance, children rarely are required to pick up after themselves, much less make a bed or do laundry. Sometimes I've seen them loudly summon a servant all the way from the other end of the house rather than get up and get a glass of water for themselves from the next room. And when they become teenagers, they generally don't get summer or after-school jobs waiting tables, delivering pizzas, washing cars, or working behind the counter at a store, as their American counterparts are often required to do.

In part this trend persists because the Brazilian underclass has millions of adults eager to perform such tasks for wages that members of the *juventude dourada*, or "gilded youth," would regard as a pittance. But another factor is the disdain that affluent Brazilians have traditionally shown for manual labor and those who perform it. Never having done that kind of work themselves, they neither appreciate its worth nor recognize the skills and endurance it requires. They consider such work inherently demeaning and thus beneath their dignity, rather than a source of important life lessons about the value of labor. All of these attitudes serve, of course, to reinforce the master–servant distinction that dates back to slavery and the colonial era.

Indeed, the members of the servant class are often treated as disposable or less than human—hence they are often called "João Ninguem," or "John Nobody." In the late 1970s, while living in a middle-class neighborhood in Rio de Janeiro, I once found myself standing in line in a butcher shop, waiting with my wife to buy meat. A woman in line ahead of us, whose imperious bearing indicated clearly that she was what Brazilians call a "madame," or person of means and airs, told the butcher she wanted two pounds of *picanha*, a prime and deliciously tender cut of beef, and one pound of *carne de empregada*, or "maid's meat." That she was there at all was odd; it must have been the maid's day off. So I was puzzled at first, but as I watched the transaction unfold, it was clear that she was referring to a very inferior cut, just a step above the scraps that a person of her station might feed a dog.

Inevitably, these class prejudices creep into public policy. Until recently, investment in public education, health clinics, and low-cost housing lagged in comparison to projects that personally benefited the powerful. Those in power could not conceive of any advantage in bettering public schools because their own children were enrolled in private schools. Similarly, they saw little point in building roads or hospitals that they and their friends would never use. The road to the weekend house in the mountains above Rio that belongs to cousins of my wife, for example, is paved only as far as the mansion of a former governor; after that, it is a rutted dirt track because he was not going to use it. And when such projects were constructed, they were regarded not as something due the poor as citizens of the republic, equal in the eyes of God and the law, but as favors expected to be repaid.

For women, the situation is more ambiguous. In formal legal terms, Brazilian men and women are equal, or at least that is what the constitution says. The realities of daily life are quite different, however. Though the position of women has improved enormously over the last generation, men continue to dominate every sphere of society that matters. Women are entering the marketplace in large numbers as workers, but they earn far less than men and they also make up a smaller part of the work force in comparison to their sisters in the industrialized world. This means that the majority of adult Brazilian women are still economically dependent on a male breadwinner—either a husband to whom they are legally married, with the imprimatur of church and state, or a partner with whom they are informally *amigado*, the word used for a common-law marriage.

Gender roles in Brazil remain more clearly defined than in the United States or Europe, whether on the street, in the household, or in the bedroom. When describing sexual intercourse, a man is said to "*comer*" a woman, meaning that he "eats" or consumes her; a woman, in contrast, is said to "*dar*," which means to give or serve. These idioms assume that the man is active and the woman passive: He dominates and she submits; he directs and she follows.

Actual attitudes about sex and sexuality, though, are often a jumble. On the one hand, Brazil has a reputation globally as a sensuous and sexually permissive place. That is why some rich Europeans, Americans, and Arabs go there on vacation: in hopes of partaking of what they believe, mistakenly, to be a libertine lifestyle. They see the images of "exotic" dark-skinned women in skimpy, dental-floss bathing suits on the beach at Ipanema or shimmying almost nude at Carnival, hear about the striptease clubs in Copacabana, and read the online advertisements for sex tours. From that scant evidence, they mistakenly conclude that throughout all of Brazil there must be that kind of licentiousness writ large.

Brazilians, of course, know better. It is true that they cultivate an image of sensuality, have made it part of their cultural identity, and seem even to take a certain perverse pride when one of their own seduces a celebrity, thereby enhancing the country's reputation for sexiness. This goes back to Carmen Miranda's days in Hollywood and continues unabated today. The model Luciana Gimenez is a celebrity largely because she seduced Mick Jagger and gave him a Brazilian son, while Jesus Pinto da Luz went from being an anonymous underwear model to a boldface name when he snagged Madonna on the rebound from her failed marriage to Guy Ritchie.

All of this celebrity intrigue is seen as evidence of Brazil's irresistible erotic power and confirmation of the physical beauty of the Brazilian people. Yet a counterpoint is provided by the concept known as *pudor*, which combines the notions of propriety, modesty, decency, and shame and is common throughout Latin America. This leads to a strain of *moralismo*, the word that Brazilians use to describe a tendency toward excessive attention to morality and the appearance of being virtuous that has great influence over romantic and sexual life in Brazil.

Because of *pudor*, certain activities and types of behavior are meant to be kept out of sight. Traditionally, the code of machismo allows Brazilian men to have greater sexual freedom than women. In fact, to be in command is seen as a basic attribute of masculinity, whereas a woman who violates the code of modesty by sleeping around—or even one who takes the initiative in pursuing a man, dresses in a gaudy fashion, or frequents bars—is likely to be classified as a slut. A word often used in Portuguese for this type of woman is *piranha*, just like the flesh-eating fish.

But *pudor* mandates that even a *mulherengo*, or lady-killer, who is married needs to exercise a modicum of discretion and should flaunt his conquests only among close friends and not in public. If he has a mistress, it is better for all concerned if he sets her up with a small business of her own and an apartment where he can visit her discreetly, rather than parade around in public and cause a scandal. This is especially true in the more conservative interior.

The dominance of the male is reinforced, or perhaps it would be more apt to say exemplified, by a certain penchant for anal sex. This is a practice that Brazilians often try to hide from outsiders or deny, since many of them consider it shameful and embarrassing. But both research and popular anecdotes indicate that such a proclivity does exist. If it can be said that American men are fixated on breasts, for Brazilian men, judging by jokes, folklore, and the nude photo essays in men's magazines, the body part of preference is the buttocks, or *bunda* in Portuguese. In 2006, I wrote an article about a São Paulo call girl named Bruna the Little Surfer Girl, who had become famous for a blog about her sex life that she then turned into a best-selling book. She told me that all of her Brazilian clients wanted to engage in anal sex, but none of her foreign customers did.

According to one survey conducted by the Institute of Market Research in the late 1990s, a majority of Brazilians consider anal sex to be "abnormal." Nevertheless, a majority of those surveyed in Rio de Janeiro and a near majority elsewhere reported engaging in anal intercourse at least "occasionally." Men between the ages of 30 and 45 were three times more likely than women to request anal sex; among married couples, it was generally the male who wanted anal sex and the female who accepted her partner's solicitation or demand.

This chapter began with a mention of Chico Buarque's song "Sin Doesn't Exist Below the Equator," the most popular version of which is probably the one recorded by Ney Matogrosso, the most flamboyantly gay figure in Brazilian pop music. That hardly seems coincidental; Brazilian ways of thinking about homosexuality are also ambiguous, and the song's title is as relevant to those often contradictory attitudes as it is to any other aspect of sin and sexuality.

Strictly speaking, the code of machismo frowns upon homosexuality and indeed any manifestation of effeminate behavior. As a gay friend of mine from São Paulo once told me, he was brought up to believe that the appropriate behavior for males was to "talk tough, spit, and scratch your balls." But it has also been argued that Brazilians have a built-in tolerance for homosexuality because of Carnival, which not only countenances cross-dressing and experimenting with sexual roles but actively encourages them. Behind the anonymity of the mask, anything goes, and within that framework, homosexuals have traditionally flourished and felt free to engage in the kind of transgressive dress and behavior that would be censured in another setting.

Certainly Brazilian homosexuals have more options and occupy more public space than their counterparts in other countries in Latin America. In large cities such as Rio and São Paulo, gay couples, male or female, can live openly and frequent their own clubs and bars. Television soap operas now feature gay couples of both sexes who sometimes are allowed to kiss on screen. Even in some smaller cities in the interior the situation is similar: The annual Miss Gay Brazil beauty pageant for drag queens is held in Juiz de Fora, an industrial center of some five hundred thousand people in Minas Gerais, with the results broadcast nationally on television.

Nationally, though, a stigma is still attached to homosexuality. In many parts of the more conservative interior, it is still dangerous for gays to express affection or even meet in public, and newspapers regularly report cases of flamboyant homosexuals who are beaten up or even killed for violating local mores. In addition, Brazilian Portuguese continues to be rich in pejorative terms for homosexuals, the most common of which are *veado*, or "deer," for men and *sapatão*, or "big shoe," for lesbians. Men from the city of Pelotas in the far south of Brazil are constantly the target of jokes and derisive comments thanks to a folk belief, dating back to the nineteenth century, that all males there are homosexuals. Before becoming president, as the leader of a left-wing party that prides itself on being socially progressive and had sponsored gay rights legislation, Lula even described Pelotas as "a factory that manufactures queers." The same superstition applies to women from the northern state of Paraíba.

In such a climate, many homosexuals prefer to remain in the closet: There is, for instance, a whole contingent of female singers who everyone knows to be lesbians but who prefer not to acknowledge their sexuality. The same goes for certain soccer players, whose careers in what is considered an extremely macho enclave would be ruined if they announced their homosexuality.

Partly for those reasons, it has always been difficult for academic and government researchers to determine how widespread homosexuality is in Brazil. But the issue is even more complicated because definitions of what constitutes homosexuality are often more fluid than in the Anglo-Saxon world. This is especially so among men: In the traditional, popular imagination, if two men are engaged in a sex act, only the passive or penetrated partner is regarded as a homosexual, a *veado* or *bicha*, which is probably the most pejorative term in the Brazilian vocabulary used to refer to gay men, corresponding to "fag" or "queer." The active participant can even make a claim to macho status because he has subjugated another male and reduced him to the status of a woman.

In a similar fashion, a man who has sex with a *travesti*, one of the transvestites who make up much of the population of prostitutes seen on the streets of Brazilian cities, more often than not is also not really regarded as homosexual. *Travestis* may have male genitalia, but they dress, act, and regard themselves as women, and as such they occupy a peculiar twilight zone between the two genders; some even take female hormones to make themselves appear more female. In recent years, *travestis* have even begun exporting themselves to Europe, where the authorities are not sure what to make of them. At home, some have become celebrities: Roberta Close, born in 1964, even posed for the Brazilian edition of *Playboy* magazine, modeled clothes, hosted a late-night talk show, and made films. She underwent a sex-reassignment operation in 1989, but, in a case that went all the way to the Brazilian Supreme Court, was prevented until 2005 from modifying her government documents to reflect the change of sex.

The increased visibility of sexual minorities, their growing unwillingness to operate in the shadows as custom demands or to have their concerns swept under the rug, may in part be a reflection of greater contact between Brazil and the outside world. The same can be said of other groups that have traditionally been marginalized and forced to rely on the *jeito*, such as women or blacks, whose situation will be addressed in the next chapter. They see that their counterparts in foreign countries make more progress through demands and campaigns that are direct, or even confrontational, than by relying on oblique stratagems like the *jeito*. And so they start to rethink their tactics and to behave in ways that may not seem typically Brazilian, such as resorting to court cases rather than informal, personalized negotiations and to publicity instead of discretion.

In the realms of civics and politics, there are some similar signs of change, especially among computer-savvy young people who have a greater acquaintance with life abroad thanks to their use of the Internet. They seem less willing to accept the corruption and hierarchy associated with the *jeito* as something immutable. And with a band of crusading young prosecutors in the lead, they have been especially vocal in protesting and prosecuting recent government scandals involving corruption and abuse of privilege. Investigations of many of those cases have gone nowhere, but the mere existence of groups unwilling to accept or submit to the "Quem manda aqui sou eu" syndrome is in itself notable.

Brazil's increased interaction with the outside world clearly has had another result, which is that Brazilians are discovering, to their confusion, that the *jeito*, Gerson's law, and the code of the *malandro* don't really work very well outside Brazil's borders. As regards the *jeito*, the world of diplomacy, where Brazilians have distinguished themselves, may be a notable exception. But Brazilian companies investing abroad, like the growing number of Brazilian tourists traveling overseas and students on exchange programs, are often startled to find that there is very little give in rules, laws, and regulations, especially in places like Japan and the Anglo-Saxon world, and that it is impossible to dribble around some problems. That too ends up requiring a reconsideration of values and behaviors, which has the potential to spill over into the internal national sphere.

Somewhere down the line, then, in some unspecified future, Brazilian society may become less dependent on the *jeito*. But for now, snapshots of daily life tell us that Brazilian society, whether in the bedroom or the boardroom, in the household or the halls of Congress, has a deep dislike for hard and fast categories. Always there must be some wiggle room, and if that does not exist, it will surely be created. Those in control, at the pinnacle of power, may demand deference and obedience, but those beneath them always will invent a way to undermine that authority, evade whatever laws or rules they do not like, or mock their values. In other words, there is always a *jeito* that can be applied, so long as one knows how to find and implement it. Or as a Brazilian saying puts it, "The sun rises for everyone, but only the crafty get to stand in the shade."

THREE

THE MYTH OF
A RACIAL PARADISE

IN 1996, A BLACK teenager named Luciano Soares Ribeiro was riding his bicycle in the southern city of Porto Alegre when he was struck by a BMW whose driver was white. Instead of coming to the young man's aid, the motorist, Rogério Ferreira Pansera, told witnesses that he had deliberately run over "a black guy on a stolen bicycle" and left the scene. When Luciano's mother arrived at the hospital four hours later, her son still had not been treated because, as a neurologist later told her, the medical staff "suspected he was a homeless person and didn't know who would pay the bill." Two days later, the young man died of cranial trauma—with the bicycle's receipt, which his parents insisted he always carry with him in case police ever accused of stealing it, still in his pocket.

Brazilians like to think of their country as a "racial democracy," and they have done a remarkable job of selling that idea to the rest of the world. Over the years, delegations from the United States, South Africa, Malaysia, and other nations with long histories of racial or ethnic tensions have gone to Brazil hoping to learn the secret of its success and to be able to transfer that formula to their own countries. An American sociologist who lived and worked in Brazil for many years even wrote a textbook, used for decades in universities around the world, concluding that racism did not exist in Brazil. The result is that Brazil is seen almost universally as a symbol of tolerance and cordiality.

But the reality of race in Brazil is far more complex and ambiguous than it appears to the casual visitor smitten by the beauty of the country and the warmth of its people, or even to the average white Brazilian who may go through life rarely, if ever, thinking about the subject. Rather than being a source of pride, race has, in reality, become Brazil's secret, hidden shame.

More than half of Brazil's nearly 200 million people claim African descent on census forms. Brazil's black population is thus not just the largest outside Africa but also bigger than that of any African country except Nigeria. Yet "Afro-descendants," the official term used in Brazil to describe people who are black or of mixed race, are excluded from important aspects of national life, confront discrimination in the details of their daily existence, and fall into the bottom group of most important social indicators. They are the biggest group, for example, among residents of *favelas*, the crime-ridden squatter slums common in the country's large cities. Brazilians with black skin are far more likely to be killed by police than their white countrymen, earn less money, have a shorter life expectancy, and have less educational opportunities than whites.

When pressed, Brazilians will acknowledge these disparities and lament them. But they are also likely to attribute such problems to class, habitually blamed for nearly all of the inequalities that afflict Brazilian society, rather than race. There is undoubtedly some foundation to this argument: Brazil has traditionally had one of the most skewed and inequitable distributions of income and wealth in the world. The gulf between the small, overwhelmingly white elite at the top of the economic pyramid and the poor mass at the bottom is enormous. Since the majority of Brazil's population is of African descent, it is only natural, or so the argument goes, that black Brazilians should constitute the bulk of the country's poor, who are victims of class prejudice no matter what their color.

But race and class are inextricably intertwined in Brazil, with the focus on class often being used as a smokescreen to divert attention and criticism from the deeper underlying problems of race and racism. As we shall soon see, even a wealthy, well-educated black Brazilian can be subjected to forms of discrimination that poor whites are not, and even the poorest of whites enjoy some privileges that black Brazilians are denied, no matter how well off they may be.

That does not mean that examples of racial tolerance and amity do not abound in daily life in Brazil, in ways that until recently would have been frowned upon, or at least considered unusual, in the United States. Traditionally, Brazilians have married across racial lines with considerable frequency, especially the lower down the social ladder one goes. According to an analysis of Brazil's 2000 census, 30 percent of households consist of couples who have married outside what in the United States would be considered their own race. Perhaps this is because poor whites and poor blacks often live in close proximity to each other, which is not the case among the wealthy.

Many times Brazilians also socialize in groups whose composition cuts across racial lines. This is true not only at Carnival, when barriers of all sorts are meant to fall, but also in the workplace and afterward, during leisure hours. On a Friday night in Rio or São Paulo, it is common to see blacks and whites who are colleagues on the job beginning their weekend by sitting around a table at a sidewalk café, drinking beer or *cachaça* together and swapping jokes and stories.

Brazilians, including those who are white, also tend to show less ambivalence than Americans do about acknowledging the African roots of their country's identity and popular culture, as expressed through such things as Carnival, music, and cuisine. To take just one example, Americans may debate whether jazz is high art or low art, or whether hip-hop is art at all, and argue whether the contributions of whites are more important than those of blacks in the formation of popular music. Brazil, in contrast, unequivocally exalts such cultural expressions as African in origin and embraces them wholeheartedly as a manifestation of the collective cultural genius of Afro-Brazilians. At Carnival, itself a mixture of African and medieval European customs and practices, it is common to see white Brazilians singing sambas that praise the African character of their country.

Other racial and ethnic groups are also part of Brazil's multicultural stew, and they too have sometimes been victims of stereotypes and prejudice. The image of the large and growing Asian population, predominantly Japanese, is that of academic overachievers who don't have a sense of rhythm, so that at Carnival each year there are inevitably condescending stories in the news about some "japonga," the slightly derogatory slang term for Brazilians of Japanese descent, trying to sing or dance samba. President Luiz Inácio Lula da Silva has been known to tell anti-Semitic jokes, and the World Social

Forum his party sponsors each year openly displays anti-Semitic literature. Indigenous peoples are routinely mocked for their speech, dress, and culture; are sometimes referred to pejoratively as "burges," a term that emerged in medieval Portugal to refer to any savage, primitive, pagan or uncouth group; and have been known to be targeted for hate crimes. In 1997, for instance, a leader of the Pataxó Hã-Hã-Hãe people, in Brasília to try to get government help to evict ranchers who had illegally occupied tribal lands, was attacked on the street by five middle-class youths who set him ablaze and allowed him to burn to death.

But these are all subsidiary conflicts. Brazil's Indian population is only 600,000, divided among dozens of tribal groups, and for both of those reasons, the country has never developed an indigenous movement that compares to those in Bolivia, Ecuador, or Peru, where the indigenous populations are much larger and more organized. Brazil's Jewish community is tiny, only some 150,000 people, and deliberately keeps a low profile. The much larger Japanese community is as much the object of admiration as of envy because of its educational and economic accomplishments, and recent Chinese and Korean immigrants, though associated in the public mind with the flourishing contraband trade, also benefit from that aura of success. So the racial question in Brazil ends up being primarily about blacks and whites and the space between them.

Brazilian attitudes about race are both complicated and contradictory. On the one hand, the national ideal is one of miscegenation, a concept so dreaded in the old segregationist American South that laws were passed to prevent it from occurring. In Brazil, even those who seem unlikely to have African blood sometimes claim it so as to seem more authentically Brazilian and less isolated from the social mainstream. As an ultimately successful presidential candidate in the 1990s, Fernando Henrique Cardoso, the son of a general and an intellectual regarded as part of the white elite, claimed to have "a foot in the kitchen," a slang term often used to denote having some unacknowledged black ancestry.

But that same phrase also reveals something about the nature of racial hierarchies in Brazil. So does another saying, this one much blunter, that Brazilian men sometimes employ to describe their ideal relationship with women: "a white one to marry, a black one to cook, and a *mulata* to screw." The "place" of black Brazilians, if we interpret the subtext common to both expressions, is not in the dining room or boardroom or classroom, but in the kitchen, garage, field, factory, or anywhere else where social inferiors are obliged to live or work.

Hedio Silva, a prominent lawyer from São Paulo who in 2005 became the first black to be appointed secretary of justice in Brazil's most populous state, once told me a story that illustrates how difficult it is for black professionals in Brazil to shed that burden. During his tenure, he was invited, along with the governor of São Paulo and several other high-ranking state officials, to attend the swearing-in of a new supreme court justice in Brasília. Arriving at the ceremony, the São Paulo group was directed to a seating area reserved for guests of honor. All of Silva's white colleagues entered without difficulty, but he was stopped and told: "This entrance is for authorities only, not for their bodyguards." When he tried to explain who he was, he was met with disbelief, and one of his colleagues had to vouch for him before he was allowed to rejoin the group.

Even though some of the security officials who tried to bar Silva were themselves black, he thought their behavior demonstrated racism. I agreed, having heard other black professionals tell similar stories, such as being confused with a waiter or parking attendant at public receptions or a bellhop or limousine driver at a luxury hotel. The notion of a black person in a position of authority is hard for many Brazilians to fathom and, especially for some whites, even more difficult to accept. It can also expose black Brazilians to subtle discrimination or blatant bigotry when they hold posts that are considered unusual for a member of their race. The case of José de Andrade, a soccer referee in São Paulo who became the center of a court case that I wrote about in 2006, offers an even more clear-cut example.

While working a police league match, de Andrade made a controversial call. A player on one of the teams, a retired police colonel, vented his unhappiness with the decision by calling de Andrade "a monkey" whose skin was "the color of shit." Citing Brazil's national antidiscrimination statute, which promises that "crimes of prejudice of race or color will be punished," de Andrade then filed a criminal complaint for defamation, slander, and "incitement to racism." But the police officers' athletic club that employed de Andrade began pressuring him to drop his suit or accept a cash settlement out of court. When he would not, police patrols began to harass him on the street, and the athletic club cut back his work hours and reduced his responsibilities.

At that point, de Andrade agreed to a meeting with the colonel who had insulted him, hoping the officer would show some contrition. Instead, de Andrade told me when I interviewed him later, his antagonist talked about how he had been the commander of the local equivalent of the SWAT team, which de Andrade took as a not-so-veiled threat. Only when de Andrade's suit was widely publicized in the press, bringing the club negative publicity, did officials there restore his job status. As for the criminal complaint, it continues to wind its way through the courts.

"All I wanted was an apology," de Andrade told me. "I always addressed him by his rank, always treated him respectfully, and he should do the same to me. Now I hope the entire black race will have the courage to denounce prejudice so that our children will not have to accept these offenses."

In 1980, I interviewed Brazil's most popular writer, the novelist Jorge Amado, at his home in Salvador da Bahia. One of the subjects we discussed at length was race. Salvador is Brazil's most African city, sometimes called "the Black Rome" because of the numerous Afro-Brazilian religious groups that have their main sanctuaries there. Amado, though not considered black himself, had spent most of his life in the city and had absorbed and adopted its African values. Raised a Roman Catholic, he gravitated to Communism as a young man. But eventually he became an *obá*, or honorary high priest, in the cult of Xangô, the deity of lightning and justice in the syncretic Afro-Brazilian faith *candomblé*, and was a frequent visitor to the temple of Ilê Axé Opó Afonjá, the spiritual home of a succession of powerful *candomblé* priestesses.

Amado's novels are models of racial tolerance, as was his life. One theme that appears in his work with some frequency is that of the European or Arab immigrant who arrives in Brazil with preconceptions and prejudices that he sheds as he is exposed to and absorbs the country's humane and open-minded embrace. Of course, Amado, who died in 2001 at the age of 88, sometimes included characters who display racial or class prejudice or use demeaning language to describe their darker-skinned neighbors. But they are the exception rather than the rule and usually end up recognizing the error of their ways.

"The United States has millions of people who are not racists, but it is a racist country," Amado told me as we sat on the patio of his beach house, shaded by palms, with the waves crashing a few yards away. "Brazil has millions of people who are racists, but it is not a racist country."

I have always been a great admirer of Jorge Amado's work, and I respected him as a person. But in this case, I think his analysis is fundamentally flawed. There is an abundance of data, drawn from both history and today's headlines, to suggest that both countries suffer from the same affliction of racism. What is different is the way that racism manifests itself in each country and the ways in which the two societies have chosen to confront that problem.

Thanks to the education they receive, the books they read, and the movies they see, most Americans have been forced to acknowledge that slavery and racism are part of their country's history and their heritage as a people. In case they do not, Brazilians are always quick to remind them of it any time a conversation turns to a comparison of the racial situation in the two countries. Even in the lifetime of many Americans, segregation by race was rigidly enforced by law in the South, and discrimination in housing and education were widespread and accepted in cities all over the country, making necessary a battery of laws to combat such practices.

Racism in Brazil, in contrast, was never institutionalized. There were never any laws that formally defined a black person as anyone with one-sixteenth African blood or established separate and inferior schools, drinking fountains, toilets, and waiting rooms for him or prohibited him from marrying across racial lines. Brazil's reality is such that there has never been a need to formalize such exclusions because they are part of an unwritten social code that Brazilians of all colors understood and have traditionally lived by.

Nor is race the simple matter of black and white that it is in the United States. Because of its history, Brazil also has a large intermediate category that may actually be the country's largest demographic group and whose existence complicates racial classifications and makes race more of a continuum than a sharp divide. I am referring here, of course, to mulattos. In Portuguese, such people are also referred to as *pardos*, or dozens of other terms, and their large numbers and varied shades of skin color make it difficult to establish where "white" ends and "black" begins.

As a result, in place of the simple black and white classification that has historically prevailed in the United States, Brazil has dozens of gradations. I once tried to do a tally and came up with a list of more than sixty different terms to designate shades of skin color, from *preto* for someone with African features and very dark skin to *brancarão* for a person with very light café au lait skin. But Brazilian friends who are sociologists or anthropologists have told me that a complete index would have to include at least three hundred terms.

Obviously, someone like Pelé or the singer Milton Nascimento would be classified in both the United States and Brazil as black. In Portuguese, various words apply and are used in daily speech, *negro* and *preto* being the most common and most acceptable. There is also the word *crioulo*, which has more than a dozen definitions in Aurélio Buarque de Holanda's *Dictionary of the Portuguese Language*, the Brazilian counterpart to Webster's dictionary, one of them being "any slave born in the house of his master." Whether for that reason or others, the word *crioulo*, once neutral, is now regarded by many black Brazilians as pejorative and has almost become the equivalent of "nigger."

But to a Brazilian, lighter-skinned people may not necessarily register as black even if they are regarded as such in the United States on both sides of our color line. When I first moved to Brazil, in the 1970s, a cousin of my wife startled me with this simple question, which forced me to think about racial categorization in the two countries: "Larry, why is Muhammad Ali called a leader of the Black Power movement when he is not even black, but is a mulatto?" Similarly, a bit later, when the singer Donna Summer, queen of disco music, became popular in Brazil, she was always referred to as a *mulata*, not black.

Late in 2008, I was in Brazil to promote a book I had just written about the country. Barack Obama had been elected president of the United States just ten days before my arrival, so naturally there was great curiosity and excitement about him in Brazil. I was asked questions about Obama at every interview I did, whether for print, television, or radio, but on several occasions, interviewers stopped me, apparently puzzled, when I referred to him as America's first black president. "But he's not black," they would object. "He is a mulatto." To which I always offered the same reply: "Both by American standards and Obama's own definition of who he is, he is black. The United States has moved past the stage in which we sought to impose our racial categories on you, so you shouldn't try to impose yours on us. These are two different ways of looking at race, and one is as valid as the other."

As this episode suggests, at least part of the debate about race and racism is cultural and reflects the difference between Brazilian norms and those that prevail in North America and parts of Europe. Racial views that in the United States would ruin a career or drive a person from public life continue to flourish in Brazil, without negative consequences for those who express them. In 2006, when I was writing just before the World Cup about Brazil's reputation as a "soccer factory" and its incredible capacity to keep churning out the world's best players, I asked commentators, players, coaches, and team executives to explain the phenomenon. Most of Brazil's best players are black or mulatto, and the most common response I heard was that since people with African blood are inherently "more athletic" than whites and Brazil has such a large black population to draw from, it is only natural that the country should dominate the sport.

Ask for an explanation of Brazil's enormous musicality and the ability of its people to create new musical genres and dance styles, as I have, and you get a similar response: blacks innately have a "better sense of rhythm," which allows Brazil to excel at music and dance. Indeed, sports and entertainment may be the only two areas of Brazilian life in which a black person's success is considered normal and goes unquestioned. In almost any other endeavor, it is likely to be viewed as an oddity or aberration.

To cite another example of different cultural standards: Brazilian soccer players are usually given one-word nicknames that appear on their uniforms, and because the star striker Edinaldo Batista Libâno is extremely dark-skinned, the name he was given is "Grafite," or "Graphite," as in pencil lead. Though that nickname makes many foreigners uncomfortable, Brazilians insist it is neither offensive nor racist, just amusingly tongue-in-cheek, and make fun of what they see as excessive political correctness. But I can't think of a countervailing example of a white player with a name that references his skin color in such a blunt way, such as "Branquinho" or "Whitey."

Even some of the regional stereotypes that Brazilians routinely express are, in all likelihood, based on race. In the popular mind, people from Bahia are considered to be slow to act, lazy, disorganized, and overly fond of partying. There is even a slang term, *baianada*, derived from the name of the state, which is applied to any task that is badly done, a grossly stupid mistake, or an abrupt and seemingly inexplicable maneuver in traffic. Since Bahia is also the state whose population contains the highest percentage of blacks, it seems to me that what we have here is a thinly veiled or barely disguised manifestation of racial prejudice directed toward blacks.

In an interview in the 1970s, the pop singer and composer Milton Nascimento told me a story about an homage that had recently been organized in his honor in a small town in his home state of Minas Gerais. During the ceremony, the local mayor introduced him as "a black man with a white heart," as if that were some kind of praise for which Nascimento should be grateful. Here you have a perfect example of the contradictions of race in Brazil. As a small child, Milton Nascimento had been adopted by a white family, a phenomenon that has always been common in Brazil but hardly existed at all in the United States until recently. But in public, he had to endure the thoughtlessly racist declarations of someone who thought his white skin gave him some sort of moral superiority.

As in the United States, racial discrimination and racism in Brazil are legacies of slavery. But the two countries experienced slavery in demonstrably different ways, so the impact is also fundamentally different.

In some respects, the heritage of slavery is even more deeply embedded in Brazil than it is in countries such as the United States or South Africa, where apartheid, as a formal, law-based system, lasted for less than a half century. The Portuguese crown first authorized the African slave trade in 1559 in an attempt to regulate and profit from a traffic that was already in place. So by 1619, when the first African slaves arrived in the United States—Angolans aboard a Portuguese ship, perhaps originally bound for Brazil, that was captured by Dutch pirates and diverted northward—slavery had already existed in Brazil for more than 60 years. Slavery also endured longer in Brazil than in the United States, being outlawed by imperial decree only in 1888, a full 25 years after President Lincoln issued the Emancipation Proclamation.

In addition, slavery in Brazil was not confined to a single region, as was the case in the United States. Though most common and crucial in the sugar-growing areas of the northeast, it was a truly national phenomenon, stretching from the Argentine border in the south to the Amazon in the north. As a result, slavery was all-encompassing: There was no equivalent to the Underground Railroad and thus no legally recognized safe haven to which slaves could flee. Many more slaves were freed in Brazil than in the United States, but there was little place in Brazilian life for blacks who wanted to live by African values and traditions, and little for them to aspire to. The only realistic alternative in colonial times was to escape Brazilian society altogether by taking to the unexplored hinterlands and forming a *quilombo*. That was the name given to settlements organized on African tribal principles, the most famous of which was Zumbi dos Palmares.

If Brazil managed to avoid the tragedy of a Civil War with the gradualist approach it adopted once it became independent, it also missed a Reconstruction or any other official effort to help newly freed slaves become economically self-sufficient or guarantee their rights, as the Fourteenth Amendment did in the United States. Brazil did have an abolitionist movement, which grew stronger as the nineteenth century wore on, but the broader society was reluctant to address the heritage of slavery once it had ended. Some official records of slavery were even burned after abolition so as to "remove this dark stain" from the national consciousness.

The most profound difference between the two countries, however, is probably a simple matter of numbers. In the United States, blacks were always a minority, and steps were taken to keep things that way. In colonial Brazil, blacks came close to being a majority of the population nationwide, and in some areas, African slaves actually outnumbered the number of people who were free. No one knows exactly how many Africans were transported to the New World as slaves, but the most common estimates are in the range of nine million to eleven million, with Brazil importing between 35 and 40 percent of that total, far more than the United States. So by the time slavery was finally abolished, blacks and people of mixed race constituted a majority of Brazil's population.

For that reason, even Brazil's embrace of miscegenation needs to be seen through a prism of skepticism. In the United States, segregationists inveighed against "race-mixing" because they feared it would degrade the white race, which they saw as superior. In Brazil, members of the white elite endorsed miscegenation because they saw it as a means of "whitening" the predominantly black population they regarded as inferior. The abolition of slavery coincided with a massive wave of subsidized immigration, mostly from Europe but also from Japan and the Middle East, not only because the elite needed new sources of cheap labor, but also because they saw immigration as a tool to dilute the presence and influence of blacks in their own society. In fact, two years after abolition, Brazil prohibited black immigration, a ban that was strengthened in the 1920s and again in the 1930s as part of the campaign to give Brazil an "injection of civilization" and "purify the race."

A famous painting from 1895 called *The Redemption of Cain*, portrayed the way Brazilians hoped the process would work. It shows a family of four gathered in front of their simple home. The husband, sitting in the doorway, is white, with features that are clearly European. His wife, in a chair, is a *mulata* dressed in formal European fashion, holding their child, whose skin color is closer to that of his father than of his mother, in her lap. The child's maternal grandmother, dark-skinned and with African features, stands off to the side with her arms raised in a gesture of thanks, as if grateful that her grandchild is white, not black.

That policy of "whitening" remained in place until the fall of the Vargas dictatorship, in 1945, and was expressed in legislation whose stated purpose was to "develop in the ethnic composition of the population the more desirable characteristics of European ancestry." From abolition onward, government funding was directed not so much toward helping freed slaves find livelihoods or gain an education as toward helping the newcomers from abroad settle and find a place in Brazilian society. As a result, many black Brazilians emerging from slavery lacked any means to advance socially or economically. They either remained in the countryside, with its limited opportunities, or gravitated to the *favelas* that were just taking shape on the outskirts of the capital, Rio de Janeiro, and other large cities.

If any one person is responsible for making official the notion of Brazil as a "racial democracy" and providing the intellectual doctrine required to buttress that concept, it would be the scholar Gilberto Freyre. In his most important work, *Masters and Slaves*, published in 1933, he seems at times to be almost an apologist for slavery. He argued that slavery in Brazil was not as morally noxious an institution as it was elsewhere and was not even as harmful to the country's character as previous scholars had thought. Instead, he "characterized slavery in Brazil as composed of good masters and submissive slaves," in the words of a critic, the sociologist Clóvis Moura in his 1988 work *Sociologia do Negro Brasileiro*. If anything was to blame for the moral depravity of the system, Freyre argued, it was "the docility of the slave woman, opening her legs to the first desire of the young master. Desire, not an order."

But at the same time, Freyre acknowledged the central role of blacks in the construction of Brazil's identity and praised miscegenation for enriching the country's culture. "Every Brazilian, even those who are snow-white with blond hair, carries in his soul, if not in body and soul, the shadow, or at least a tinge, of the Indian and/or the black," he wrote. The result, he predicted, would inevitably be a unified, hybrid race in which opportunity for advancement would be available to all. In addition, since social classes were based on economic and not racial differences, it was poverty, rather than prejudice, that created social inequality.

It would be easy to dismiss Freyre's doctrine as a historical relic were it not for the fact that it is constantly being updated and repackaged. As a consequence, its pernicious influence continues to dominate the discussion of race in Brazil today. The most recent reworking took the form of a book called *We Are Not Racists*, a best-seller that was first published in 2006 and continues to be cited in debates about race. In contrast to "a segregated society like America," the book argues, Brazil is "completely open to people of all colors, our judicial and institutions framework is completely colorblind, and all forms of racial discrimination are combated by law."

The book's author, Ali Kamel, who comes from a Syrian immigrant family, also maintains that since "races do not exist," Brazil cannot really be considered a country in which the majority of the population is black. Any effort to develop racial consciousness among black and brown Brazilians, therefore, will only lead to "racial hatred" and other problems like those in the United States, he argues. "When I see the Black Movement disparaging Gilberto Freyre, belittling him as if he were an enemy, it makes me crazy," Kamel writes. "Our problem is not racism, but poverty and an economic model that over the years has only concentrated income."

Not by coincidence, Kamel is the news director at Rede Globo, Brazil's most powerful television network. Globo has often been a prime target for black activists, who complain that the casts of both its entertainment and news programs exclude blacks, failing to reflect Brazil's racial composition. The heroes and heroines of the network's popular telenovelas are almost always white and often blue-eyed and blond, as are the star reporters who appear on its nightly newscasts, including the married couple who are the anchors.

To change that situation, black groups have in the past tried everything from vowing boycotts to threatening to file discrimination suits, but to little effect. Brazil has a comprehensive antidiscrimination statute, which was passed in the mid-1990s. But the growing number of groups advocating equal rights for blacks point out that though offenders have occasionally had to pay fines or perform community service, no one has ever served jail time for violating the racial provisions of the law.

Under pressure, Globo and the newspapers and magazines it controls have conceded a bit of ground in the past couple of years. For the first time, black actors have been able to break out of the ghetto of racially stereotyped roles such as maids and drivers and be cast in the lead roles of prime-time soap operas. But so far, that status has been granted only to one actress, Thaís Araújo, and one actor, Lázaro Ramos. On the news side, the formula is much the same: One black male reporter, in Brasília, occasionally anchors weekend news broadcasts, and one black female reporter got the plum stories on the Sunday night show that is Brazil's equivalent of *60 Minutes* (until she decided to retire). That has not been enough to satisfy black advocacy groups, who want to see more black and brown faces in roles as teachers, businessmen, or scientists, as newscasters, and featured in television and magazine advertisements.

When I first moved to Brazil in the 1970s, I was struck when I read the classified ads in local newspapers by the number of job announcements that stipulated "good appearance required" of applicants. When I asked Brazilian friends and relatives what that meant, they explained to me that it was a code phrase that warned blacks not to apply. There was no need to be more specific because all Brazilians, whether black or white or somewhere in the middle, understood what was going on and acted accordingly.

Those days are now gone, in part because the complaints of the black-consciousness movement drew unwelcome attention to the practice and embarrassed those who used it to hide their discriminatory hiring practices. But blatant discrimination still occurs in various forms and continues to go unpunished. One revelatory example occurred in Rio de Janeiro in 2005, and it drew a brief burst of attention because a celebrity was involved, Carlinhos Brown, a popular singer, songwriter, and percussionist.

Born in Bahia, Antônio Carlos Santos de Freitas adopted Carlinhos Brown as his stage name in an homage to his idol, James Brown. He is married to one of the daughters of Chico Buarque de Holanda, Brazil's most celebrated songwriter and a member of one of the country's most distinguished families of intellectuals. One day when Brown was taking his children to visit their grandfather, a doorman stopped them in the lobby of the apartment building in which Chico Buarque lived and told Brown that they would have to use the service elevator, since the "social elevator," as it is called in Brazil, is reserved for residents and their guests. Brown tried to explain his situation, but to no avail, and later he made such a fuss that the incident found its way into the newspapers.

It is hard to imagine such an incident going unpunished in the United States, but that is what happened in Brazil. No discrimination suit was filed, no damages were paid, and no apology was issued, though there was some tsk-tsking in the press. The epilogue turned out to be nearly as revealing. Soon after the episode, during Carnival celebrations in Bahia, Brown, hurt and stung by his experience in Rio, sharply criticized Brazilian attitudes about race, calling them hypocritical and complaining of what he called "vile apartheid" in the way Carnival is organized. But his remarks drew a gentle rebuke from Gilberto Gil, another of Brown's idols, who at the time happened also to be minister of culture, so Brown apologized for his outburst.

Yet Brown was clearly on to something in suggesting that Carnival celebrations in Brazil's blackest city offer a kind of template for the undercurrent of prejudice and bigotry that can pervade race relations in daily life. Over the past decade, a spate of complaints of racial discrimination against blacks, which have led to court cases and official investigations eliciting detailed testimony, have been filed against the private social clubs that are the focal point of the weeklong series of Carnival parties and parades in Salvador.

In one case that caught my attention, two female college students, one white and one black, who were close friends went to sign up to parade in the costumed Carnival procession being organized by a well-known club. The white woman's application was immediately accepted, while the black woman's was summarily rejected. Afterward, the white woman told me, a leader of the club, one of the more than a hundred such associations that enroll revelers in return for membership fees of several hundred dollars, approached her and said: "Are you crazy? Blacks can't join this club." Another club member, whom she has known since childhood, scolded her, asking, "How many more darkies are you planning to bring around?"

From this system, practices that appear even more discriminatory have evolved. As the private clubs parade down the streets of Salvador during the Carnival festivities, they use giant cords, wielded by burly security guards, to prevent non-members from entering their parade space, dancing with members, or taking advantage of the free drinks and snacks that are offered to those who are members. Anyone who is black is almost always automatically assumed to be an outsider and blocked from participating, which is the practice that Carlinhos Brown found so infuriating. In one instance, which led to a court case, a black teacher married to a white man was prevented from joining her lighter-skinned child at a ball when a private security officer grabbed her by the arm and commented sarcastically to onlookers, "Look at this darkie trying to get in."

"Everyone knows racism exists here, but when you go to talk about it, nobody wants to recognize it exists, much less recognize that it is structural," Juca Ferreira told me. He is a former Salvador city councilman who initiated an inquiry into discrimination during Carnival and later served as minister of culture. "The myth of racial democracy is so strongly ensconced here that it has become an instrument of social hypocrisy and stratification, which is precisely why we need to undertake this exercise."

As part of their defense, the traditional white-run clubs complained that they were victims of a double standard because Ilê Aiyê and a score of other black Carnival groups known as *blocos Afro* forbid the entry of whites. But when I interviewed Antônio Carlos dos Santos, the founder of Ilê Aiyê, at the group's headquarters, he described that policy as a response to the racism that he and other black residents of Salvador had encountered not just during Carnival but throughout the year.

"We formed this group as a reaction to the separation of the races, to the perverse cultural apartheid that exists here, and we are not going to give up our black-only policy until we achieve our objectives and prejudice no longer exists," he said. "If we let whites and foreigners join, do you think that is going to improve conditions in the neighborhood or get the police to change their attitude toward blacks?"

At the official level, some significant strides have been made in recent years toward bettering the situation of Brazilian blacks. Lula appointed three blacks to the cabinet that took office with him in 2003, as well as a fourth minister who is clearly of mixed racial descent but did not define herself as black until leaving the cabinet. Prior to Lula's taking power, the highest ranking black government official had been Pelé, the world's most famous soccer player, who served as state secretary of sport in the previous administration. Lula also named the first black justice to the Supreme Court and created a new ministry of racial equality to deal with problems of discrimination and ensure that Afro-Brazilians were given equal opportunities.

Of course, two of Lula's black cabinet ministers, both of them women, later had to step down after it was determined they had used government funds to pay for personal expenses such as travel. That had the unfortunate effect of reinforcing certain racial and gender stereotypes. Since other officials who have engaged in similar abuses—but happened to be white and male— have sometimes been spared the kind of public flogging and humiliation that marked this scandal, it doesn't seem unreasonable to conclude that a double standard may also have been at work in singling out two black women, one of humble social origins and the other renowned for her militancy.

During Lula's first term in office, I met several times with his minister of racial equality, a black social worker from São Paulo named Matilde Ribeiro. She was a controversial figure in Brazil because she didn't mince words in criticizing racism when she saw it in daily life. Among her controversial statements was, "I'd rather have whites resentful, with blacks in the universities, than whites happy and blacks out of universities," referring to affirmative-action quotas for college admissions. She also sparked a storm of criticism when she said, "It's not racism when a black person rises up against a white." That declaration, she said, was intended to urge black Brazilians to be more assertive in demanding their rights. But the national press interpreted the statement as an invitation to a racial bloodletting.

Personally, I always found it instructive to listen to Ribeiro when she analyzed racial issues, compared the different ways in which Brazil and the United States had dealt with racism and the legacy of slavery, and suggested what each could learn from the other. One particularly vivid story she told me had to do with a trip she took to Washington, D.C., during the Bush years to meet with Condoleezza Rice and other black American leaders. Late on a Sunday afternoon, Ribeiro happened to find herself at the Kennedy Center, watching the audience arrive for a concert there. Most of the spectators were black, she noted, dressed elegantly, driving late-model automobiles, and, she concluded from listening to their conversations, obviously well educated.

"That's what we need in Brazil," she told me in her office in Brasília one day in 2004, "that kind of black middle class." She was not arguing that Brazil should copy everything that the United States has done to alleviate centuries of institutionalized racism. But she believed that some of the experiences and mechanisms developed in the United States could be relevant to Brazil—if Brazil truly wants to combat its own racial problem. And perhaps affirmative action is one such tool, even though the mainstream press constantly attacked and ridiculed her for offering that suggestion.

Indeed, the clearest sign that race has become an issue that Brazilians can no longer ignore is the national debate about affirmative action, which in recent years has gone from being an issue on the fringes of Brazil's national awareness to one that is endlessly discussed. The principal battleground has been college admissions, specifically a plan by Lula's government to set aside 40 percent of admissions to some of the country's most prestigious universities for high school graduates who qualify as "Afro-descendants."

Brazil has always had a shortage of spots in its colleges and universities. But that situation has worsened in the past 15 years, ironically because of an economic boom that has enabled children from poor families to stay in high school through graduation instead of dropping out to go to work. As a result, each year as many as 2.5 million students now take college admission qualifying exams, which are costly and often demand an entire year of cram courses to prepare, for barely a million openings. So any government policy that favors one group, such as blacks, at the expense of another is bound to provoke controversy.

An additional problem with such quotas is that racial categories are so much more flexible and ill defined in Brazil than in countries like the United States. As a result, it is hard to determine who is black and who is not, or to come up with a workable legal definition. That, in turn, means that deciding who is eligible to benefit from affirmative action and who is not can be extremely tricky.

Even Lula has often seemed confused. When the question of affirmative-action policies came up during a presidential debate in 2002, he suggested that a scientific test be used to determine who is black and who is white. Even if such a test existed, it would be almost useless in Brazil, where centuries of interracial marriages and coupling have left most "black" people with some white blood and most "white" people with some black blood. According to a recent DNA study done by the University of Minas Gerais, 87 percent of Brazilians, or nearly 175 million people, have genes that are at least 10 percent African in origin.

In recent years, the Brazilian press, which for the most part opposes any form of affirmative action based on race, has focused on cases of people trying to game the system or stories that otherwise suggest affirmative action is an illogical policy. One example much commented on was the case of a young woman in Rio de Janeiro who came from an immigrant family but, in hopes of bettering her chances to be admitted to a prestigious private university there, claimed to have African ancestry when she clearly had none.

But the most notorious instance is the case of identical twin brothers, with a black father and white mother, who applied to different departments of the same public university in Brasília in 2007, hoping to be admitted under the racial set-asides for "Afro-descendent" students. In order to qualify, though, their academic records had to be examined by a panel whose duties also required them to look at pictures of the teenagers to determine whether they were "black enough" to be eligible. One brother was ruled to be black and was admitted under the quota, but the other was declared not to be black and was rejected. After he threatened to take his case to the courts, which have final jurisdiction over the issue, the university reversed its decision. "There is no way to understand the criteria the university used," complained the twin who had originally been ruled white. "How can they consider my brother black and not me?"

In response to the clamor, Lula's government tried to walk back its original support for a quota system that would specifically benefit blacks. During his second term, which ran from 2007 through 2010, the focus shifted from an explicitly race-based system to one that uses family income as its main criteria, on the assumption that that would diminish opposition. The effect is much the same, since the overwhelming majority of those who are poor are also black, but the packaging is considerably less controversial.

But attempts to impose quotas in other areas of Brazilian life continue to generate controversy. Television networks and advertising agencies, for example, have lobbied intensely against bills that would require them to choose more blacks for the casts of their programs and commercials. Those proposals do not aim to require producers of visual media to exactly match the composition of the Brazilian populations, but only to give black and mixed-race actors a larger and more representative share of roles, typically about 30 or 40 percent. The main result, however, has been to harden the opposition of television networks to affirmative action in general, with Globo and its allies portraying any kind of quota in any area as an assault on the Brazilian way of life.

Historically, Brazilians have tended to counter any criticisms of their inadequacies on the race issue with finger-pointing, citing the existence of institutionalized racism in the United States and South Africa. In the past, they may well have been justified in doing so. Over the past 50 years, however, both the United States and South Africa have successfully acknowledged their failings and begun to redress them. While continuing to affirm its moral superiority, Brazil has also made advances, but at a slower, more timid pace, and in a piecemeal rather than systematic manner.

But the election of Barack Obama as president of the United States seems to have encouraged an unusual degree of reflection and self-examination among Brazilians and to have shaken some of their assumptions. For example, a journalist friend of mine who works at a major daily told me that his newspaper's editorial board had concluded early on that Obama could not possibly beat John McCain, since "Americans are racists and will never vote for a black candidate." At the same time, black advocacy groups and some Brazilian intellectuals began to take note of the paucity of black mayors, governors, legislators, and cabinet ministers in their own country and to wonder, as some of my Brazilian friends have asked me, "Why hasn't an Obama appeared here?"

In any society, the first step in addressing the problem of race is to recognize that it exists. The United States has undertaken that painful process, reluctantly at first but with greater tenacity in recent years. Brazil has not been forced, or forced itself, to own up to its blemishes and shortcomings, and so it continues to cling to myths that conflict with the more complicated realities of daily life. Until Brazil demonstrates the courage to face its racial problem head on, the myth of a "racial democracy" will continue to flourish, and Brazil will continue to lag behind countries that have been more forthright in confronting the sordid aspects of their past and in making amends to those groups that suffered the most from it.

FOUR

THE TROPICAL LIFESTYLE

IT IS A HOT AND humid Sunday morning in Rio de Janeiro in the middle of January, the midpoint of summer in the Southern Hemisphere. The beaches at Ipanema, Copacabana, and Barra da Tijuca, already jammed, are getting more crowded as buses disgorge riders who have made the long trip to the seashore from the city's northern suburbs. At kiosks near the sidewalks, groups of friends sip chilled beers or coconuts and watch the volleyball games. Restaurants and bars are packed, too, as clusters of city residents, the men largely shirtless and in Bermuda shorts, the women in bikinis and flip-flops, gossip about politics, celebrities, and neighbors.

By mid-afternoon, many of the beachgoers are leaving, not because of the broiling sun, to which they are accustomed, but because there are so many other attractions. Three P.M. is a good time for a *churrasco*, the outdoor barbecue grills where typical extended Brazilian families meet to cook steak, chicken, and sausage. At five o'clock, there may be a soccer match at Maracanã, the world's biggest sports stadium, that will draw tens of thousands of fans of the city's four main clubs. And once darkness falls and the temperature cools, the samba associations begin rehearsal for the upcoming Carnival.

Leisure time, called *lazer* in Portuguese, is important in any society, but Brazilians cherish it and fill their days with abundant opportunities to kick back. Unlike in the United States, workaholics who sacrifice the pleasures of private life in the name of work and wealth are not admired and do not become cultural icons. If anything, they tend to be the butt of jokes. The *cariocas*, as natives of Rio de Janeiro are called, make fun of *paulistas*, residents of São Paulo, who are seen as too serious and excessively concerned about their jobs. In Brazil, work may be a necessity and can sometimes bring satisfaction. But learning to enjoy one's time on earth is an art, and those who have mastered that art are held in high esteem.

Even the language Brazilians use makes this predilection clear. As spoken in Brazil, Portuguese has at least six different verbs for "play." *Divertir* can be applied to any activity that is fun, like going to the movies or a party. *Brincar* is what children do with their toys or, in some usages, what adults do in bed. The verb applied to playing a musical instrument is *tocar*, but when playing a sport like soccer, volleyball, or basketball, the proper word is *jogar*. If you're playing the horses, slot machines, or the lottery, the word you want is *apostar*, while the term for playing a role in a film or the theater is *desempenhar* or *representar*.

Because Brazil's tropical climate encourages so much of public life to be lived out of doors, the human body is also on display much more than it would be in a temperate climate. People dress to be comfortable, which necessarily means fewer clothes, and two very different attitudes result. For some, the constant exposure of the body in a public setting leads to vanity and pride. They want their bodies to be trim and fit, no matter what the toll, and so they diet and exercise, sometimes to extremes, or undergo plastic surgery. Brazil has a reputation as the world capital for such procedures, which may be a bit exaggerated. But the country's body-oriented culture has made tummy tucks, liposuction, nose jobs, face lifts, and chemical peels commonplace and accepted, and it has transformed top surgeons like Ivo Pitanguy into global celebrities with an international clientele that includes Hollywood stars. Middle-class professionals have also flocked to Brazilian clinics from abroad, drawn by the country's reputation and by prices that are considerably cheaper than those they would find at home.

Many ordinary Brazilians, however, either cannot afford the time or the money to have cosmetic surgery, don't want to make the effort, or are simply indifferent to how their bodies look to others. But they display them nonetheless; one of the things first-time visitors often notice is how even corpulent people, especially women, expose vast expanses of flesh to the public gaze. This is in part because ideals of physical beauty are not the same as in America: Brazilian men say they like women with a body "like a guitar," with lots of curves and plenty of flesh on the bone, especially on the rear end rather than the chest. "Those huge breasts you see in the United States, like in *Playboy*, were always considered ridiculous in Brazil," Pitanguy once told me. But many Brazilians who do not conform to that ideal also have learned to be comfortable in their own bodies, take pleasure from their own corporality, and seek relief from the heat by literally "letting it all hang out."

Each of the three most visible and popular activities enjoyed by Brazilians places the human body front and center—beach culture, Carnival, and soccer—and all three activities both reflect and shape the values that help make the country vibrant, colorful, and exciting. In the United States, when two strangers meet for the first time, they are likely to ask one another what kind of work they do, where they live, or where they went to school. Brazilians ask similar questions when first introduced, but they have an additional battery of inquiries to help determine a person's status, interests, and loyalties: What is your soccer team? What samba club do you support during Carnival? What beach do you frequent? For both the native and the visitor, being able to answer those questions convincingly helps mark the difference between really being part of Brazil and merely being present in a Brazilian space.

BEACH

In 2008, archeologists working at a site in northeastern Brazil found shards of pottery and other evidence indicating that Tupi-speaking Indians had created settlements on the coast as early as 9500 B.C. For nearly as long as human beings have inhabited Brazil, they have turned their back to a potentially hostile interior of jungle and mountains and gravitated to the sea.

Those Indian cultures have vanished today, but more than three-quarters of Brazil's 200 million people still live within a hundred miles of the coastline, which runs for more than five thousand miles. And where there is no sea, Brazilians create beaches and a beach culture on the banks of mighty rivers. Though inhabitants of Manaus or Santarém may be more than a thousand miles inland, they too like nothing better than to spend a weekend lying on the sand at the edge of the Amazon or the Tapajós, eating the same snacks, playing the same games, wearing the same fashions, and singing the same songs as their more privileged countrymen in the south.

Certain aspects of life in Brazil adhere to predictable rhythms. As the weather warms and the end of the year approaches, enrollment in gyms and exercise academies rises sharply as future beachgoers struggle to get back in shape. Women predominate in the spinning and yoga classes and the work-outs with personal trainers; in early December, the newspapers name some attractive young woman as the "Summer Muse" and publish long articles in their Sunday supplements about fashion for the Christmas-to-Carnival season: Pink or lilac bikinis? Beach mats or blankets? Hairy or shaved chests for men?

Brazilians conceive of the beach in much the same way the ancient Greeks regarded the agora. It is the most public of public spaces, and for largely that reason it is also considered the most democratic. The beach has traditionally been seen as a great social leveler, a "place where the general, the teacher, the politician, the millionaire, and the poor student" are all equal and coexist harmoniously, in the words of Roberto DaMatta, an anthropologist and author who is one of the country's most astute social observers and commentators. "There, bodies were all made equally humble" by the near naked proximity of "one body with others, all of them without defense or disguise."

If you don't consider the cost of a gym membership, that assessment is mostly true. Beaches here were never formally segregated by race, as they were in parts of the United States and in South Africa. Nor have they been privatized to keep out the riff-raff and hoi polloi: The 1988 constitution even contains a provision that declares all beaches to be public land, held by the nation in trust for all Brazil's people.

But this is only part of the story. Look past the placid surface, and the reality of beach life becomes far more complicated, marked by differences based on class, race, age, sexual preference, and even regional prejudices. This is particularly the case in Rio de Janeiro, the city most identified both in Brazil and abroad with beach culture, thanks to songs like "The Girl from Ipanema."

Rio de Janeiro has 59 different beaches, spread out along 110 miles of oceanfront sand. The most famous and elite of these beaches are Ipanema and its extension, known as Leblon, and Copacabana and its extension, called Leme. Both beaches are informally divided into sectors, which are demarcated by a dozen lifeguard stations, called *postos*, each about a half-mile from the next. The *postos* are numbered 1 through 12, and each has a culture of its own, which appeals to a different socio-economic "tribe," and which can be unwelcoming to those who are considered outsiders.

One notorious video, widely viewed on YouTube, shows a group of New Year's Eve revelers throwing raw eggs from the balcony of one of the most prestigious and expensive buildings directly overlooking Copacabana beach at pedestrians below. In the video you can hear that the egg throwers, many of whom were celebrities or children of wealthy or famous families, were deliberately targeting those whose appearance suggested they were poor.

Over the years, a hierarchy of prestige among the lifeguard stations has been delineated and is known to all regular beachgoers. Posto 9, in the heart of Ipanema, is clearly at the top and has been since I first visited Brazil in the early 1970s. The military dictatorship was in power in those days, and this stretch of the beach, alongside a pier that has since vanished, was one of the few places hippies could congregate without fear of harassment by the police. Nowadays, it's a magnet for celebrities, left-wing intellectuals (who signal their presence by flying the flag of the ruling Workers Party), and other bohemian types, including former hippies who have now aged into upper-middle-class respectability. Slightly to the left of the lifeguard station itself, gays and lesbians mark their territory with a rainbow flag.

In contrast, Posto 7, at the eastern end of the beach, is the redoubt of outsiders, many of them dark-skinned, who have come from working-class suburbs that may be as far as three hours away by public transportation. This is especially the case on weekends, when entire families ride the bus to Posto 7, the first bus stop in Ipanema, and station themselves on the sand. These visitors used to be pejoratively known as *farofeiros* because instead of buying food from vendors or kiosks, they brought picnic lunches that include *farofa*, a toasted flour made from yucca that is a staple in the diet of the Brazilian masses. The slang terms for them have changed, but they continue to be the butt of jokes because they often sit on drab straw mats rather than colorful towels and apply a cheap red tanning lotion rather than a more expensive sunscreen.

Segregation at the beach is now self-imposed, not the result of a law, and is based on class. But a racial component is clearly involved. The poorer interlopers from working-class areas on the north side of the city tend to be darker skinned. The young habitués of Ipanema who determine fashion trends do not seek to emulate the outsiders in behavior or dress and certainly do not want to look like them. Listen to the conversations of the beach elite, and it becomes clear that the skin color they are striving for, with the help of their lotions and creams, is a toasted golden brown. They look with disdain on both the tourists, whose pasty white skin marks them as outsiders, and their opposites, those native-born *cariocas* whose skin happens to have a darker hue. There is nothing to be gained in being too white or too black.

Compared to American beachgoers, fewer Brazilians go in the water, aside from surfers, even on a sunny day when the water is calm and the waves weak. A Brazilian beach is not just for recreation but is also a public, social space, much like a square or plaza or street corner. Brazilian courting rituals are on view, and candidates for political office know that the beachfront is a good place to campaign. So do advertisers: The skies above the most popular beaches are filled with airplanes trailing banners, and on the sidewalk, attractive young people offer samples of new products ranging from hand lotions to beverages. Musicians and comedians perform there, too, as if they were buskers at a subway station.

But just as elsewhere in Brazilian society, the beach cannot function without what can only be described as a servant class. When beachgoers arrive and select the spot where they intend to spend the day, operators of kiosks compete to rent them chairs and an umbrella; sometimes a proprietor will already have set things up for a regular, long-time customer. While they are sitting on the sand, they are served by strolling vendors, many of whom sing or chant the praises of the products they are selling, which include soft drinks, ice cream, sunglasses, T-shirts, and tanning lotion. Typically, these vendors have made the long trek from the working-class suburbs where they live with their families who depend on their income. Sometimes they enlist the help of their wives and children at home to make the fruit ices, juices, or kabobs they sell. During the summer season, however, some of them sleep and cook on the beach all week long and go home only on Monday, the slowest day of the week.

In large coastal cities such as Rio, Salvador, Recife, and Fortaleza, there may also be beaches near some of the neighborhoods where this servant class lives. But almost inevitably, those beaches will in some way be inferior—polluted, rocky, pounded by waves, or infested with jellyfish—for that is the lot of the lower classes. In Rio, for example, the beaches on the north side of the city face Guanabara Bay, not the Atlantic Ocean, and that makes for an enormous difference. Guanabara Bay is ringed by oil refineries, chemical plants, docks where giant container ships load and unload their cargo, and shipyards, all of which dump their untreated waste into the bay. Only the poorest residents of a *favela* will go to a beach such as Ramos, which regularly has the highest count of fecal matter and bacteria of any beach in Rio de Janeiro.

At the start of the last decade, the municipal government built a large swimming pool, quickly dubbed the Big Pool, in one of the poorest neighborhoods on the north side. Initially, the new attraction drew huge crowds, mostly people who were relieved not to have to spend the time and money to get to elite beaches of the Zona Sul, where they might feel unwelcome. Even some of the well-heeled residents of Ipanema and Leblon made the trip north—slumming, as it were—to see what all the fuss was about. For a while, it was a chic thing to do on weekends for members of the elite.

But eventually the realities of life began to intrude, and the glow faded. The pool was in an area being fought over by two gangs. The dominant group decreed that no one could wear beach attire with the colors of their rivals and began to harass and threaten those who defied or were not aware of that edict. Then, after the next election, a new, more conservative mayor took office, the money to maintain the project dried up, and eventually so did the Big Pool. Funds were poured into modernizing refreshment stands and lifeguard stations along the elite beaches of the Zona Sul. Those beaches supply the views seen on the postcards of Rio and from the apartments of the city's wealthiest citizens. So it seems only natural to those in power that the beaches of the rich should get preferential treatment. That is the nature of the social contract in Brazil.

Yet Brazil's social problems manage to penetrate even elite havens on the shore. The rapid growth of the *favelas* on the hillsides overlooking Copacabana, Ipanema, Leblon, and São Conrado has resulted in garbage and waste being spewed into the ocean in front of those elite beaches. Even body parts—of victims in the wars between drug gangs—have washed up on these beaches, much to the chagrin and anger of authorities eager to project Rio's image as a laid-back vacation destination. I once wrote a story about a rash of such incidents on the beach next to the Sheraton Hotel, for instance, and city tourism authorities were so furious with me that they threatened to cancel my credentials to cover the next year's Carnival.

In recent years, beaches have also suffered from mass muggings, in which large groups of young men from the hillside *favelas* descend to swarm the shoreline and rob beachgoers of their money, jewelry, radios, and other belongings. Anyone who tries to resist is simply knocked to the ground or pummeled, and though fatalities are rare, some victims have had to be hospitalized. The petty criminals indiscriminately sweep up everything in their path, making no distinction between tourist and native, foreigner and Brazilian. The resultant clamor from veteran beachgoers in Rio (and elsewhere as the practice spread) has led to a police crackdown, which substantially has reduced the frequency of the attacks. But one consequence of the crackdown is that any group of young, dark-skinned men, especially if they have bleach-blond hair or certain types of tattoos—markers common among *favela* residents or gang members—are regarded with suspicion.

But the beach can also be a stage on which experiments in social change are announced and ratified, or at least attempted. Back in the early 1970s, the actress Leila Diniz, a leading sex symbol at the time, created enormous controversy because she dared, while quite visibly pregnant, to wear the tiniest of bikinis on the beach at Ipanema; in retrospect, that action is sometimes cited as the start of the feminist movement in Brazil. In 1980, after returning from exile in Sweden, the writer and social activist Fernando Gabeira—who had been given amnesty for his role in the kidnapping of an American ambassador—outraged both social conservatives and his former revolutionary comrades-in-arms by wearing a crocheted lilac thong to the beach. That act was seen by many as announcing the birth of the New Left in Brazil, less dog-matic, more pragmatic, and more tolerant on social issues.

A decade ago, a group of young women created a media sensation when they went topless at Ipanema on a summer weekend, when the beach was at its most crowded. They were protesting an incident a few weeks earlier in which a 20-member police squad, armed with machine guns, ordered a 34-year-old saleswoman at another Rio beach to put her top back on and then roughly hauled her off to the police station when she refused. Despite Rio de Janeiro's reputation as a hub of licentiousness, and the presence of bare breasts on numerous telenovelas and other television programs, a municipal ordinance at that time prohibited women from going topless at local beaches. For their efforts, the demonstrators were rewarded with insults and showered with beer. But their protest, combined with the wave of public ridicule that followed the police action, led the mayor to sign a decree that permits women to shed their tops at the beach.

Everything indicates that the beach will continue to be a social laboratory, changing as Brazil changes, reflecting the society's strengths and weaknesses. This was again illustrated during the summer of 2009–2010, when the municipal authorities in Rio announced what they called a "shock of order" and began enforcing a prohibition on the cooking or manufacture of food on the beach. The ban had long existed, but was never enforced—until powerful companies decided that they wanted to eliminate competition from the freelance vendors, those who dealt in beach equipment as well as those who sold food, and force beachgoers to buy from their kiosks.

But the authorities and their well-connected business allies pressed too hard, leading to public resistance and disobedience. Beachgoers who had been going to the same stretch of beach for years found to their dismay that they could no longer buy shrimp or cheese on a stick or rent beach chairs or umbrellas from vendors with whom they had longstanding, cordial relationships. Consumers of fresh coconut water were outraged at being told they could only purchase that refreshing, healthful delicacy in plastic bottles or paper containers. In the end, a typically Brazilian solution was found: While the law remains on the books, enforcement has been reduced and the traditional social order restored, at least until next summer, when the battle will most likely be resumed.

CARNIVAL

Carnival is the best-known aspect of Brazilian life. Films such as *Black Orpheus* depict it as a five-day extravaganza and free-for-all during which people don masks, shed sexual inhibitions and social identities, and engage in otherwise forbidden behavior. The poor man is king, the rich mingle with their servants, men can dress as women, women can act with masculine audacity, and racial and class barriers come down, all in a kind of Dionysian frenzy.

All of this is more or less true, as any outsider visiting Carnival in Brazil for the first time quickly discovers. Beginning late on the Friday before Ash Wednesday and extending until noon of that Wednesday, which is the Roman Catholic day of fasting and abstinence marking the start of the penitential season of Lent, official formal life in Brazil shuts down and gives way to the people's festival. Business, school, and other normal daily activities cease. Bands of ordinary people, many dressed in costume, take to the streets to dance, sing, and drink. At social clubs and community centers, fancy dress balls are held, each varying in opulence according to the wealth and social class of those involved. There is much casual or anonymous sex, which is why billboards go up in the weeks before the start of Carnival warning revelers to use condoms when they frolic.

But that is only a part of the picture; dig deeper, and other, seemingly contradictory aspects emerge. For Carnival is also a fierce competition, and as Brazil modernizes and becomes more prosperous, Carnival has become an industry. In Rio, large corporations that seek publicity and profit are pushing aside the shadowy underworld elements that have traditionally helped finance Carnival. There has also been a backlash in recent years against the industrialization of Carnival and a desire, at least among purists and the nostalgic, to return to the era when Carnival was a festival of, for, and by the people.

Carnival is something ancient, a "farewell to the flesh" that dates back to the Middle Ages and the Roman Catholic Church's creation of Holy Week, but it also draws from even older European pagan sources. In its modern Brazilian form, however, Carnival is most closely linked to rites and practices that are African in origin. In 1930, the mayor of Rio de Janeiro sought for the first time to regulate longstanding Carnival activities, inadvertently creating a space for groups that had recently been formed in the city's poor black neighborhoods to propagate a new style of music developed there, the samba. These "samba schools" took their rhythms, their songs with satirical lyrics, and their elaborate costumes to the streets and quickly found favor among the city's other residents. As a result, other rhythms and other activities were pushed into the background, and the samba gradually became synonymous with Carnival.

Over the years, that tradition has evolved into two nights of fierce competition, held at a specially constructed "Sambodrome" on the outskirts of downtown Rio, near the city's leading brewery, and televised live all over Brazil. Each night, before an exacting audience of seventy thousand sitting in a grandstand, seven samba schools parade for an hour, to be graded by four judges in ten categories ranging from the beauty of their costumes to the effectiveness of their percussion sections. The dancers and drummers are for the most part ordinary people, bus drivers and housewives and other members of Rio's working class, who yearn all year long for this moment of glory and have devoted months of rehearsal to mastering their steps and rhythms. The results are announced on the afternoon of Ash Wednesday, after Carnival has officially ended, in a ceremony that is also broadcast live.

Just as in Olympic gymnastic and ice skating competitions, the difference between finishing in first place and being the runner-up is often tenths or even hundredths of a point. As a result, tension and nervousness mount as the results are tabulated, especially for supporters of those schools in danger of finishing last. The punishment for that failure is to be bumped down to the second division, while the winner of that category ascends to the glory of competing in the "special group." For the next year, the special group winner basks in the contentment of being recognized all over Brazil as the best of the best; faithful fans of the last-place finisher, in contrast, must endure the constant gibes of others.

Certain samba schools, such as Beija-Flor ("Hummingbird") from the poor, crowded, violent working-class suburb of Nilópolis, have developed a strong winning tradition. Others, such as Mangueira ("Mango Tree"), the oldest and most traditional of samba schools, have enjoyed days of glory in the past but have been supplanted by newcomers and are struggling to regain their former grandeur. Others win only rarely, if at all, and aim not for victory but merely to avoid relegation to the second division: Unidos da Tijuca's surprise victory in the 2010 competition ended a drought of 74 years for them. To achieve their varied goals, the samba schools draw from a small, exclusive, and well-paid group of professionals known as *carnavalescos* to organize, design, and direct their presentations.

Some of these *carnvalescos*, such as Fernando Pamplona and Joãozinho Trinta, have become national celebrities. Pamplona is an intellectual, a scenographer, and a lifelong student of Brazilian folklore who focuses on daily life or Brazilian history in his performance. Trinta has enjoyed his greatest successes leading the Beija-Flor group. He is most famous for his response in the 1970s to criticism that Carnival wasted money that could be used on education, housing, and medicine for the poor. "The poor like luxury," he said. "It's intellectuals who like poverty."

With so much at stake, the leading samba schools have in recent years opted for ever larger and more extravagant presentations. In part, they're financed by the city government, which wants to support what has become a major tourist attraction. For many years, a good chunk of money also came from the city's most prominent *bicheiros*, the bookies who run the flourishing illegal numbers game called the *jogo do bicho*, or "animal game." In fact, it was almost a civic obligation for the game bosses to finance the samba schools in their neighborhoods, since much of their wealth came from the same local residents who participate in the Carnival competition.

But as their ambitions have gradually come to outstrip the capacity of the *bicheiros* to subsidize Carnival presentations, the samba schools have had to seek other sources of financing. Some nouveau riche residents of the slum alleged to be drug kingpins have stepped up to fill part of the need. Large corporations have also increased their donations, in return for samba schools' putting the company's logo on their musical instruments and costumes. Agencies of the federal government, such as Petrobras, the state oil company, have also supplied funding, with the understanding that the samba school it supports will choose for its presentation a theme that praises the benefactor.

Even Venezuela's populist strongman Hugo Chávez, recognizing the importance of the competition as a public relations tool, has emerged as a patron of Carnival. In 2007, his government supplied a reported $1 million to the Vila Isabel samba school, the theme of whose presentation was "I'm Crazy About You, America: In Praise of Latinity." After Vila Isabel unexpectedly and narrowly won the competition, amid speculation that Carnival judges may have been paid off, Chávez declared Vila Isabel's triumph to be "a victory for Latin American integration" and sponsored an international tour by the group.

Numerous samba schools have over the past decade also begun selling tickets to foreign tourists to take part in the parade down the Sambodrome. Although this practice helps raise the money the schools need to mount their presentations, it rankles traditionalists, and not just because most of the outsiders can't dance the samba. Purists argue that the presence of outsiders devalues the Carnival experience, diluting the bond between the samba school and the members who work hard all year long to learn the dance steps, memorize the samba *enredo* or theme song, sew the costumes, and attend the rehearsals.

The ordinary people who have traditionally provided Carnival with its inspiration and character are also being squeezed out in other ways. Tickets to the Sambodrome competition are now beyond the price range of many knowledgeable samba fans, the result of increased interest by tourists. And since the two nights of samba competition are televised nationally, they provide a stage on which entertainers and other celebrities can reach a mass audience and promote their careers. As a result, Carnival has been inundated with armies of C-grade actresses and models who seem to view the event as an audition—a chance to strut their well-toned bodies for the television cameras and make their way into the gossip magazines.

This trend may have reached a nadir in 1994, when an aspiring model was photographed dancing at the side of Brazil's president at the time, Itamar Franco, in the "box of honor," where he was watching the Carnival parade. She happened not to be wearing any panties at the time, as the pictures taken by photographers shooting the couple from street level made quite clear the next day, when they were published in newspapers and shown on television. The incident was a major embarrassment for Franco, but it provided a boost for the model, Lilian Ramos, who later emigrated to Italy and now has a television show there.

For many years, the trend had been for the women marching at the head of samba schools to reveal more and more of their bodies and wear less and less clothing. TV Globo, a media conglomerate with a monopoly on televising the Rio Carnival, helped encourage this attitude with its broadcast spots promoting the Carnival competition, featuring a gorgeous *mulata* dancer named Valéria Valenssa. Known as the *Globeleza*, or "Globo beauty," she was shown on the air with breasts bared and paraded down the avenue undressed as well, with nothing but a few strategic dabs of paint covering her crotch. Since Carnival in Rio is extremely competitive, other models and dancers tried to emulate or even outdo her.

But by the start of the last decade, when some beauties were daring to parade completely naked in public, a backlash began. The offenders were criticized for vulgarizing the spectacle and diminishing its splendor and creativity, and Carnival organizers finally passed a resolution formally prohibiting complete nudity. TV Globo dropped Valéria Valenssa a few years ago, and she became an evangelical Protestant. She no longer participates in Carnival and has in fact become a fierce critic of the event. "Carnival is a festival of the flesh, a worldly festival," she said in an interview in 2008. "The people who are there are committing a sin."

In the face of this growing glitziness and elitism, some Brazilians are taking Carnival back to its popular roots. In Rio, the *blocos*, the smaller semi-organized neighborhood groups that were all but moribund when I first arrived in the city in the 1970s, have been resurrected and injected with new life. There are not only more of them, but they are also more active, beginning their marches through the streets as early as two weeks before the formal competition at the Sambodrome. And true to Carnival's irreverent origins and traditions, they march in the gaudiest and most absurd of costumes, singing songs that criticize authorities and celebrities in a hilariously irreverent manner. The result is a growing gulf between this popular, chaotic Carnival in the streets and the formal, structured event at the Sambodrome.

True fans of the event are also gravitating toward Carnival celebrations in other cities, especially Salvador, Olinda, which is just north of Recife, and other places where efforts are made to protect the original flavor of Carnival and retain public involvement. In Olinda, the musical foundation of Carnival is not the samba but the *maracatu* and the *ciranda*, two other traditional rhythms popular in the region. Similarly, the focus of the festivities there is not a competition among groups, with a single winner, but raucous street parades featuring giant papier-mâché puppets, some standing more than 20 feet high, that caricature local or national celebrities.

The leading creator of puppets, Sílvio Botelho de Almeida, born in 1957, is so talented that his work has been exhibited in museums abroad, and he is constantly being offered commissions from Carnival schools in Rio de Janeiro to design floats for them. But he has turned all of those proposals down—not because he doesn't need the money, but because he believes that the festivities in Rio have been hijacked by commercial interests and turned into a mere "spectacle" for tourists.

"Carnival in Rio is like going to the theater just as a spectator and leaving as soon as the play ends," he told me in 2004, "whereas here, you are part of the show that's taking place out on the street." The intensely competitive aspect of Rio's parade, with one samba school walking away with all the glory, also strikes him as contrary to the true spirit of Carnival. He prefers Olinda's collegial atmosphere, which culminates on Shrove Tuesday in an event, which Botelho sponsors, to honor all of the local puppet makers.

Salvador's Carnival has emerged as the biggest rival to Rio's. There the focal point of celebrations is the "electric trios," sponsored by companies or hired by neighborhood associations, that lead the parades from seaside streets to a square on the edge of downtown. First seen in 1950, these ensembles, some of which have grown into full-fledged orchestras but still retain the "trio" name, now draw hundreds of thousands of revelers from all over Brazil and the outside world who dance, march, sing, drink, and, yes, have sex to the thunderous sounds emanating from speakers atop specially designed trucks; think of Led Zeppelin, only with music that is much, much louder and faster and mixes both Brazilian and rock sources. As in Olinda, and in sharp contrast to Rio, the emphasis is on mass participation, not competition.

Carnival so appeals to the Brazilian imagination and love of festivities that some locales have created their own unauthorized versions, held during the offseason. The town of Parintins, on an island in the middle of the Amazon River, offers perhaps the best-known example every year at the end of June and beginning of July. Thousands of people come hundreds of miles by boat from the surrounding region to witness or take part in the celebrations, whose focus is two groups, the Reds and the Blues, who compete to stage the most extravagant retelling of a local legend about the resurrection of a mythical ox. But commercialization is creeping in here too, as beverage companies eager to capitalize on this new opportunity fight to sponsor the rival groups.

The singer and composer Caetano Veloso once wrote a song about Carnival in Bahia called "Rain, Sweat and Beer," in which he urged revelers to "come, see, let it happen, kiss, be, whatever God wills." That title conveys the frenetic, chaotic quality of Carnival at its purest, while the lyrics capture the almost fatalistic "anything can happen" attitude with which Brazilians celebrate their most important festival, one that exceeds even Christmas and Independence Day in popularity. Carnival will always be valued as an outlet to express Brazil's mischievous spirit and the joy in living that its people feel. But how long it can retain its underlying anarchic, anti-authoritarian character in the face of the mounting pressures to commercialize, centralize, and standardize is now a valid question.

SOCCER

Brazilians play soccer so passionately and skillfully, with such grace, dexterity, and panache, that it is easy to think that they invented the game. Though Brazil has clearly perfected the world's most popular sport, winning the World Cup a record five times, and has almost turned it into an art form, the reality is that soccer was brought to the country only in 1894, when Charles Miller, a young *paulista* of English and Scottish descent, returned from studying in Britain. Initially, the sport was played primarily by a small, mainly white, and highly Europeanized urban elite who were not interested in seeing their pastime taken up by the unwashed masses. Reflecting the prejudices of that era, the writer Graciliano Ramos even went so far as to argue that the game would never become popular in Brazil because the physique and mentality of the typical Brazilian were ill suited to such an intellectually sophisticated and physically demanding "European" game.

But just as they have done repeatedly in the arts, Brazilians soon demonstrated their extraordinary ability to take a foreign import and make it over into something very much their own. On the athletic fields of Eton, soccer was highly disciplined, even stiff, an exercise in order and strategy. As it came to be played in open lots on the outskirts of Brazilian cities and in pastures and fields in the countryside, the game was transformed into a show of agility and creativity, almost an extension of the nimbleness that is required of the best dancers in Carnival. At the same time, the focus shifted from team play to individual expression and accomplishment. Rather than execute a military-style collective attack, Brazilian teams preferred to let their players improvise on the spot, a strategy that has led over the decades to innovations in kicking, passing, heading the ball, decoying and feinting, and offensive and defensive alignments.

For those who were black or poor, which, as we have seen, often amounts to the same thing in Brazil, soccer also offered one of the few paths to social acceptance and financial advancement. That added to the game's allure and helped it take root as the sport of the masses. Many of the early teams were sponsored by companies that viewed soccer as a way to advertise their products, and many of those teams' players were recruited from the factories of the sponsoring company. Those who played well were rewarded with bonuses, promotions, or transfers to departments where the workload was less onerous. "A worker who played soccer well enough to guarantee a spot on the starting team soon found himself in the cloth department, doing lighter work," Mário Rodrigues Filho wrote in *The Negro in Brazilian Soccer*, which was published in the 1950s but is still the authoritative book on the subject. "And if he continued to merit the confidence of the factory owners, things could get even better. There was the office, where the work was even more pleasant, and the salary higher."

That phenomenon has continued into the contemporary era. The soccer star Pelé (whose given name is Edson Arantes do Nascimento), is recognized everywhere except perhaps Argentina as the greatest player in the history of the sport and is today probably the most revered sports celebrity in the world. But he was born into humble circumstances in a small town in Minas Gerais and raised on the outskirts of São Paulo. Scores of other players have risen to wealth and fame in much the same way, including many of the dominant players of recent years, such as Romário, Ronaldo, Rivaldo, Roberto Carlos, and Ronaldinho. An analysis of the 2002 and 2006 national squads that competed in the World Cup revealed that three-quarters of the players came from poor or rural backgrounds or both, or were sufficiently dark-skinned to be considered non-white in Brazil's complicated but informal system of racial classification.

But in sharp contrast to beach life and Carnival, where the presence of women is welcome and even necessary, soccer has been an almost exclusively masculine realm, at least until recently. Women may root for a team, watch its games on television, and follow it in the press or even wear its colors, especially when the national squad is playing in the World Cup. But they traditionally have been discouraged from both playing the game and attending matches. A woman considered too athletic or too interested in sports is likely to be classified as a *sapatão*, or "big shoe," the slang term for a lesbian. And while Brazil does have a women's national squad, it has never won the World Cup, and interest has been minimal, even when it reached the finals for the first time, in 2007, against Germany, a fierce rival when the men's teams are playing. In some previous tournaments, games of the women's team had not even been televised.

"In Brazil, soccer has a strong gender demarcation that makes it a masculine domain par excellence," the anthropologist Roberto DaMatta once explained to me. "It is a sport that contains all of the various elements that are traditionally used to define masculinity: conflict, physical confrontation, guts, dominance, control and endurance."

In fact, some of the verbs used in popular speech to describe possession of the soccer ball are the same words used in the street to describe sexual intercourse. A player is said, for example, to "eat" the ball, just as a man who has seduced or conquered a woman is said to have "eaten" or consumed her. In addition, all nouns in Portuguese have a gender, and the most common word for ball, *bola*, has connotations that are as feminine as the voluptuous roundness of the ball itself. In cartoons in newspapers and men's magazines, for example, a woman's body is sometimes represented by soccer balls where the breasts and buttocks would be.

"You see players out on the field kissing or caressing the ball all the time," Renata Cordeiro, one of the first Brazilian women to be a television sports announcer, once pointed out to me. "There really is an erotic component to this, and it is all tied up with the idea of the man subduing the ball, just as he would a woman."

These gender taboos long extended to watching the game when it was played in a public setting. The stadium, with all its ritualized violence and swagger, both on the field and in the stands, was traditionally seen as off-limits to women. Not that many women were eager to endure the churlish behavior that often occurs in the stands, which at times can rival that of Britain's famous hooligans for outrageousness: Games can be marred by fights between *torcida*s, the highly organized fan clubs that root for a team, many of which prohibit women from membership. One favorite trick, called a *mijada* and practiced by fans in the upper deck, is to urinate into a paper cup and then pour the liquid onto the rival team's supporters sitting in seats below. But sometimes the violence escalates to melees in which fans are beaten or stabbed to death. More often than not, this occurs after the match, when all it takes to trigger half-drunk fans of the losing team is a single mocking remark.

Today, soccer so dominates Brazilian athletic life that to describe it as the king of sports would be an understatement. In the United States, fans of baseball and football are always arguing which deserves the title of America's national game, and basketball and hockey also claim large and devoted followings. But those sports are all seasonal, and they compete with each other for the fan's dollar and loyalties. In Brazil, however, soccer, played year round, faces no such competition. Even the most ardent supporters of volleyball and automobile racing, which probably have the largest popular followings after soccer, recognize that those sports are contending for a distant second place.

In fact, soccer has become an integral part of the Brazilian psyche and landscape, generating metaphors and slang expressions that are deeply embedded in the Portuguese spoken in Brazil. In my travels around the country, I have found soccer fields even in the poorest and most remote places, including tribal reservations in the Xingu where Indians wear nothing but a penis sheath and a T-shirt with the colors of a popular team, such as Flamengo or Palmeiras. President Luiz Inácio Lula da Silva, a long-suffering fan of Corinthians, one of São Paulo's four traditional teams, peppers his speeches with references and analogies to the game. His predecessor, Fernando Henrique Cardoso, was one of those rare Brazilians who does not follow the game, but even he felt compelled to hide his lack of interest, fearful it made him seem like he was not a man of the people. When the national squad won the World Cup for a record fifth time, in 2002, he made sure to greet the players on their return to Brazil, following the practice of his predecessors.

The relationship between soccer and politics is often a complicated one, with presidents and other elected officials cast in the role of supplicants to soccer stars seemingly exempt from many of the prohibitions that apply to other Brazilians. Before the 1970 World Cup, for example, General Emílio Médici, the military dictator in power at the time, criticized the coach of the national team, João Saldanha, for failing to add a player that the president admired. "I don't tell him who to choose for his cabinet," Saldanha, who was also a journalist and a member of the Communist Party, shot back, "so he shouldn't be telling me who to pick for my squad."

Saldanha was given the nickname Fearless João for daring to talk back to the president at a time when public dissent of any kind could be punished. Though he was not jailed because of his defiance, he did pay a price: Médici was already irritated because Saldanha had declined an invitation to bring the national team to lunch at the presidential palace in Brasília, citing a conflict with the team's training schedule, and shortly after he made his critical remarks, the coach was fired. Yet Médici, whose nickname was the Executioner, also gained from his devotion to the sport. Images of him with his ear glued to a transistor radio, listening to Brazil's matches, helped humanize him, and when Brazil won the World Cup that year, the dictatorship's propaganda machine hailed the accomplishment as proof that Brazil was prosperous, confident, stable, and moving into the ranks of world powers.

World Cup play can also have a significant impact on the economy. Statistical analyses have show that when Brazil wins the competition, which now always occurs during a presidential election year, Brazilians feel happy and proud, and they respond by spending more money, which bolsters growth and, by extension, confidence in the government. All bets are off, though, if Brazil finishes anything but first. In his memoirs, former president Cardoso noted that when he first ran for that office, in the World Cup victory year of 1994, he, the reluctant soccer neophyte, took the risk of hitching his fortunes to the national squad, while his rival, Lula, the die-hard fan, kept his distance from the team, fearing negative consequences if Brazil was eliminated. "Was it a slightly hammy bit of political theater?" Cardoso wrote. "Yes, of course. But it was also quite dangerous. If I was to be identified publicly with the team, what would happen to me if Brazil lost?"

Soccer players and soccer officials are aware of their exalted status and do not hesitate to take advantage of it, for purposes both good and bad. Occasionally they speak truth to power in a way that others cannot, as Saldanha did, but at other times they behave as if they are above the law. After the 1994 team's World Cup victory in the United States, players and coaches returned on a chartered plane that was weighed down with tons of computers, household and electronic appliances, jewelry, and other luxury goods. When they landed and customs officials demanded they pay duty, the squad threatened to boycott the official celebrations, and top government officials were forced to intervene to get the customs department to relent. And in 2006, when Lula twice suggested that Ronaldo, the national team's star forward, was overweight, the player took offense and fired a salvo right back at the president. "They say he drinks a whole lot," the player told Brazilian reporters. "Everybody says that I'm fat and he drinks. Since it is a lie that I'm fat, I think it must also be a lie that he drinks." After that, Lula backed down from any further confrontation, sending Ronaldo what was described as a letter of apology.

This sense of privilege and lack of accountability permeates the business side of soccer, which has become a symbol of all that is wrong and unsavory about Brazil. As a result, the health and integrity of "the beautiful game," as Pelé famously called it, has been challenged. Corruption, nepotism, cheating, and dishonesty all flourish, especially among the elite, incestuous coterie of executives that administers the country's leading teams and controls player contracts. Known as *cartolas*, or "top hats," because of their imperious behavior, high living, and self-indulgent spending habits, these sports bosses manage to prosper personally even as their teams verge on bankruptcy and as one corruption scandal after another engulfs them.

Like Carnival, soccer has been transformed from a mere entertainment into a big business, offering all kinds of new and ingenious ways to make money for those who are cunning. In 2005, for instance, two prominent referees acknowledged accepting more than $4,000 a match from gamblers in return from making calls on the field to favor one team over another. As a result, 11 games were nullified and replayed, and standings in the national championship had to be altered.

A few years earlier, the head coach of the national team was dismissed after a spurned mistress accused him of naming some players to the 22-member squad in return for secret payments from their agents. Prior to the scandal, the national team was thought to be one of the few areas of Brazilian life where choices were made on the basis of talent and merit instead of connections. Because of the team's prestige, the market value of its players soars, and they command higher transfer fees when later sold to teams in Europe. The coach, Wanderley Luxemburgo, was also said to have received a percentage of the transfer fee, which he then laundered and used to purchase apartments, paintings, and luxury automobiles. Despite the allegations, no official legal action was taken against him, nor was he banned from the game. On the contrary, since the scandal broke, he has coached five different domestic teams and one in Spain.

Questions have also been raised about the Brazilian Soccer Confederation, the entity that supervises the national squad. In 1996, for instance, the federation signed a $160 million sponsorship agreement with Nike in what was hailed at the time as the largest single sports transaction in history. The deal was renewed for another decade in 2006, four years after Brazil won its record fifth World Cup. But no public accounting of the monies was ever made, and to this day, no one knows in detail where or how it was spent. As a correspondent in Brazil, I made inquiries in 2002 and 2006, but the confederation simply ignored me, precisely as Brazilian colleagues had predicted.

When the contract was originally signed, there was jubilation at the windfall and predictions that huge amounts of money would be invested in new instructional programs, training facilities, and equipment to provide more opportunities to the poor. There is no evidence that this has happened on anything but the smallest scale, and even a pair of congressional inquiries into the federation's handling of the money were thwarted. In the meantime, the gap between Brazil and its leading European challengers, such as Germany, Spain, Italy, and France, appears to be narrowing. Brazil remains the best in the world and is the leading source of talented players, but that has become part of the problem.

Agents scour the back-country and slums for promising but extremely young players who they can then sign to long-term personal service contracts, which make the player personal property of the agent, not an employee of the club in whose uniform he performs. Although this system has been criticized as a modern and disguised form of chattel slavery, hardly any steps have been taken to prohibit or even regulate such practices. The commercial interests involved are so powerful and entrenched that even the protests and warnings of Pelé, who served as the government's top sports official in the 1990s, have gone unheeded.

Another consequence of this system is that since agents are constantly looking for the highest transfer fee, increasing numbers of Brazil's best players are being sold to foreign clubs and spending most of their careers playing abroad, not at home. Because of Brazil's reputation as a soccer powerhouse, even run-of-the-mill players are sought by teams abroad, both as box office attractions and because their skill level is seen as higher than those of local players. As a result, the export of soccer players has become a lucrative source of income for Brazil, if not necessarily for the players involved. In his 2002 book, *Futebol: The Brazilian Way of Life*, the British writer Alex Bellos calculated that more than 1,000 Brazilians were playing for foreign clubs. (The Brazilian soccer federation recognizes 783 teams as professional, each of which has a maximum of 22 players, which gives a total of about 17,000 professional soccer players in Brazil.) Many were in countries famous for the high quality of their club play, such as France and Italy. But others were playing in places such as Qatar and Malaysia, or even the cold and remote Faeroe Islands, between Iceland and Norway. A few have even changed their nationality so that they can play on the national teams of their adopted countries. Since the publication of Bellos's book, the numbers have only grown, and today a veritable exodus is taking place.

That outflow of players has both lowered the quality of play in Brazil and made it harder for the national squad to come together cohesively, since clubs in Europe are sometimes reluctant to let their Brazilian players return home for the series of national team qualifying matches that precede the World Cup competition. Of the 22 players on Brazil's 2006 World Cup squad, defeated in the quarterfinals after winning the competition four years earlier, only two were not "foreigners," that is, playing for teams overseas; a similar pattern occurred with the equally ineffective 2010 team, which, despite being favored to win a sixth trophy, was again eliminated in the quarterfinals after losing 2–1 to the Netherlands.

From the outside, Brazilian soccer appears to be a well-oiled machine. That is because of the obvious talent of the players, who continue to emerge in large numbers, like cars rolling off the assembly line in a factory. But up close, organized professional soccer is not just corrupt but chaotic. That sharp contrast—between flair and supremacy on the field and incompetence and utter dishonesty in the executive suites—is an obvious liability and mostly the fault of greedy *cartolas*. But Brazilian fans are to blame, too. They seem perfectly content to accept the status quo and ignore abuses as long as the national team wins and continues to bring glory to Brazil. Only a major World Cup disaster—being eliminated in the opening round of play, for instance, as has happened to arch-rival Argentina—seems capable of generating a constituency for the reform of Brazilian soccer. And since a debacle of that magnitude seems improbable in the near future, the prevailing laissez-faire attitude is likely to persist, making the chances for significant change slim. After all, "sin doesn't exist below the equator," especially when it delivers success after success and makes the people happy.

FIVE

CREATIVITY, CULTURE, AND "CANNIBALISM"

WHEN THE EUROPEANS FIRST began to colonize Brazil in the 1500s, Portuguese, French, German, and Dutch mariners or adventurers were sometimes taken captive by Indian tribes. We don't know much about what went on during the captivity because most prisoners never made it out to tell their story. However, one such hostage, Hans Staden, escaped. In 1555, he returned to Europe and wrote a book that became an international best seller, describing in vivid, even shocking, detail how the Tupinamba tribe killed and consumed the flesh of their captives.

Similarly lurid stories about Brazil's early history, which may or may not have been true, spread widely, carrying with them the popular notion that Brazilian culture was characterized by anthropophagy. In the world of academia, that is merely a fancy technical term for cannibalism. But ever since a group of critics and intellectuals gathered in São Paulo in 1922 to attempt to plot a course for the modern arts in Brazil, the term *antropofagia*—in essence, cultural cannibalism—has also been applied metaphorically to a doctrine that is used to explain, codify, and encourage Brazil's prodigious artistic production.

Brazil's culture is without doubt the country's pride and glory, its greatest achievement, and its main calling card around the world. The amazing vitality and variety of Brazilian artistic expression provides an entry point to get to know Brazil and its people, but has also made the country a cultural power. Is there anyone around the world within reach of a radio, television, or record player who has not heard "The Girl from Ipanema" at least once? Or who does not know of the brightly costumed musicians and dancers sashaying down the street at Carnival? Or who has not seen images of the broad avenues and towering glass and concrete buildings of Brasília jutting up from the grassy savannah?

To Brazilians, all of this can only be explained by the phenomenon of *antropofagia*. From the start, their culture has been a blend of European, African, and indigenous elements. But as they see it, their relationship with the rest of the world is one in which they avidly consume and digest artistic artifacts coming from abroad—whether French novels in the nineteenth century or Hollywood movies and British pop music in the twentieth—and in doing so transform them into something different, something that acquires a uniquely Brazilian character and flavor, and is then re-exported to the rest of the world. The bossa nova, for example, was born largely out of Antônio Carlos Jobim's fascination with American jazz and romantic classical composers such as Chopin, but he absorbed those influences and produced something new that is quintessentially Brazilian.

"Antropofagia is a Brazilian state of being," argues Caetano Veloso, the singer and songwriter who has enjoyed the most international success of any Brazilian artist of his generation. Indeed, Hans Staden's story and its symbolic implications remain fresh and vital in the contemporary Brazilian imagination, having been the subject of novels, songs, paintings, and a pair of films. Dressed up as a manifesto, the notion of "cultural cannibalism" provides a theoretical framework for virtually every important development in modern Brazilian culture. That includes the Tropicalismo movement that Veloso himself spearheaded in the late 1960s and in recent years has become an important influence on artists in the United States and Europe.

Though Brazilians have reached a consensus on the nature of the artistic process in their country, they are hard pressed to explain the reasons for the torrent of creativity that surrounds them and have advanced numerous theories in an effort to do so. One popular argument is that the very unpredictability of daily life in Brazil, the tendency for things not to occur as planned or to go off track unexpectedly, requires Brazilians to be agile and inventive and gives them an innate capacity to improvise. Maybe, maybe not.

After all, many other countries in which life can be even more chaotic and disorganized are nowhere near as productive as Brazil.

Brazilians excel at those creative activities in which the ability to adjust on the spot and improvise is most useful and highly valued, such as music and dance. It probably makes sense to add soccer to the list, too. The Brazilians took a stodgy, often physically clumsy sport born on the playing fields of the oh-so-proper British public school and transformed it into a joyous spectacle of dance and theater appreciated around the world.

In the arts, Brazilians have cannibalized and added their own character to everything from music to architecture. Where but in Rio de Janeiro, birthplace of the samba, would the managers of a beachfront restaurant feel it necessary to warn clients that "it is expressly forbidden to pound out rhythms while eating at the tables"? In how many other countries do passengers on buses spontaneously break into song and play a samba beat on the vehicle's windows, seats, and rails? But that is life in Brazil, a country where an explosion of creativity always seems about to erupt.

"When it comes to popular music, the only three places that really count for anything are Brazil, Cuba, and the United States," the bossa nova composer Antônio Carlos Jobim said in an interview I did with him in 1980 in the garden of his home in Rio. "All the rest is just waltzes."

Jobim's statement was meant to be provocative, but in an amusingly roundabout way he was making two fundamentally unassailable points: Brazil is a musical superpower, and it has become so thanks mainly to the seemingly inexhaustible ability of its musicians and songwriters to invent new rhythms and harmonies and avoid the plodding predictability of the European song tradition.

The samba and its gentler offshoot, the bossa nova, are obviously the best-known examples of the Brazilian popular music tradition. But while the casual listener may not be aware of it, lesser-known Brazilian styles, ranging from the *maracatu* and the *maxixe* to the *frevo* and *forro*, not to mention *axé, baião,* and *pagode,* have insinuated themselves into the work of some of the most influential international pop stars of recent decades, including (but not limited to) Paul Simon, Michael Jackson, the Rolling Stones, Talking Heads, Peter Gabriel, Sting, Eric Clapton, Beck, Earth Wind & Fire, Nelly Furtado, and

Devandra Banhart. And that's just in the English-speaking world; in places such as France and Italy and Spanish-speaking Latin America, the impact probably runs even deeper.

Brazilian artists have also made a mark for themselves abroad, led by Caetano Veloso and Gilberto Gil, the founders and theorists of the movement known as Tropicalismo. Jazz ensembles such as those of Miles Davis and Chick Corea, as well as jazz-rock bands such as Chicago, have had Brazilian members who left their stamp on the music both rhythmically and in determining the band's repertoire. More recently, Brazilian DJs such as Gui Boratto, DJ Marlboro, Sany Pitbull, DJ Marky, DJ Patife, and Amon Tobin have toured the world and become major influences on the electronica, house, trip-hop, and drums 'n' bass movements. Enchanted by the music coming out of Brazil, foreign artists ranging from M.I.A. and Asian Dub Foundation to Diplo of Hollertronix have visited Brazil, hoping to sample the wellspring of innovative sounds directly at its source.

For all we know, this creativity may date back to colonial times, when the original mixing of European, African, and indigenous elements that make up Brazilian culture was first taking place, in relative isolation from what were then the main centers of global culture. But it was only the arrival of the twentieth century and the possibility of mass diffusion and reproduction of culture through a series of newly developed technologies, starting with the phonograph and continuing with the Internet, that permitted Brazil to become one of the world's leading exporters of music, whose innovations are admired and copied by others.

That process has occurred gradually over the past hundred years, with technology helping to spread the new sounds. One of the first beneficiaries of the birth of big international record companies able to distribute sound recordings around the world on discs was the samba composer and flute and saxophone player Alfredo da Rocha Viana, known as Pixinguinha, who was invited to tour Europe with his group Os Oito Batutas as early as 1922, not long after the first 78 rpm recordings of his music became available there.

To define the samba is a challenge because it is not only a feeling and a beat but a way of looking at life and also one of the main symbols of Brazilian national identity, with associated styles of clothing and even its own slang and cuisine. The samba's basic rhythm is 2/4, but over the years musicians and singers have developed seemingly infinite variations to shift and vary accents and syncopate that deceptively simple beat. Samba is played in many forms, from bands with rock-style instrumentation led by the electric guitar to orchestras with large horn sections.

In its simplest and purest form, however, samba is played by small acoustic ensembles. Traditionally, these feature string instruments such as the ukulele-like *cavaquinho* to state the melody, accompanied by a host of percussion instruments with exotic names (*agogô, cuica, ganzá, pandeiro, reco-reco, surdo, tamborim, xequerê*) to establish the irresistible beat. As the old saying goes, inevitably incorporated into a hit song, "Anyone who doesn't like samba is either sick in the head or crippled in the feet."

No one knows for certain how the samba was born, just as the exact origins of jazz and the blues are shrouded by questions that can never be answered with any certainty. Nevertheless, Pixinguinha can be considered a Brazilian counterpart to Louis Armstrong: a brilliant instrumentalist, improviser, and bandleader who synthesized various African-based musical streams into a new and swinging style that captivated the world. Pixinguinha didn't write or record the very first samba: That occurred in 1916, with "Pelo Telefone," or "By Telephone," whereas Pixinguinha didn't make his first recording as a bandleader until 1919, when he was twenty-two. But he came to personify the samba's popularity in Rio de Janeiro, just as Armstrong will forever be associated with New Orleans and jazz.

The samba is the fountainhead of nearly all the other genres of popular music developed in Brazil to this day, just as critics and musicologists regard the blues as the main source of subsequent American popular music styles from jazz to hip-hop. This is not an accident: Both the samba and the blues have their roots in West Africa and were brought to the New World aboard slave ships whose destination would be Charleston, South Carolina, on one voyage and Salvador or Recife on the next. The result is a kinship and commonality of values, especially an emphasis on rhythmic complexity and syncopation, that helps explain why musicians the world over are interested in the music.

The emphasis on rhythm has even seeped into Brazil's classical music tradition. Heitor Villa-Lobos, who was active during the first half of the twentieth century, is the most frequently played and influential composer ever to come from Latin America. Born in Rio in 1887, he played in street and movie-house bands, absorbing the influence of the samba and especially the *choro* before undertaking long expeditions to the interior to collect folk melodies and rhythms. Those found their way into symphonic poems, chamber pieces, concertos, string quartets, and a dozen symphonies, in which Villa Lobos, a nationalist, sought to demonstrate that purely Brazilian themes were not incompatible with the European art music conventions.

But it was the emergence of Pixinguinha that marked the start of what has become a constant dialogue between Brazilian and American pop music. When he and his band returned from their 1922 tour of Europe, where he saw American jazz bands play live, he began to play the saxophone. Pixinguinha was sometimes criticized in Brazil for giving the saxophone equal footing with the flute, and some of his subsequent recordings, such as the world-renowned "Carinhoso," were attacked for being "too jazzy" or "too Americanized." But jazz musicians adored his music and over the decades have covered many of his songs.

The American public truly began to succumb to the samba's charms only after Carmen Miranda arrived in the United States in 1939. Thanks to a series of nightclub engagements and musicals that made her a Broadway star, she was offered the movie contract that would take her music to cinema screens around the world and eventually make her the highest-paid actress in Hollywood. The Brazilian Bombshell, as Carmen Miranda was called, made fourteen movies between 1940 and 1953, mostly campy studio items with titles such as *That Night in Rio* and *Copacabana*.

The samba presented in these productions was a much watered-down version, far from the authentic style that thrived at Carnival. But the beat and Carmen Miranda's energy were irrepressible and helped to establish the samba as a popular ballroom dance in America and Europe.

Back home, however, Brazilians were of two minds about Carmen Miranda. They were pleased that she brought international attention to Brazil and its music but irritated that she did so by playing a scatterbrain and reinforcing every condescending stereotype the Anglo-Saxon world has ever had about Latin Americans. Because Miranda was born in Portugal and never acquired Brazilian citizenship, others questioned her right to sing a music whose origins were black and accused her of bastardizing the country's image and culture for personal gain and the amusement of foreigners. She scoffed at such criticisms but was clearly sensitive to them; during an unhappy trip home in 1940, she even recorded a dismissive reply in a song called "They Say I've Come Back Americanized."

By the time of her death, in 1955, Brazilian music had left Carmen Miranda behind and had already begun moving toward the next innovation to have global popularity, the bossa nova, or "new trend." The roots of the bossa nova were in the samba, but a group of young musicians working in the nightclubs of Rio de Janeiro, with Antônio Carlos Jobim and João Gilberto in the lead, had also been listening to American cool jazz, especially recordings by Stan Kenton, Nat King Cole, Miles Davis, and Frank Sinatra, as well as classical composers such as Chopin, Debussy, and Ravel. Mixing all that together, they came up with a sound that retained the infectious rhythm of the classic samba but opted for a quieter, gentler approach in which the piano and softly strummed acoustic guitars were given precedence over horns and percussion instruments.

The very first bossa nova recording, an initially unsuccessful LP on which the pianist Jobim and guitarist Gilberto played as sidemen, hit the market early in 1958. A couple of months later, Gilberto's versions of "Chega de Saudade," known in English as "No More Blues," written by Jobim and the poet Vinicius de Moraes, and "Bim Bom," which Gilberto wrote himself, followed. Gilberto sang so quietly, and with such sparse accompaniment, listeners had to strain to hear him. But Brazil was in a particularly upbeat mood, thanks to the prosperity created by newly elected president Juscelino Kubitschek, and the bossa nova seemed to capture the optimism of the moment. Within months, it had become a national sensation.

By 1960, word was already spreading abroad about this delicious new sound emanating from Rio de Janeiro. The movie *Black Orpheus*, whose soundtrack included lilting bossa nova songs such as "Manha de Carnaval" and "A Felicidade," was enjoying international success. Jazz musicians the world over were particularly fascinated by the bossa nova, especially its complex harmonies, which offered them a platform for improvisation when they began to perform bossa nova songs themselves. In 1961, a tour sponsored by the U.S. State Department brought guitarist Charlie Byrd and other American jazz musicians to Brazil, and they returned to the United States excited by what they had heard and determined to record in the bossa nova style themselves.

What came next was a kind of quiet explosion or chain reaction. Byrd and saxophonist Stan Getz made an album together called *Jazz Samba*, which generated the Jobim-written hits "One Note Samba," which won a Grammy for Getz, and "Desafinado," or "Out of Tune." The next step was for Getz to go directly to the source: He collaborated with João Gilberto and his wife, Astrud, and Jobim to make another album, which was called *Getz/Gilberto*. The first single from that record, Jobim's "The Girl from Ipanema," became one of the biggest-selling records in history, won Getz some more Grammys, and convinced the two most renowned singers in the United States, Frank Sinatra and Ella Fitzgerald, to record bossa nova albums of their own.

Bossa nova was dominating the American pop charts and even looked like it might become the most popular form of pop music worldwide when it was abruptly pushed aside in the mid-1960s by the British invasion. This immediately had an impact in Brazil, where rock 'n' roll had gained a foothold with the emergence of Elvis Presley and had stimulated a movement called the Jovem Guarda, or Young Guard, led by the singer Roberto Carlos. Young Brazilian pop musicians quickly began to use electric instruments and incorporate rock rhythms into their songs, much to the disgust of the traditionalists, who accused them of "selling out" their Brazilian identity and heritage. By the time psychedelia appeared in London and San Francisco in 1967, Brazil was already preparing a response to the 1960s pop explosion in the form of the homegrown movement that came to be known as Tropicalismo.

Tropicalismo had its roots in Bahia in the early 1960s among a group of arts-minded university students and their friends, led by Gilberto Gil, Caetano Veloso, his sister Maria Bethânia, Gal Costa, Tom Zé, and Torquato Neto. They were deeply interested not just in Brazilian culture but in the whole range of international expression that was emerging then, from French nouvelle vague cinema and Andy Warhol's pop art to the Beatles and Bob Dylan. After Maria Bethânia was invited to perform in a play in São Paulo, the others gradually followed and formed friendships with kindred spirits there, such as the pop group Os Mutantes and the arranger Rogério Duprat.

Initially, there was strong resistance to what the Tropicalistas were doing. Their eclecticism, especially their enthusiasm for the electric guitar and their embrace of rock 'n' roll, scandalized the musical old guard. For much the same reasons, the orthodox political left saw them as pawns of American imperialism working to undermine the integrity of Brazilian culture and weaken the political resolve of young people. Televised song festivals were very much in fashion at this time, and the Tropicalistas often were drowned out by boos when they performed and eviscerated in reviews afterward.

Still, they persisted and in 1968 delivered a record that was both an artistic masterpiece, named by *Rolling Stone* magazine in 2007 as the second-best Brazilian album ever made, and a manifesto. *Tropicália, or Bread and Circuses* had a dozen tracks, the majority written by Gil and Veloso—together, alone, or in partnership with others—that drew on all the disparate influences that Tropicalismo embraced. Those ingredients included mainstream rock 'n' roll, European pop filtered through a Bahian sensibility, psychedelia, and even a reworked version of a tearjerker ballad from the 1930s, included precisely because it was so camp.

"I suppose I was the one who decided we needed to do a record-manifesto, a collective record that would announce that our work was intended as a movement," Veloso wrote many years later in his memoir *Tropical Truth*. "One characteristic of *Tropicália*, perhaps its own indisputable historical success, was precisely the broadening and diversification of the market, achieved through a dismantling of the order of things, with a disregard for distinctions of class or level of education."

Though Tropicalismo was not an explicitly political movement, the military dictatorship then in power correctly saw its anarchic aesthetic as a threat to the repressive order the armed forces were trying to install. For although Tropicalismo's primary concern was artistic expression, it also advocated unrestricted personal freedom as a means to that end, including a permissive attitude toward drugs and sex that the country's rulers saw as a Communist plot. Late in 1968, Gil and Veloso were arrested in São Paulo and sent to a military prison in Rio de Janeiro. After several weeks, they were released on condition that they agree to go into exile, and early in 1969, they were bundled off to London, where they spent the next three years, far from the roots that had nourished their music.

That episode illustrates two points: just how effective a tool of resistance to the dictatorship popular music, always the public's favorite means of communication, had become; and how determined the military was to suppress that resistance. Scores of songs were heavily censored, and some, like Geraldo Vandré's "So As Not to Say I Didn't Talk About Flowers," Chico Buarque's "In Spite of You," and Gil and Buarque's "Chalice," would be prohibited from broadcast or performance altogether. But they spread by word of mouth and became anthems of opposition, sung at clandestine meetings of student and political groups or even at public demonstrations against the regime. YouTube has rare archival footage of a 1973 performance of "Chalice" at a show in São Paulo, with Gil and Buarque mumbling new nonsense lyrics or humming the melody, leaving the audience to fill in the blanks. The military censor present at the concert understood exactly what was going on: He responded by cutting electric power to the microphones.

In a strictly formal sense, the exile of Gil and Veloso marked the end of Tropicalismo, since many of the artists remaining behind became more cautious, hoping to avoid the fate that had befallen them. But Gil has spoken almost nostalgically to me of how the experience of exile affected him in a positive way, exposing him to new influences such as reggae, Pink Floyd, and Jimi Hendrix. Rather than forcing Gil to close in on himself, exile ended up making him and Veloso even more receptive to what was going on outside Brazil and more convinced that Brazil had a rightful place at the table of an emerging global youth culture. When Gil and Veloso returned to Brazil in 1972, they promptly injected that attitude and the new sounds they had heard during their exile into the bubbling cultural stew, what Gil has called the "general jelly" of pop.

During the absence of the leading Tropicalistas, the singer Milton Nascimento and a circle of musicians and composers closely linked to him, known as "the club on the corner," emerged as an important new creative force. Initially based in Minas Gerais, Nascimento recorded a couple of jazz- and bossa nova–inflected albums in the late 1960s and also wrote several songs recorded by other artists at that time. But he had his first big commercial success only in 1972, with an album called *Club on the Corner* that moved him away from those flavorings and more in the direction of mainstream pop and rock. In fact, one of the songs on the breakthrough record was called "For Lennon and McCartney," and later in the decade Nascimento would record an idiosyncratic version of "Norwegian Wood."

Nascimento's chief attributes were his voice, an agonizingly pure tenor that he often allowed to slip into an ethereal falsetto, and his sophisticated harmonic sense, which quickly made him a favorite of jazz musicians. That quirky harmonic inventiveness, he told me in an interview in 1991, was largely a byproduct of growing up in a small and isolated town deep in the interior of Minas Gerais, where he was an avid listener to radio stations in Rio and São Paulo that played the latest Brazilian and foreign hits but had their signals partially blocked by a mountain range.

"You couldn't hear the harmonies because the radio reception wasn't strong enough," he said. "They'd play a song we liked and we'd copy the lyrics and the melody, but we had to invent the harmonies out of our own heads. Months later, we'd get to a big city to play the song and see that our harmonies were completely different from the original."

That inventiveness led to an invitation in 1974 to collaborate with Wayne Shorter, the jazz saxophonist associated with Miles Davis and Weather Report, on the album *Native Dancer*, today considered a classic of the jazz fusion genre. In the years that followed, Nascimento would work not just with jazz performers like Pat Metheny, Herbie Hancock, Ron Carter, George Duke, and Quincy Jones but also with some of the biggest stars in the pop music firmament, including Jon Anderson of Yes, Duran Duran, Peter Gabriel, Paul Simon, Sting, Cat Stevens, and James Taylor.

"Milton Nascimento has a beautiful, beautiful voice, and in his tunes you hear things that are almost like folk melodies," Sting told me in an interview in 1991, shortly after he and Nascimento had performed together on television in Brazil. "The idea that there can be truth in beauty is kind of missing in modern rock 'n' roll and jazz, but the Brazilians have kept it, and Milton is its finest exponent."

The other towering figure in the generation of musicians who came of age in the ferment of the 1960s is the singer-songwriter Chico Buarque, who in a 1999 magazine poll was voted the most important Brazilian musician of the twentieth century. Sometimes called the Bob Dylan of Brazil because of his gift for language, Buarque had first emerged in the mid-1960s as a "national unanimity," in the words of one critic, popular among all groups and classes. Musical traditionalists liked him because his music flowed out of the samba and bossa nova tradition, with which he seemed comfortable. Politically engaged people, especially on the left, were fond of him because his lyrics showed social awareness and often contained criticisms of the status quo wrapped in poetry. Young girls considered him as handsome as a movie idol, especially because of his striking green eyes, and their parents found him acceptable because he came from one of the most prominent families in Brazil, with numerous intellectuals and artists in his family tree.

Over the next few years, Buarque's lyrics, which had been agile and clever from the very start of his career, grew more and more sophisticated and subversive, and when military censors banned several of his most popular compositions as part of the December 1968 crackdown, he thought it best to go into exile. He went to Italy, and after he returned home, in 1970, many of the new songs he wrote, full of untranslatable puns and double meanings, continued to address social issues, and he also began writing plays and novels to express his concerns. Increasingly, however, he also turned into a writer of undulating sambas and love songs brimming with romance.

In the cultural debates of the late 1960s and early 1970s, Buarque was often held up as a kind of anti-Tropicalista defending traditional Brazilian values against the onslaught of foreign-influenced barbarians. That was a distinction always more artificial than real, and it became even less plausible after Buarque came back from his European exile, wrote and recorded with Gil, Veloso, and Maria Bethânia, and proved willing, as the decade wore on, to embrace some of the same techniques the Tropicalistas had been advocating. He, too, electrified his band, mixed and matched genres, sometimes in the same song, and incorporated foreign influences into his work, most notably in adaptations of Kurt Weill's "The Threepenny Opera" and the Brothers Grimm's "The Musicians of Bremen."

As a result, the Tropicalista experiment remains Brazil's dominant musical aesthetic even today in one important sense: Over the past four decades,

Brazilian popular music has been a delicious free-for-all in which anything goes. When reggae found its way south from Jamaica in the 1970s, for example, musicians in Bahia ingested it to create a new style called samba-reggae. Every new development in Anglo-American rock or dance music, from punk and disco to hip-hop, emo, and electronica, has also been incorporated into Gil's "general jelly." With the rise of the Internet, which makes such exchanges quicker and easier, that process has become almost instantaneous.

The Internet has also altered what might be called the terms of trade between Brazilian artists and their counterparts in the more prosperous and powerful countries of the North, or at least it has altered the footing on which they face each other. In 1991, Gilberto Gil complained to me that the outside world's fascination with Brazilian music was leading to what he called "cultural safaris," a modern-day version of the same exploitative colonial system that "enabled the Portuguese to come and remove all our brazilwood, and later for others to take away our sugar and coffee, more for their own benefit than ours."

When I asked him specifically about the wave of pop stars then mining Brazilian pop as part of the world music movement, he returned to the "cultural safari" analogy. He was troubled, he said, by the "attitude of the adventurer, the guy who comes in search of novelty, who comes in his air-conditioned Land Rover, his weapons cocked, and enters the jungle saying, 'Where are all the rare specimens? Oh, there they are.' And then it's *bang, bang, bang,* all of this without leaving the comfort of his vehicle, equipped with radio and computer."

By 2007, however, those practices had "changed completely," he argued, thanks in large part to technological advances. "Today the hegemony of the North has, in a certain form, been broken," he told me in an interview at his home in Salvador. "Local tendencies are allowed to manifest themselves and adopt their own languages and forms of packaging. It is no longer that vision of transforming some regional raw material into a single, standardized product. Today you have all kinds of local scenes that utilize universal elements."

As a result, Brazilian popular music today, respected worldwide, is bursting with energy and creativity on all fronts, a glorious pandemonium in which every style imaginable flourishes and is accepted. The Tropicalistas, now the elder statesmen of the scene, continue to produce work that resonates with audiences at home and abroad, as do Chico Buarque, Milton Nascimento, and Roberto Carlos. The process of fusing soul music with Brazilian pop, begun by the late Tim Maia, Jorge Ben, and Luiz Melodia, has been continued by Ed Motta, Luciana Mello, and Max de Castro. Longstanding rock-based bands and performers like Arnaldo Antunes, Os Titãs, and Paralamas do Sucesso also flourish, as do a younger generation of bands such as the poppy Los Hermanos, punk-inspired bands like Charlie Brown Jr. and Jota Quest, and reggae-influenced groups like Skank and Cidade Negra. In Rio, home-grown funk bands are especially influential in slum areas but have also had their work sampled by artists visiting from abroad.

Particularly impressive is the large crop of female singers that has developed in recent years, ranging from Joni Mitchell–style balladeers to hard-rocking band leaders. Unlike the female performers of past generations, from Carmen Miranda through Astrud Gilberto to Gal Costa and Maria Bethânia, this recent generation also writes their songs and often plays instruments on stage. Adriana Calcanhotto, Ana Carolina, Cássia Eller, Maria Rita, and Vanessa da Matta have already achieved stardom in Brazil, and the example they have set is stimulating other young women to follow suit.

Brazil's landscape of jungle, mountains, sea, and sky is so stunning, with colors so vibrant and attractive to the eye, that no one should be surprised that Brazilians have also shown a sensitivity to their surroundings that has translated into a vocation for the visual arts. This manifests itself not just in painting, sculpture, woodcuts, and architecture, but through film, especially in recent years.

During the early decades of cinema's emergence as an art form, Brazil was more a subject for outside filmmakers than a producer of behind-the-lens talent that could be exported. Hollywood's fascination with the notion of Brazilian glamour and exoticism led to movies such as *Flying Down to Rio*, made on the back lots of Hollywood rather than on location, and to Carmen Miranda's stardom. In 1942, Orson Welles was even inspired to come to Brazil after the success of *Citizen Kane* to film *It's All True*, a feature about Carnival and fishermen that was never completed. But the Brazilian film industry itself was at that time largely limited to formulaic comedies of little sophistication called *chanchadas*.

That began to change in the early 1960s, with the emergence of the movement that came to be known as the *cinema novo*, or new cinema. Inspired by Italian neo-realism and the French nouvelle vague, a group of young directors and screenwriters, working with virtually no money, produced a series of films that examined the political and social reality of Brazil in a way that had never been done before: with seriousness, using the most experimental, even avant garde, cinematic techniques available.

The first of these films to register internationally was Alfredo Dias Gomes and Anselmo Duarte's *O Pagador de Promessas*, a drama of poverty in the northeast, which in 1962 became the first Brazilian movie to be nominated for an Oscar and to win the top jury prize at the Cannes Film Festival. But the main leader and ideologue of the cinema novo was Glauber Rocha, who saw the movement as a Third World response to the monolith of Hollywood and preached an "aesthetic of hunger" based on the notion that the only things needed to make a film are "a camera in hand and an idea in the head," not a huge Hollywood budget. His debut, *Barravento*, came in 1962 and was followed in short order by three films that won prizes at Cannes and made him the enfant terrible of world cinema: *God and the Devil in the Land of the Sun*, *Earth Entranced*, and *The Dragon of Evil Versus the Holy Warrior*.

But the 1964 military coup essentially destroyed the cinema novo just as its most talented exponents were entering their prime. First came censorship, which limited the subjects that directors and screenwriters could address, especially with respect to political and social themes. The government soon followed by establishing a quota of locally made films that theaters were obliged to show. Perhaps paradoxically, this worked to the advantage of those looking for the lowest common denominator, and throughout the years of military rule the market was flooded with soft-core sexual comedies known as *pornochanchadas*. The impact on makers of artistic films, some of whom gave up or even moved abroad, was enormous, and even after the fall of the dictatorship in 1985, the Brazilian film industry remained in the doldrums, dependent on government largesse to stay alive.

But the years of dictatorship also witnessed the flowering of a television genre known as the telenovela, which provided a refuge for some of those no longer able to make the films they wanted, such as Dias Gomes. The telenovela is often described as a Latin American version of the soap opera, and while there are many similarities, there are also important differences, beginning with structure. While some American soap operas have been running for more than fifty years, a Brazilian novela always has a beginning and an end, and normally they run for 150 to 180 episodes.

Nor is the novela consigned to the ghetto of daytime programming. The United States has had prime-time soap operas such as *Dallas* and *Dynasty*, and in Brazil, novelas are similarly glossy, but they are on the air five or six nights a week. As such, they attract the biggest audiences, demand the highest advertising rates, and thereby are entitled to the biggest production budgets, with the cost of a single episode sometimes exceeding $100,000. Indeed, novelas are so popular that nighttime broadcasts of soccer, the country's other great passion, are delayed until the last novela is over.

The novela was invented in Cuba for radio and first came to popularity in Mexico, but it is often argued that Brazil perfected the genre and gave it style, heft, and occasionally seriousness. Under a frothy exterior, writers and directors of telenovelas used the genre during the dictatorship to make pointed social and political criticisms that would have been censored had they been working in another medium. For example, Dias Gomes's *The Loved One*, shown in 1973, focused on a corrupt and egoistic politician, while his *Roque Santeiro*, made two years later, used religious zeal as a metaphor for ideological fanaticism of any form.

Both of the novelas just mentioned were produced for the Globo television network, which has used its mastery of the form to become the largest commercial television network outside the United States. Globo's formula combines glossy production values and technology with improbable but appealing story lines that always have a romantic element. That has helped the network sell its telenovelas to markets as diverse as China, Turkey, Russia, and the Philippines. That commercial success, however, has led to a certain rigidity and predictability of form and a lack of artistic innovation, which makes the novela less attractive to new, emerging talents with a desire to experiment and tell stories in new ways.

Perhaps as a result, beginning in the late 1990s a new generation of film directors began to emerge, and with them, Brazil was able to reclaim a place on the world stage. The first movie to break through was Walter Salles's *Central Station*, the story of the love that develops between an embittered old woman and an orphaned boy as they travel across Brazil trying to locate his relatives. Released in 1998, it became a worldwide hit and earned Fernanda Montenegro an Academy Award nomination as best actress in 1999. Because of the dexterity he showed in making a road movie, Salles was then hired abroad to first direct *The Motorcycle Diaries*, based on the diaries Che Guevara kept as he traveled through South America as a young man, and then the film adaptation of Jack Kerouac's *On the Road*, which is scheduled for release in 2012.

But it was Fernando Meirelles's 2003 crime drama *City of God* that has really forced Hollywood and the rest of the international film industry to pay attention to Brazil. An unblinking look at the violent lives and deaths of drug lords in the *favelas* of Rio, the movie was a worldwide hit and earned four Academy Award nominations, but its biggest impact was aesthetic. Meirelles filmed simultaneously with 16- and 35-millimeter cameras and then converted the film to digital video and tinkered with the color tones before transferring the video back to 35-millimeter film. The resulting hues looked washed out and drained of life, as if bleached by a searing sun. Combined with the extensive use of hand-held cameras, that effect gave *City of God* a deliberately dizzying and disorienting feel.

"When you see the movie from start to finish, it seems like the director and crew are unlearning everything you are supposed to know about making a film," Meirelles told me in 2002. "I wanted it to look like we were losing control, because as time went on, the state was losing control of the area to the drug dealers, and that only leads to chaos."

Back in the era of the cinema novo, Glauber Rocha had declared that "we Brazilian filmmakers need to abandon the Kodak chart and discover the secret light of the tropics." Meirelles had done just that, and the rest of an increasingly globalized world film industry responded immediately. Meirelles himself has gone on to have a successful career directing the film adaptations of John le Carré's *The Constant Gardener* and Jose Saramago's *Blindness*. But perhaps even more important, his cinematographer, César Charlone, and his film editor, Daniel Rezende, took the techniques that Meirelles pioneered with them to their projects, where they have now been incorporated into the vocabulary of filmmakers everywhere, from feature films to advertisements and music videos.

But Brazil's struggle to create its own style and tradition is perhaps most clearly seen in arts such as painting and sculpture. During colonial times, isolation from the main centers of world culture actually helped Brazil forge its own unique variation on the baroque style then prevailing, in the form of a remarkable sculptor and designer known as Aleijadinho, or "the little cripple," because of the disease that caused him to lose his fingers and eventually left him unable to walk. Born in Minas Gerais, Aleijadinho, the son of a black woman slave and a Portuguese architect, worked in both wood and stone to create richly ornamented and painfully evocative statues of saints and Biblical prophets to adorn the churches of what was then Brazil's richest province. Contemporary critics such as Carlos Fuentes and José Lezama Lima consider him "the maximum expression of the Latin American baroque," and much of Aleijadinho's work, done in Ouro Preto and nearby towns, has been designated part of the "patrimony of mankind" by the United Nations.

In the nineteenth century, however, after independence was won, Brazil turned to France as its model in painting and sculpture and many other forms of expression, and creativity that drew primarily on local sources of inspiration was stifled. Any trip to a Brazilian museum that covers that period can be disheartening, since so much of the work from that time is so clearly imitative and derivative. It was only with the arrival of the twentieth century that Brazilian artists, encouraged by critics like Mario and Oswald de Andrade and an emerging class of newly rich collectors interested in national themes and scenes, felt confident and comfortable enough to throw off those shackles.

The key moment in the visual arts is the Modern Art Week exposition in São Paulo in 1922 and the manifesto that resulted from it. Young painters just starting their careers, such as Tarsila do Amaral and Anita Malfatti, were immediate beneficiaries, having exhibited works at the show that won them praise for the first time after years of critical mockery. Emiliano Di Cavalcanti, then twenty-five, designed the program for the exhibition and also had canvases on display; Candido Portinari, though somewhat younger than the others, attended the show and absorbed its ethos and aesthetic in his future works, which include *The Coffee Worker.* Together, these four modernists are the most important Brazilian painters of the twentieth century.

Tarsila do Amaral is especially interesting, for both aesthetic and commercial reasons. A canvas of hers painted in 1928, called *Abaporu,* an indigenous word that means "man who eats meat," is the single most valuable Brazilian painting ever. It sold for $1.5 million in 1995 to the Argentine collector Eduardo Constantini, who took it to Buenos Aires to form the centerpiece of his Museum of Latin American Art. More important, the oil painting, a semi-abstract landscape showing a seated man, a scorching sun, and a cactus, inspired her husband, the critic and writer Oswald de Andrade, to write his *Manifesto Antropófagico,* or "cannibalistic manifesto," in which he postulated that the principal characteristic of Brazil's culture is its ability to "eat," by which he meant absorb and digest, European culture and transform it into something distinctly, uniquely Brazilian.

Many of Brazil's other most distinguished twentieth-century painters and sculptors were not native sons or daughters but immigrants whose work reflects a sense of wonder and even disorientation at the brilliant colors, heat, and lush exuberance that life and nature demonstrate in the tropics. Lasar Segall was born in Lithuania, while Fayga Ostrower and Frans Krajcberg came from Poland; Manabu Mabe, Tomie Ohtake, and Tomoo Honda were all born in Japan; and Alfredo Volpi and Mira Schendel were both citizens of Italy when they arrived in Brazil. In one way or another, all of them were inspired by what Segall, whose best-known paintings include plantation landscapes as well as scenes of urban poverty and prostitution, called "the miracle of light and color" they saw in Brazil.

The modernists dominated Brazilian art until the late 1950s, when another manifesto led to a new explosion of creativity, controversy, and prominence for a new generation of artists and critics led by Lygia Clark, Lygia Pape, Franz Weissmann, and Ferreira Gullar. These so-called Constructivists, based in Rio, rejected formalism and sought to create works in various media that would blur the distinction between creator and observer and force the spectator to react in both a visceral and palpable way. By touching an object that has been freed from the shackles of strict compositional rules, they argued, the observer becomes a part of it and the true functions of art are recovered.

"We wanted to work intuitively, unencumbered," Lygia Pape explained in an interview years later. "In sculpture, the idea was to destroy the base and make an object that could be called such and placed in any position. Painting would also no longer be wrapped up in a frame, it would advance into space. . . . This sense of invention, of creation, was what really characterized the movement. At that time, it was still thought that a painting should be a picture on a wall, merely for contemplation. There was no sense of participation, of the use of different materials, so all this gave us a huge sense of freedom."

This was a quintessentially Brazilian attitude, which is why the country's leading art critic, Mario Pedrosa, described the movement as representing, despite its avant-garde characteristics, a return to "the pre-history of Brazilian art." Before the Portuguese arrived, Brazil's original Indian inhabitants created objects, which today are considered works of art and displayed in museums around the world, from the natural materials they found around them: feathers, animal hides and bones, plant dyes, wood and leaves, and grass and straw. These objects, ranging from headdresses and masks to pots, baskets, fans, and canoe paddles, were meant to be handled, felt, touched, and manipulated in daily life or in religious rituals and ceremonies. And when African slaves were first brought to Brazil, they arrived with similar notions, which seeped into the Brazilian consciousness and in modern times found expression in the costumes and instruments of Carnival.

Though all of the principal members of the group went on to have international careers, in retrospect the most influential seems to have been the youngest, Hélio Oiticica, born in 1939. In the early 1960s, he began creating what he called "penetrables," which today would be classified as multimedia installations. Oititica's penetrables were elaborate interactive environments, sometimes labyrinthine in form, and when they were first shown in London and New York, they caused a sensation among other artists. The most famous of these installations was *Tropicália*, which included banana trees, parrots, sand, and a television set broadcasting novelas; it ended up directly inspiring the musical movement that came to be known as Tropicalismo.

Gilberto Gil, Caetano Veloso, and the other founders of Tropicalismo felt a natural kinship with Oiticica and his ideas. "Purity is a myth," he wrote on one of his penetrables, and that was also the basic operating principle of the Tropicalistas. Early in 1968, Oiticica published an essay arguing that "the myth of 'tropicality' is much more than parrots and banana trees. It is the consciousness of not being conditioned by established structures, hence highly revolutionary in its entirety. Any conformity, be it intellectual, social or existential, is contrary to its principal idea." Each of those notions was also appropriated by the Tropicalistas and applied to music.

Oiticica died in 1980, but his "anything goes" doctrine continues to dominate Brazilian art, which today is a mélange of influences and tendencies in which no single school or approach dominates. The only orthodoxy is that there is no orthodoxy, as can be seen just in a quick survey of the current scene. Vik Muniz the subject of the Oscar-winning documentary "Waste Land," explores the relationship between drawing and photography with his melancholy gelatin prints; Rivane Neuenschwander makes installations with found materials from domestic settings; Marepe prepares ready-mades in the Marcel Duchamp tradition, often using materials acquired from street vendors in his native Bahia; and Tunga is a multimedia creator who mixes elements of sculpture, design, video, and performance art in his three-dimensional installations.

Far from the increasingly rarefied and academic world of formal art, Brazil has also developed a vibrant folk-arts tradition that is particularly strong in two fields. Working in both clay and wood, Brazilian folk sculptors have long excelled in depicting scenes from daily life and portraying archetypal figures and mythical beasts from folk tales and legends. Many such pieces have found homes in museums of folk and naïve art around the world. On visiting one such collection on the outskirts of Rio, at a museum called the Casa do Pontal, the Portuguese Nobel laureate José Saramago described it as "a national treasure, more important than Corcovado" and later cited the pieces he saw there as the inspiration for his novel *The Cavern*.

But in recent years, Brazilian woodcuts have become even more prized by collectors. The center for both of these forms of popular art is the arid interior of the northeast, particularly the state of Pernambuco and the city of Caruaru and environs. Born in 1909, Vitalino Pereira dos Santos, later known as Mestre Vitalino, began producing these figures of baked clay in the 1930s, and as his neighbors took note of the success of his efforts, they eventually followed suit. As demand and competition grew, the artisans began to paint the figures with bright and even gaudy colors after they had been baked in kilns, hoping to make them more attractive to customers.

Mestre Vitalino's much-imitated tableaux show musicians playing at dances, wedding ceremonies, families fleeing droughts, visits to the dentist or lawyer, domestic cooking scenes, cowboys and bulls, funerals, farmers' encounters with wild boars or jaguars—the whole range of life in the backlands from birth to death. There are also brilliantly colored life-size statues of Padre Cícero Romão Batista, a Roman Catholic priest born in 1844 whom many Northeasterners consider a saint because of the many miracles attributed to him, and of Lampião, a bandit active in the 1930s who even today is regarded by many peasants as a kind of Brazilian Robin Hood, and his wife, Maria Bonita.

The woodcuts draw on many of the same themes for their subject matter and indeed began as an offshoot of a form of folk poetry known as *literatura de cordel*, or string literature. Since the nineteenth century, unlettered folk poets have roamed the remote backlands of the northeast, reciting elaborately rhymed verses about real and imaginary events and characters, such as the Mysterious Peacock. Traditionally, they have sold the same poems, transcribed, at fairs and markets, with the woodblock prints as covers for the chapbooks.

Beginning in the 1960s, however, enlarged, folio-sized versions of the black-and-white woodblock prints, produced on old-fashioned hand-pulled presses, have emerged as a freestanding art form of their own. The most renowned woodcut practitioner is José Francisco Borges, an elementary school dropout and former herb seller, bricklayer, potter, and carpenter whose work has been displayed at the Louvre and the Smithsonian Institution. "Thanks to Borges and others like him, the popular graphics tradition is alive and well in Brazil in a way that you don't see in other countries," said Marion Oettinger, director of the Center for Latin American Art at the San Antonio Museum of Art, who also described Borges's work as "very powerful, moving and sophisticated."

Borges, who works with just a knife and a block of wood, often gives whimsical titles to his bold prints, which now sell for hundreds of dollars at galleries in the United States, Europe, and Japan. His subjects range from slices of local color, like *The Hillbilly's Honeymoon* and *The Goat Herder*, to purely fanciful titles like *The Woman Who Put the Devil in a Bottle* and *The Monster of the Backlands*.

"I carve what I see, not just legends and imaginary things that come to my mind, but also scenes from daily life or working in the fields, things that are linked to religion or society," Borges told me once during a visit to his workshop near Caruaru, where his prints were available for less than $20. "No one ever taught me how to do this, but I've got more than two hundred titles to my name, and I'm still coming up with ideas."

Critics have been saying for decades that the demise of the woodcut and other forms of folk art is inevitable, if not imminent. But, just like more celebrated manifestations of Brazilian popular culture, the folk arts continue to evolve, adapt, and absorb new materials and influences, which would seem to ensure their survival.

"The younger artists live in a hybrid world, and their work reflects an amalgam of styles," Candace Slater, an expert on Brazilian folklore at the University of California at Berkeley, explains. "They have taken art courses and they are in no way ignorant of who Picasso is. But at the same time, they are drawn to traditional themes like the Mysterious Peacock and Lampião. I take a long view: Their work remains immediate and deeply felt because the creative force and energy is still very much there."

Brazil's vast open spaces, tropical climate, and lush vegetation have also offered a canvas to architects, foreign and domestic. The most famous of these is Oscar Niemeyer, born in 1907 and still active as of 2011. Niemeyer is a national hero to Brazilians and has designed both public buildings and private residences in many of the country's major cities. Though considered the most Brazilian of architects, he began as a disciple of Le Corbusier, the Swiss-French founder of the modernist international style, but later developed a strongly nationalist manifesto to justify his singular aesthetic choices.

"I was attracted by the curve, the liberated, sensual curve suggested by the possibilities of new technology, yet so often recalled in venerable old baroque churches," Niemeyer, who also helped design the United Nations headquarters in New York, wrote in his memoirs, *The Curves of Time*, published in 2000. "I deliberately disregarded the right angle and rationalist architecture designed with ruler and square to boldly enter the world of curves and straight lines offered by reinforced concrete. . . . This deliberate protest arose from the environment in which I lived, with its white beaches, its huge mountains, its old baroque churches, and the beautiful suntanned women."

Niemeyer's love of curves is pleasing to the eye and is displayed in projects such as the Pampulha Complex, a church, casino, museum, and yacht club in Belo Horizonte, the UFO-like Niteroi Contemporary Art Museum across the bay from Rio de Janeiro, and the sinuous auditorium and memorial to Latin America at Ibirapuera Park in São Paulo. But his fondness for concrete sometimes undermines the grace of those curves and gives his work a clunky, heavy feel that it might not have if other materials were used. In addition, those who are forced to live or work in Niemeyer's buildings often complain that the rooms in his concrete structures are hot and annoyingly prone to echoes. Form, in other words, has prevailed over function.

Along with the urban planner Lúcio Costa and the landscape architect Roberto Burle Marx, Niemeyer was also one of the designers of Brasília, the capital city built in the middle of nowhere that has become the embodiment of Brazil's "can-do" spirit and ambition and a magnet for tourists. Many first-time visitors leave Brasília disappointed, however, and not sure what all the fuss is about. The passage of time has not been kind to the city: Reminiscent of the Epcot Center at Disney World, Brasília has a dated feel to it and seems like exactly what it really has become, a passé 1960s vision of what the future would be like rather than the future itself. It is also a city unfriendly to pedestrians and socially segregated, with poor people relegated to so-called satellite cities, not at all the monument to egalitarianism it was meant to be.

Niemeyer's renown and prestige, combined with his amazing longevity, have led to a kind of stifling orthodoxy in Brazilian architecture that has been hard to shake. One effort to counterbalance Niemeyer's influence is the so-called Paulista school of architecture, exemplified by Paulo Mendes da Rocha, who is the only Brazilian other than Niemeyer to have won the prestigious Pritzker Architecture Prize, architecture's equivalent of the Nobel. Also known as Brazilian Brutalists, the Paulistas share Niemeyer's preference for concrete but favor more geometric shapes, exposed materials, and rougher finishes.

Practitioners of the Paulista school, especially Joaquim Guedes, perhaps Niemeyer's fiercest critic in Brazil, are also known for their emphasis on an architecture that meets the needs of ordinary people. Mendes da Rocha, for example, has overseen the renovation of the Pinacoteca do Estado, an arts complex in a rundown area adjacent to downtown São Paulo, while Guedes, who died in 2008, focused on single-family homes that are resident friendly. Few would apply that characterization to Niemeyer's work, which may be its greatest flaw: Though he is a Communist who says he wants a classless society and claims to be a critic of elitism in any form, his own buildings tend to be grand personal statements that do not have the user in mind.

Because Brazil so excels in other art forms, its contribution to world literature is often overlooked. That lack of awareness may in part also be a function of the language in which Brazilian authors are obliged to write. Even though more people speak Portuguese than French, German, or Arabic, Portuguese is not often regarded as a global language, and while the numbers of translations of Latin American novelists, poets, and playwrights who write in Spanish have soared in recent decades, their Brazilian counterparts have lagged behind.

Brazilians also like to argue that theirs is "not a country of readers." Historically, there is some truth to this: It has often been claimed that Buenos Aires, Argentina, has more bookstores than all of Brazil, and even most of Brazil's greatest novelists and poets wrote as a sideline or avocation, forced to earn their living as teachers, diplomats, journalists, doctors, engineers, or government bureaucrats. But their words have always carried a weight in real life that is far out of proportion to actual sales, with sensitivities being especially acute among those who hold political power: During the era of Getúlio Vargas and again during the last military dictatorship, some of the country's most prominent writers, including some poets with hardly any popular following, were forced into exile because their work offended the authorities.

Few Brazilians would disagree that their country's greatest literary figure is Joaquim Machado de Assis, the nineteenth-century novelist known as the wizard of Cosme Velho, after the Rio neighborhood in which he lived. Machado de Assis is to Brazilian fiction what Mark Twain is to American literature: the model, touchstone, and wellspring who defined a national style; found and developed a truly native subject matter; and set the standard by which all who come after him are inevitably compared. The two men were contemporaries, with Machado being slightly younger and dying two years before Twain, and Machado de Assis even translated some of Twain's work into Portuguese.

Stylistically, though, Machado is one of a kind. His favorite subjects were jealousy and envy, which he wrote about with elegant irony and biting wit, both in his short stories and the five novels from the final years of his life that are considered his finest work. His prose flows with great beauty and poetry, but he is also an incisive social critic of the habits, customs, and behavior of the last years of the empire and the first decades of the republic. It is the combination of those two traits that leads critics even today to argue that *Dom Casmurro*, a study of sexual jealousy in a marriage, and especially *The Posthumous Memoirs of Brás Cubas*, a mordant analysis of the upper classes supposedly dictated by a dead man, are probably the best novels ever written by a Brazilian.

The English-speaking world has come late to Machado de Assis, but as translations have finally begun to appear in the past two decades, the accolades have grown and his reputation with it. The critic Harold Bloom describes Machado de Assis as "the supreme black literary artist to date," while Susan Sontag, another ardent admirer, called him "the greatest writer ever produced in Latin America," surpassing even Jorge Luis Borges. American novelists and poets have been just as enthusiastic: Philip Roth has classified him with Samuel Beckett as "a great ironist, a tragic comedian" who "underlines suffering by making us laugh," and Allen Ginsberg once called him "another Kafka."

To find their own voice, novelists writing after Machado de Assis, who died in 1908, had to veer off in an entirely different direction. The search for a new path led, in 1922, to the issuance of a modernist manifesto in São Paulo and, somewhat later, to the publication of the allegorical novel *Macunaíma*, written by Mário de Andrade, one of the leaders of the 1922 movement and perhaps the most brilliant Brazilian intellectual and critic of the twentieth century. Using a language embedded with popular and indigenous locutions instead of a high-flown Portuguese, *Macunaíma* recounts the misadventures of an Indian, "a hero without character," but nonetheless "the hero of our people, born in the virgin jungle of the fear of the night," as he travels from the countryside to São Paulo and Rio de Janeiro and back again. "Oh, what laziness!" is the character's catchphrase, one that has passed into daily usage, often used to criticize sloth in government and business.

Beginning in the 1930s and continuing for more than fifty years, Jorge Amado's work further advanced the notion of a truly Brazilian literature based on themes and language drawn from the streets. His many novels focused on his home state of Bahia rather than the two more cosmopolitan metropolises in the south, and through skillful use of that formula, he eventually became the country's most popular novelist. Thanks to hit film versions of his novels *Dona Flor and Her Two Husbands* and *Gabriela, Clove and Cinammon*, he is also well known outside of Brazil. Amado's critics, and there are many of them, complain that he favors a romantic exoticism over gritty social realism, but there is no question that his work captures various recognizable social types and explains the influence of African beliefs and customs on their worldview and values. His characters have also popped up in telenovelas and advertisements and have influenced fashion and culinary trends.

The reputations of two writers who were contemporaries of Amado but never enjoyed his commercial success have grown enormously, both in Brazil and abroad, since their deaths. Brazilians sometimes call João Guimarães Rosa "our James Joyce," and the comparison seems apt: His 1956 masterpiece, *Grande Sertão: Veredas*, is a dense stream-of-consciousness epic in which he plays with language, inventing new words and phrases to describe life in the arid backlands known as the *sertão*. That makes him difficult to translate, though a serviceable English-language version, called *The Devil to Pay in the Backlands*, does exist.

But the emerging literary star of recent years has been the novelist Clarice Lispector. Born in Ukraine in 1920, she came to Brazil as an infant and was raised in Maceió, Recife, and Rio, where she died in 1977 after spending many years abroad as a diplomat's wife. Lispector specialized in highly introspective psychological studies, exemplified by *Near to the Wild Heart*, a stream-of-consciousness rendering of the shifting emotional states of a young woman named Joana, and *The Passion According to G.H.*, in which an upper-class Rio woman undergoes an existential crisis while cleaning out her maid's living quarters. Lispector has become something of a feminist icon in recent years: Her English-language translator, Gregory Rabassa, has memorably described her as "that rare person who looked like Marlene Dietrich and wrote like Virginia Woolf," and other critics have compared her to Kafka and Dostoevsky.

Though they write in radically different styles, one thing that Amado, Lispector, and Guimarães Rosa have in common is an awareness of the suffering and poverty of their countrymen in the northeast (where both Amado and Lispector grew up) and the arid interior (the home turf of Guimarães Rosa). This has been a constant theme in Brazilian literature since the publication in 1902 of Euclides da Cunha's *Rebellion in the Backlands*, considered the country's greatest work of non-fiction, and has often fueled the political debate about how to rectify those yawning economic and regional inequalities. Amado is direct and colloquial about such matters, Lispector usually more subtle and oblique: "The room was the portrait of an empty stomach," is how she describes the maid's quarters in *The Passion According to G.H.* Her last novel, *The Hour of the Star*, however, is the painfully humorous account of a naïve immigrant from the northeast trying to make her way in Rio de Janeiro and has become a cultural reference point.

Among contemporary novelists, the enormously popular Paulo Coelho, who first came to prominence in the early 1970s as a writer of pop song lyrics with a mystical flavor, exists in a category all his own. He favors a spare, stripped-down prose style, which lends itself to translation, and writes slender fables and parables of spiritual growth and fulfillment, including "The Alchemist," one of the best-selling novels around the world in recent years. Yet some Brazilian critics seem not to know what to make of him because, by design, his stories take place in far-away lands (the Middle East, Spain, the Balkans, the United States) rather than Brazil and do not feature specifically Brazilian characters.

As Brazil has modernized and urban life has become more complicated, one of the main trends in recent decades has been to steer away from Amado's folksy and colorful regionalism to a kind of gritty and transgressive hyperrealism. Perhaps the leading exponents of this dark style are a pair of reclusive writers notorious for their focus on violence and other manifestations of aberrant behavior: Rubem Fonseca, a former police official who lives in Rio de Janeiro, and Dalton Trevisan, nicknamed the Vampire of Curitiba, which is both the title of one of his books and a reference to his home city in the south, which he rarely leaves.

Fonseca is primarily a novelist, and works such as *August*, the acerbic *High Art*, and *Vast Emotions and Imperfect Thoughts* have been translated into English. Trevisan, a lawyer by training, specializes in short stories that examine the underbelly of city life. Their work shares a common focus on human psychology and the suffering and anguish that daily life in urban Brazil can generate. Both men, but especially Trevisan, also write in a concise, unadorned style, at times as deliberately flat and unemotional as a police report, which seems designed to reject anything that smacks of being ostentatiously and consciously literary.

A similar process has occurred in poetry. The leading poet of the nineteenth century, Antônio Frederico de Castro Alves, was politically a progressive committed to the twin causes of abolition and a republic. But he wrote in a florid Romantic style, heavily influenced by French poets such as Victor Hugo, that was derivative and introspective and anything but experimental. Even poems written in defense of the abolitionist cause, such as "The Slave Ship," today seem ornate and overwrought—especially when recited by the Brazilian schoolchildren who are still forced to memorize them.

But the major poets of the twentieth century, though differing widely in the subjects they chose, generally sought a more stripped-down and precise style, closer to the vernacular. The American poet Elizabeth Bishop, who lived in Brazil for nearly twenty years and still stands as one of the superb translators of modern Brazilian poetry, was particularly fond of Carlos Drummond de Andrade and Manuel Bandeira, both of whom comfortably fit that description. In fact, Bandeira, who died in 1968, once said that he envisioned his poems "saying the simplest and least intentional things."

It is Drummond de Andrade, however, who has come to be regarded by his countrymen as probably their greatest modern poet—to the point that there is a statue of him, seated on a bench at Copacabana Beach, which was one of his favorite spots for resting and observing the passing human comedy. Drummond, who died in 1987, was an ironist who was capable of seeing life in the bleakest of terms, as in "José," perhaps his most popular poem, which begins: "And now what José? / The party is over / The lights have turned off / The people have gone / The night is chilly" and continues, "Key in hand / You want to open the door / There is no door."

Modern Brazil has also produced one world-class playwright, Nelson Rodrigues, who, the film director Bruno Barreto once said to me, "would be as important, had he only written in English, as Tennessee Williams, O'Neill, or Pinter, such is the universal, timeless, and subversive quality of his work." Rodrigues, who died in 1980 at the age of 68, also wrote novels, short stories, and journalism, but his subject was almost always the same: Rio de Janeiro's lower middle class, whose moral hypocrisy, especially regarding sexuality, he recounted with unsparing glee.

That choice of subject matter made for a turbulent career: During his lifetime, his plays were considered so disturbing and offensive that censors banned one of them, innocuously titled *Family Album*, for 21 years, and at the premiere of another, an irate spectator drew a gun. But over and over again, Rodrigues, famously derided as "a degenerate in suspenders," found himself returning to the themes of sexual repression, obsessive jealousy and rage, and deception, usually with a dose of shame, guilt, self-loathing, and physical decay thrown in for good measure.

"My plays have an aggressive moralism," Rodrigues wrote in *The Flower of Obsession*, a collection of his aphorisms and essays. "In my texts, desire is sad, pleasure is tragic, and crime is hell itself. The spectator goes home terrified by all his sins, past, present and future. In an age in which the sexual behavior of the majority is like that of a mongrel dog, I transform a simple kiss into an act of eternal degradation."

Though Nelson Rodrigues remains a marginal figure in global popular culture, Brazil is increasingly at the center of the action, even when its presence goes unperceived. In 2010, for example, the popular Cirque du Soleil troupe from Canada was touring the world with a show called "OVO," the Portuguese word for egg, to commemorate its twenty-fifth anniversary. From start to finish, the performance, designed and directed by the Brazilian choreographer Deborah Colker, was permeated with Brazilian styles of music and dance, from samba and ciranda to forró and baião. Yet spectators seem completely unaware that they are watching what is an essentially Brazilian show. The same goes for the hipsters in New York nightclubs dancing to Diplo's baile funk compilations from the favelas of Rio.

Ironically, these are examples of cultural cannibalism in which Brazilian culture is being cannibalized abroad by the very same people who in the past would have been furnishing Brazil with the material it would consume and transform. So, as Gilberto Gil correctly forecast, the roles of supplier and consumer are blurring and shifting, to Brazil's advantage. We are likely to see more and more examples of this in the future. Through the concepts of sampling and the "mash-up," the Brazilian tradition of cultural cannibalism is now firmly established as a global aesthetic.

Brazil may very well be poised, in fact, for another burst of innovation and creativity, this time with immediate implications for consumers of the arts worldwide. Brazilian culture remains nimble, comfortable with improvisation, and warmly receptive to all sorts of outside influences. Thanks to the Internet and the rise of digital technology, these can now be absorbed, adapted, and altered almost instantaneously, instead of coming to Brazil's attention years or even decades later. With 200 million "cultural producers" to draw on, it could mean the start of a golden age for the arts in Brazil.

SIX

INDUSTRIAL GIANT, AGRICULTURAL SUPERPOWER

THROUGHOUT THE SECOND HALF of the twentieth century, Brazil was one of the biggest and most frequent clients of the International Monetary Fund (IMF), which became a source of national dismay. Every time a crisis got out of hand, the authorities in Brasília ended up negotiating a belt-tightening standby agreement that required them to crimp expenditures, growth, employment, and investment in order to be allowed to tap into the IMF's credit lines for the money needed to keep the Brazilian economy afloat. As recently as late 1998 and early 1999, a run on Brazil's currency, the real, forced Brazil to turn to the IMF and other international lenders for what at that time was the biggest financial rescue package in history, more than $41.5 billion in loans and guarantees.

Nowadays, in contrast, Brazil is one of the IMF's creditors, not a debtor. Punctuating that shift was Brazil's 2009 offer to purchase $10 billion in bonds the IMF was issuing to help developing countries deal with the types of problems Brazil used to have. In addition, Brazil's foreign currency reserves, the product of a growing trade surplus, now exceed $350 billion. Much of that money is held in U.S. Treasury notes, making Brazil, which during most of its history has been accustomed to sending delegations to Washington hat in hand to ask for bailouts, the fourth-largest creditor of the United States.

"Don't you think it's chic for Brazil to lend to the IMF?" Luiz Inácio Lula da Silva, the president of Brazil, gleefully asked reporters in April 2009. Bursting with pride and maybe even a bit of hubris, he recalled the time less than two decades ago when he, as a labor leader, led demonstrations calling for the organization to be thrown out of Brazil, adding that he relished having the opportunity to "go down in history as the president who lent a few reals to the Fund."

Forty years ago, when Lula was working as a lathe operator at an auto plant in São Paulo, Brazil was regarded as a "developing country," the euphemism that had just recently replaced the phrase "underdeveloped nation." Today, the country is inevitably described as an "emerging economy," having left behind its Latin American neighbors and rivals, and is often lumped together with Russia, India, and China to form the so-called BRIC group. It is hard to avoid that term, which was invented by analysts at Goldman Sachs as a kind of shorthand for those four nations, which drew attention because of their size and potential, and continues to be used in investment banks and brokerage houses on Wall Street. The coinage is an artificial one, and while the term seemed apt at the start of the last decade, the countries' economies have since lurched in different directions.

Brazil is never going to have a domestic market as large as that of India or China, each of which has a population of more than a billion. To affirm itself as one of the world's leading economies, however, Brazil does not need to match them in size. For all the complaints about poverty and income inequality in Brazil, serious though those problems may be, the country started its modernization process at a higher level of development than either of the Asian giants, as measured both in terms of per capita income and the strength of its institutions.

Brazil's economic surge over the past decade can be gauged in numerous ways. Depending on what standard of measurement is employed, the Brazilian economy now ranks as either the sixth- or eighth-largest in the world and has passed countries such as Canada, Italy, and Great Britain on its recent climb. Over the past four decades, per capita annual income has zoomed from barely $1,000 in 1970 to nearly $11,000 in 2011. In recent years, thanks to nearly a decade in which trade has been growing by 20 percent a year, Brazil has exported more than $200 billion annually. Sometimes manufactured goods such as airplanes and automobiles lead the list, but other times it is traditional raw materials such as soybeans or iron ore that are at the top.

Today, Brazil has one of the most balanced and diversified economies in the world. As in most countries that have attained some degree of development, commerce and services account for the bulk of economic activity. And though people outside Brazil do not often think of the country as a manufacturer of machines, equipment, and durable consumer goods, industry in fact accounts for more than a quarter of Brazil's annual gross domestic product (GDP) of more than $2 trillion. Agriculture and mining, though highly developed and responsible for the bulk of Brazilian exports, each accounts for less than 10 percent of GDP, a pattern that represents a sharp break with the first 450 years of Brazilian history.

How did this dramatic turnabout take place? In large part, it is the result of 16 years of increasingly market-friendly policies that have emphasized financial discipline and opening the Brazilian economy to the outside world to make it more competitive. Fernando Henrique Cardoso, a Social Democrat, made that process the centerpiece of his government program when he took office in 1994, and Lula, despite his admiration for Fidel Castro and his repeated promises to lead a "rupture" with the capitalist model of economic development, continued and extended Cardoso's policies after being elected in 2002. Brazil always had the potential to become an economic dynamo, as evidenced by the excited reports of the early Portuguese explorers and its modern eternal reputation as the next world power. What was lacking until recently, however, was the political will, economic intelligence, and consistent policies required to put that enormous potential to work for the benefit of Brazilians.

The main challenge Cardoso faced when he became president in 1995 was to bring inflation under control. Since the proclamation of the republic, in 1889, spiraling prices had been a chronic problem, vanquishing one president after another. While some countries, like Weimar Germany, or Zimbabwe in the late stages of Robert Mugabe's rule, have suffered from short bouts of hyperinflation, Brazil's challenge was constant, which made it more severe. During the twentieth century Brazil had a cumulative inflation rate of more than a quadrillion percent yet somehow managed to stagger on and avoid an economic apocalypse. Over time, however, the problem seemed to grow more serious, owing to the phenomenon economists call inertial inflation, which in laymen's terms means that inflation tends to lead to more inflation, which leads to even more inflation.

In the early 1970s, during the military dictatorship, the government tried to grapple with the problem by instituting a program of indexation. In hopes of maintaining steady purchasing power for consumers, prices, interest rates, and salaries were all adjusted on a regular basis in an effort to keep up with the official rate of inflation. The figure was announced in newspapers and broadcasts, and people would take out their calculators to determine how much of an increase they would receive. That helped contribute initially to confidence and to a spurt of double-digit growth that for a while led to talk of "the Brazilian miracle." But as the decade wore on, indexation merely locked in inflation at double- or even triple-digit rates rather than eliminating or checking it. By the time the military handed over power to a civilian government in 1985, the situation was veering out of control.

For the next decade, one finance minister after another struggled unsuccessfully to bring inflation, which came to be known in Brazilian slang as the dragon, under control. Between 1986 and 1990, six different government plans were announced, each with great fanfare, each representing a different approach to the problem. But inflation continued to surge, reaching 2,700 percent during one 12-month period in 1989 and 1990.

Between 1940 and 1995, Brazil had to resort to eight different currencies, from the cruzeiro to the real. That in itself was a reflection of how badly inflation was eroding the value of money: Rather than print banknotes in astronomical denominations, as other countries sometimes did, governments would simply lop off three or more zeros when the situation got out of hand and adopt a currency with a new name. It was in part a psychological trick meant to convince Brazilians that the government was starting afresh, with new, more disciplined policies, but the result was always failure. Four of these eight different currencies were used between 1986 and 1990, when the problem was at its worst, generating distortions that threatened to sink the entire economy.

During that period, workers rushed to spend their entire paychecks as soon as they received them, knowing that if they did not, the value of their wages would erode so quickly that by the end of the month basic food staples such as rice, beans, or eggs could easily double in price. Some people even took to buying durable goods such as television sets or air conditioners as a form of investment, since those products would increase in price even as the value of a savings account would slide drastically. And though the law prohibited the practice, many professionals, such as doctors and architects, began charging for their services in dollars, payable in Brazilian currency at whatever exchange rate happened to prevail the day the bill was due. Companies played the overnight market, shifting their money from one bank to the next on a daily basis depending on who was offering the best interest rate. Often they earned more of their profits from such financial machinations than from the products they manufactured and sold. A samba song popular at the time posed the predicament this way: "What good does it do me to have a shopping bag full of money if all I can buy is just a kilo of beans?"

As he took office in March 1990, the newly elected president, Fernando Collor de Mello, announced the most radical of the plans to halt inflation. He froze not only prices and wages but also bank accounts and imposed high taxes on financial transactions. All of these were measures meant to restrict the flow of money so as to end inertial inflation. At the same time, he adopted a floating exchange rate, decreed trade liberalization, and ordered the privatization of some government-owned entities and the extinction of others, hoping to shock the Brazilian economy into a more competitive position. Inflation dropped sharply in the first few months, but so did economic activity. As a result, the government was unable to restart the economy without inflation once again taking off. The problem still had not been solved by September 1992, when Collor de Mello was impeached after his involvement in an influence-peddling scheme was revealed.

For all his many faults, which resulted in his being banned from public life for a decade (he returned to government with a Senate seat in 2006), in retrospect Collor de Mello deserves credit for helping open the Brazilian economy to the outside world. He increased competition through such trade liberalization measures as lower tariffs and reduced restrictions on imports of computers and other high-tech products. He also encouraged modernization of industry and tried to reduce government indebtedness. Each of those measures would prove important over the next decade as the economy began to surge.

But it took the Real Plan to kill the dragon of inflation for good and finally put the Brazilian economy on the road to the kind of stability that made long-term planning and broader structural reforms possible. The plan was introduced in mid-1994, while Fernando Henrique Cardoso was still finance minister. Its initial success provided the vehicle that took Cardoso to the presidency later that year. That provided the continuity of policy necessary to ensure there would be no backsliding to the bad habits of the past, when a new president would routinely undo the policies of his predecessor. Simultaneously, he plunged ahead during his first term with additional reforms, such as privatizing inefficient government-run companies that were a drag on the budget and thus a source of inflationary pressure.

One example was the state-owned communications company Telebras, which operated the telephone system. Because it lacked capital and was restricted in the rates it could charge, Telebras was never able to keep up with demand for phone lines, and people who wanted a line ended up spending years on a waiting list. That led to a flourishing black market in which phone lines were sold for as much as $1,500 apiece. Cardoso's solution was to break Telebras up into regional chunks and sell them to the highest bidder, foreign or domestic. The result was more competition, improved service, and a huge increase in the availability and use of telephones, including cellular phones. Today, such service exists even in remote corners of the Amazon, and Brazilian cell phone companies claim that per capita Brazilians talk more on cell phones than any people in the world.

The main feature of the Real Plan was the creation of a new currency with that name. Initially valued at parity with the dollar, the real was allowed to appreciate in value as large amounts of foreign currency began to flow into Brazil, attracted by the higher interest rates the government had also decreed. That made imported goods cheaper, which dampened inflationary pressures by forcing Brazilian companies to sell their products at lower prices out of fear of losing market share. At the same time, the government restricted its own expenditures, which helped reduce the deficit spending that had also contributed to inflation. The Cardoso administration also concentrated on building up reserves in foreign currency, which helped Brazil immensely when the real was finally taken off a fixed exchange rate with the dollar and allowed to float in early 1999.

Over the past 16 years, the stability brought by the Real Plan has transformed the Brazilian economy in ways both large and small. Perhaps the most important long-term achievement is that it turned millions of working- and lower-middle-class families into full-fledged consumers. In the past, those groups had been confined to the margins of the economy, living from one meager paycheck to another. They were unwilling to open bank accounts because inflation would only erode the value of their savings, and they were unable to buy on credit because they could never be sure how much their monthly payments would increase because of inflation. Suddenly, all of that changed with the assurances of stability brought by the Real Plan. The country experienced a boom in purchases of appliances and big-ticket items like refrigerators and air conditioners, as newly empowered consumers took advantage of their status.

Though the initial pent-up demand was eventually satisfied, that pattern of consumerism has continued through the inevitable ups and downs of the economic cycle over the years. Under Lula's administration, government programs meant to reduce the horrendous gap between rich and poor have also put disposable income into the hands of the very poor and helped them become consumers. For the first time in Brazil's history, nearly all of its citizens are incorporated into the economy, and the number of those living at the subsistence level continues to decline. The result has been a strengthening and widening of Brazil's domestic market. That has encouraged Brazilian companies to increase investment and hire more employees, which leads of course to further consumption.

During the Great Recession of 2008–2009, the continued vitality of that domestic market helped shield Brazil from the worst of economic turbulence abroad and was cited as one of the main reasons why Brazil's economy suffered far less than almost any other nation. In contrast to a country such as Chile, which has only fifteen million inhabitants and therefore must depend on exports to lead growth, producers in Brazil can find ways to prosper even without having to compete beyond their own borders. Since 1950, the country's population has essentially quadrupled, jumping from fifty-one million people to just under two hundred million, offering vast new opportunities. So while foreign trade has grown rapidly, to more than $380 billion a year, it constitutes only 15 percent of gross domestic production.

And since a market of nearly two hundred million consumers is inherently interesting to almost any producer, the stability brought on by the Real Plan has also encouraged a surge of outside investment in Brazil. In recent years, foreign companies have poured as much as $45 billion annually into Brazil, making it in some years the second-largest recipient of foreign investments among developing countries (behind only China). That has been a boon to every sector of the economy, from commerce and services to the two areas that are the main source of Brazil's wealth and growth: industry and agriculture.

As much as its leaders would like it to be, Brazil is not usually thought of as an industrial power. In the words of the old Frank Sinatra song, "There's an Awful Lot of Coffee in Brazil," and that is the product that foreigners still associate most closely with the country. Yet each year, Brazil's factories, most of which are concentrated in the São Paulo–Rio de Janeiro–Belo Horizonte triangle in the southeast or in the far south of the country, manufacture millions of cars, television sets, refrigerators, and cellular telephones. Brazil is also among world leaders in the production of chemicals and fertilizers; transportation equipment such as ships, rail cars, and locomotives; steel, cement, footwear, electronics, automobile parts, and paper products. Even allowing for all the advantages that Mexico enjoys from its proximity to the United States and its membership in the North American Free Trade Agreement, three-fifths of all of Latin America's industrial production occurs in Brazil.

As in so many other things, Brazil came relatively late to the industrialization process, which makes the spurt of the past half century all the more remarkable. Though the country manufactured items such as textiles, matches, and leather goods from the time it gained independence, the first modern steel mill, in Volta Redonda, was only built in the 1940s after the United States agreed to supply financing as a quid pro quo for Brazil's distancing itself from Nazi Germany. In reality, industrialization began in earnest only in the 1950s and took off when President Juscelino Kubitschek pushed for the domestic manufacture of automobiles. He also tried to encourage related industries such as steel, aluminum, heavy machinery, electric equipment, cement, cellulose, chemicals, and plastic.

This push to industrialize made sense because Brazil is blessed with enormous reserves of the metals and minerals essential to modern manufacturing, giving the country a strategic advantage that remains important even today, amid growing fears elsewhere of looming scarcities in crucial raw materials. Deposits of iron ore, for example, are believed to be more extensive in Brazil than anywhere on earth. The same may be true of bauxite, the raw material from which aluminum is made. Significant reserves of copper, lead, manganese, nickel, tin, tungsten, uranium, and zinc are also known to exist and are being developed for use in domestic manufacturing rather than for export to traditional industrial centers in the Northern Hemisphere. Coal may be the only substance vital to industrial production that is in short supply, but Brazil has found and developed substitutes that are cheaper and cleaner, as we shall see in the next chapter.

All of this was part of an import-substitution model meant to allow Brazilian industry to take root and diversify by protecting local producers from outside competition through high tariffs. That approach is very much out of fashion today, criticized as unfair and inefficient in a globalized world. But at the time, it seemed the most appropriate way for the government to give Brazilian industry, which obviously could not yet compete against wealthier and more experienced foreign companies, a chance to get on its feet and develop its own technology. And Brazil did not totally close its doors to those outside companies; rather, it encouraged them to come to Brazil and invest and build locally. One result was that Brazil eventually became the first country in the world in which every major automobile manufacturer built a plant. More immediately, import substitution led to a burst of growth, with industry expanding at 9 percent a year or more during the Kubitschek years, double the growth rate of the then dominant agricultural sector.

For three decades, Brazilian manufacturers continued to operate behind high tariff walls. That guaranteed them dominance in a domestic market that was growing rapidly but also allowed inefficiencies to creep into their business practices. When the 1990s arrived and the economy was opened to the outside world, some companies and industries prospered, but others faltered or disappeared. For instance, during the 1980s, Brazil had tried to encourage development of a domestic computer industry by virtually prohibiting imports of both hardware and software. But that policy was junked when Collor de Mello took office. He realized that Brazilian companies were falling behind the rest of the world in efforts to develop computer technology and would never be able to catch up if the restrictions continued. With trade barriers removed, the main computer manufacturers flocked to Brazil. The result is that today Brazil has more computers and more users with broadband and wireless connections than all the rest of Latin America combined, giving Brazilian companies significant gains in productivity.

Other Brazilian companies, however, continued to flourish in the new, more competitive environment. For instance, Estrela, a popular toy manufacturer, has managed to fend off Mattel. Domestic supermarket chains such as Sendas and Pão de Açucar have withstood the incursions of European giants such as Carrefour of France. The paper and cellulose producer Klabin has prospered despite the challenge of Georgia Pacific and has even expanded into Argentina. Some companies have taken another route, selling a controlling interest to multinational companies in order to modernize and receive new injections of capital. The oven and refrigerator manufacturer Brastemp, for example, is now a part of the Whirlpool Corporation, and, in order to compete with Nestlé, the ice cream and candy maker Kibon has become the local affiliate of Unilever.

In recent years, as Brazil has become integrated into the larger world economy, numerous Brazilian companies have expanded into international markets with notable success. An instructive but little known example is that of AmBev, a beer and soft drink conglomerate formed when Brazil's two largest breweries, Antarctica and Brahma, merged in 1999. Five years later, AmBev merged with the giant Belgian brewery Inter to form InBev. In 2008, that company bought Anheuser-Busch in the United States, becoming the largest brewing company in the world. As a result, a Brazilian from São Paulo, Carlos Brito, now runs the company that makes America's most famous brand of beer, Budweiser.

Internationally, Brazilian companies are especially strong in the area of raw materials. Petrobras, the country's largest company, is discussed at length in the chapter on energy. But the Companhia Vale do Rio Doce, known as CVRD, or just Vale, is another formerly state-owned company that has prospered since being privatized in the 1990s. Originally focused on extracting iron ore for steel mills, it has diversified within Brazil and abroad to become one of the three largest mining companies in the world. And in the space of one generation, the Gerdau company has gone from being a small steel producer in the south of Brazil to a world player with mills throughout Latin America and a growing presence in the United States, where it has bought up numerous American companies.

The biggest success story may be Embraer, the aircraft manufacturer based in the city of São José dos Campos, about an hour's drive from São Paulo. Founded in 1969, Embraer began by manufacturing training aircraft for a single client, the Brazilian air force, which owned and ran the company. Within a decade, it was making jet fighters for export to air forces in Third World countries in Latin America, Africa, and Asia and had also moved into production of civilian aircraft, first for Brazilian airlines and then for airlines abroad. But the company never turned a profit, and in 1994, it was one of several money-losing state companies sold to private interests.

Today, Embraer is the third-largest aircraft manufacturer in the world, following Boeing and Airbus. After delivering a record 244 aircraft in 2009, it began 2010 with a backlog of confirmed orders for 265 aircraft, representing contracts worth $16.6 billion. The company owes much of its success to an initial decision not to confront its two larger rivals head-on by manufacturing a wide-body aircraft. Instead, it concentrated on making smaller commuter jets for short-run regional flights. That sector of commercial aviation has boomed with deregulation and Open Skies policies around the world; chances are that if you are on a flight from New York to Indianapolis or Manchester to Turin, you are flying on an Embraer plane. During the 2008 presidential campaign in the United States, in fact, Sarah Palin, despite her "America first" rhetoric, flew around the country in an Embraer 108-seat jet, the largest that the company makes. That niche strategy has proven so successful, in fact, that Embraer has expanded into production of executive jets for corporations, presenting a growing challenge to Lear.

It is not by accident that Embraer and many other of Brazil's most successful companies, including most of the leading automobile manufacturers, are located in São Paulo. Though the outside world regards Rio de Janeiro as Brazil's showcase metropolis, the city and state of São Paulo are the country's real economic engine—in fact, some business leaders there have been known to complain that São Paulo is like a locomotive pulling twenty-six empty wagons, referring to Brazil's other states.

With a population approaching 45 million, slightly larger than California's, São Paulo accounts for 22 percent of Brazil's population. But it generates more than one-third of Brazil's economic output and accounts for nearly half the country's tax base. If the state of São Paulo were an independent country rather than Brazil's most prosperous and populous state, its population and GDP would surpass those of Argentina and Colombia, which are South America's most populous countries and biggest economies after Brazil.

Though the interior of the state is dotted with thriving cities that produce a wide variety of industrial and agricultural products, São Paulo's real center of gravity is the city of the same name, which over the past 140 years has had "the fastest long-term rate of big-city growth in human experience," according to a paper published by the Fernand Braudel Institute of World Economics, a research group in São Paulo. With a population of just over 11 million and another nine million people in the industrial suburbs ringing the city, greater São Paulo is, according to United Nations figures, the third-largest urban area in the world, after Tokyo and Mexico City. In 1870, by contrast, only thirty-one thousand people lived in São Paulo.

Like New York, modern São Paulo, both the city and the state, has been built largely by immigrants and owes its wealth and cosmopolitan character to them. That flow started in 1888 when Brazil abolished slavery and required new sources of labor. Paulistas like to boast that São Paulo has more people of Japanese descent than any city outside Japan, more people of Syrian-Lebanese descent than any city outside the Middle East, and more people of Italian descent than any city outside Italy. Millions more, like President Lula himself, who worked in auto plants before becoming a union leader, are peasants who have migrated from the poor and arid states of the northeast, just as poor blacks migrated en masse from the American South to the factories of

Chicago and Detroit. Today that thriving working class constitutes not only the backbone of industrial production but also an increasingly important consumer market for producers.

What most distinguishes Brazil, however, from other members of the BRIC group as well as those of advanced nations such as Japan and Germany is its unequalled agricultural potential and production. Put simply, Brazil has the ability to be the planet's breadbasket, feeding not only itself but much of the rest of the world. The country has always been a leading producer of crops ranging from coffee and sugar to cocoa and tobacco, dating back to colonial times. Over the past generation, though, Brazilian agriculture has dramatically diversified and modernized, with noticeable increases in both yields and the variety of crops grown. No wonder, then, that when then U.S. Secretary of State Colin Powell visited in 2004, he described Brazil as an "an agricultural superpower" rivaling the United States and even surpassing it in some areas.

Agriculture is, of course, the oldest method of food production known to mankind other than hunting, and it admittedly lacks the glamour and guaranteed profits associated with the latest high-technology conquests. But while industry and technology are often subject to fads and sudden, unanticipated changes—the iPod is created, the typewriter vanishes, whole areas of manufacturing are wiped out by some innovation—people will always need to eat. Brazilian government planners realized long ago that agriculture, if properly developed, offers a solid and less capricious foundation for sustained economic growth. As a result, they have always encouraged the production of foodstuffs and other products that can be grown on farms, plantations, and ranches, such as cotton, cellulose, and rubber. No wonder, then, that Brazilians sometimes refer to agriculture, which accounts for 40 percent of the country's exports, as "the green anchor" of their economy.

In this respect, Brazil has a clear competitive advantage not only over densely populated and heavily industrialized countries such as Japan, Germany, Italy, France, and Great Britain but also the other members of the BRIC group. With their massive populations and varied terrains that include deserts and mountain ranges, neither China nor India can spare the land that would be needed to support a massive expansion of agricultural production.

Russia does have such expanses, but they are largely in places where the climate is hostile to expanded cultivation. That stands in contrast to Brazil's tropical climate, which favors a year-round growing season in which two or sometimes even three crops can be harvested annually. Aside from the United States, which also parlayed profits from agriculture into the construction of a manufacturing base, perhaps only Brazil has the possibility of becoming simultaneously both an agricultural and industrial powerhouse.

Until recently, however, Brazil was usually hurt by its tendency to focus almost exclusively on one crop at a time, a process known in Portuguese as "the cycle of monocultures." In the late nineteenth century, for example, a boom in coffee production quickly earned a great deal of money for a few large growers and companies in São Paulo, which the smartest of them used to fund the industrialization of the state and build commercial family empires that stand today. But the coffee boom soon gave way to a surge in the production of rubber, which enabled a small group of rubber plantation owners and middlemen in Manaus to accumulate fortunes almost overnight. That boom also collapsed after production spread to Southeast Asia and was replaced by a brief cocoa boom in Bahia (the subject of novels by Jorge Amado). In each case, high profits created a feverish get-rich-quick mentality that encouraged overplanting, which led to overproduction. That in turn allowed intermediaries, most of them abroad in financial centers like London and Chicago, to manipulate crop prices to Brazil's detriment.

But beginning in the 1970s, Brazil began an effort, with both the government and the private sector involved, to diversify the crops it produced. Even when I first came to Brazil in 1972, coffee was by far the main agricultural export, and to an alarming extent the country's economic fortunes still depended on two factors that Brazil could not control: the prices set at the London coffee exchange and the weather forecasts for São Paulo and Minas Gerais every July and August, when a strong overnight frost could wipe out most of the crop and force Brazil to take out loans to meet its international obligations.

Today, in contrast, Brazil no longer depends on any single crop to keep its trade balance healthy. In barely one generation, Brazilian agricultural production has diversified to the point that the country is now among the world's leading producers and exporters of at least a dozen different food products, an extraordinary feat. Soybeans, for example, have boomed since the mid-1990s—thanks in large part to the emergence of a new middle class in China and other parts of Asia that wants and can afford a more varied protein-rich diet—and are now Brazil's leading agricultural export. In some years, in fact, soybeans are the number one export product overall, competing with airplanes for that distinction. While the United States remains the largest producer of soybeans, Brazil has passed it as the largest exporter of the product. That helps explain why the U.S. Department of Agriculture closely tracks every development in Brazil's main growing areas and why Brazil itself, as part of a joint effort with China, streams data from a satellite that, among other things, monitors the soybean harvest in the United States. A few years ago, the main farmers group in Iowa, Brazil's biggest rival in global soybean markets, even put together a presentation for its members called "Should Brazil Give You Heartburn?" The answer was a not-so-qualified yes, and in recent years, farmers from all over the American Midwest have been flocking to the interior of Brazil to buy up vast expanses of land, taking advantage of lower prices and a climate that, because it varies little the year round, allows multiple harvests annually.

But in contrast to the past, the soybean boom has not come at the expense of other crops. Traditional products such as sugar and cacao also rank high on the list of agricultural exports, as does coffee. In fact, Brazil remains the world's largest producer and exporter of coffee, even though that product has fallen from first to seventh on the country's list of exports. At the same time, Brazil also has become a world leader in the production and export of oranges, pork, cotton, tobacco, oilseeds, corn, and, above all, chicken and beef. Wandering about the Amazon, for example, I have met up with Brazilian cowboys taking herds of cattle all the way to Lebanon, where they are ritually slaughtered according to Muslim custom so that the faithful there can consume the meat. Brazil has the largest commercial herd in the world, more than 185 million head of cattle, double the size of the American herd. It also exports more beef than any other country, earning more than $5 billion a year, with Russia as its largest single customer.

This diversity helps to insulate Brazil from the inevitable ups and downs of international markets and has also given the country greater flexibility and strength in negotiating contracts. If the price of soybeans falls, as it did in the middle of the last decade, rising prices for grass-fed beef and soy-fed chicken, an outgrowth of the mad cow scare in Europe, help compensate for that drop and prevent damage to Brazil's overall balance of payments. If Brazil had already invested more in storage facilities for its crops, as farmers in the American Midwest have long done, its bargaining power would be even greater. But that improvement is also in the works, as rural cooperatives, especially in the fertile states of the Center-West, become more prosperous and invest in their own future. So Brazil looks to gain an even stronger market position in the next few years.

Much of the surge in soybean and other agricultural production has come from the cerrado, a vast savannah that stretches for more than a thousand miles across central Brazil, just south of the Amazon. Written off for centuries as useless, the cerrado region has been transformed in less than a generation into Brazil's grain belt. That is thanks in large part to the pioneering work of agronomists at the Brazilian Agricultural and Livestock Research Company, a government agency known in Portuguese as Embrapa. Beginning in the mid-1970s, Embrapa scientists made advances in two important areas. First, after experimenting to find the proper mixture of chemicals, they determined that the soils of the cerrado could be made fertile by dousing them with phosphorous and lime to reduce their natural acidity. At the same time, Embrapa scientists also developed more than forty tropical varieties of soybeans, which until then had been thought of as a crop to be grown only in temperate climates, and provided technical assistance to the farmers who planted those seeds.

Today, three-quarters of Brazil's cotton production also comes from the cerrado, which provides pasture land for nearly half of Brazil's cattle herds as well. In addition, Embrapa has bred a variety of tropical hog that is lower in fat and cholesterol than its American counterpart and has a higher yield of loin and ham, resulting in a surge in Brazilian pork exports. Encouraged by those results, Embrapa scientists in recent years have focused on adapting other temperate-zone crops, such as wheat, to the tropics. Brazil has historically imported most of its wheat from nearby countries like Argentina. But Embrapa has already developed several varieties of wheat for planting in the tropical cerrado, with yields comparable to those in places such as Canada or Australia, and is also investigating ways to adapt barley to the region.

Already a world leader in research in the increasingly promising field of tropical agriculture, Embrapa in recent years has also begun to moving aggressively into cutting-edge areas like biotechnology and bioenergy. In 2007, Embrapa and BASF, the German chemical maker, announced a partnership to develop a genetically modified, herbicide-resistant soybean. That product is likely to be on the market by 2012 and is expected to compete with Monsanto's Roundup Ready brand, which currently dominates the market. And though Embrapa remains a government entity, in 2005 it gained authorization from the Brazilian Congress to form joint ventures and retain profits from those commercial undertakings, a step meant to help Embrapa overcome Brazil's chronic shortage of investment capital.

With the support of the World Bank and other international development bodies, Embrapa has also become more active in Asia and especially Africa. In 2007, it opened an office in Ghana to help transfer Brazilian technology and methods to countries that have savannahs with soil and rain conditions similar to the cerrado and would like to duplicate Brazil's success. In the long term, that could mean commercial possibilities and royalties for Brazil in assisting nations that want to raise their yields of soy, beef, corn, and especially cassava, a starchy tuber that is a staple in the diet of people in tropical areas all over the world. Dr. Norman Borlaug, father of the so-called Green Revolution and winner of the Nobel Peace Prize, told me in 2007 that having "transformed a wasteland into one of the most productive agricultural areas in the world," Embrapa and its scientists deserve recognition for "one of the great achievements of agricultural science in the twentieth century."

Considered together, Embrapa and Embraer are examples of a strategy that has served Brazil well as it tries to claw its way up the economic and technological ladder in a globalized and increasingly competitive world. As a latecomer to development, Brazil has found that the quickest way to become competitive is to find a niche that others have ignored and exploit it aggressively. The consortium known as FAPESP, which is an acronym for the Research Support Foundation of the State of São Paulo, offers another example. It has chosen to focus on genomics and has become a world leader in that field. Brazilian researchers funded by FAPESP were the first to sequence the genome of sugarcane; others have sequenced the genome of plant pests that afflict fruit trees and of the eucalyptus tree, favored by the Brazilian paper and cellulose industry because it grows faster than other trees. Those research efforts have obvious economic importance because Brazil is the world's leading exporter of those products.

For all the bounty Brazil has reaped from its soil, though, agriculture continues to pose riddles the country has been unable to resolve. In 1940, 80 percent of Brazil's population lived in the countryside and only 20 percent in cities. By the turn of the century, those percentages had exactly reversed. But that still means 40 million people live on and from the land, many of whom are sharecroppers, tenant or subsistence farmers detached from world and even local markets, barely eking out a living from their efforts. This may be primarily a social problem, and is seen as such, but it is also a challenge to the economy.

Land ownership in Brazil has always been concentrated among a small elite. But the inexorable logic of modern agribusiness, with its emphasis on the economies of scale that come with large farms and ranches, exacerbates that tendency even further, as does Brazil's focus on production for export. According to figures released in 2009 by the Brazilian Institute of Geography and Statistics, a government body, the concentration of land ownership has worsened, rather than improved, over the past decade. More than 1.3 million farmers abandoned their livelihood during that period, but of those who remain, nearly 40 percent can neither read nor write. As might be expected, this problem of inequality is most severe in the country's poorest states, where the most land is owned by the fewest people.

So Brazil at some point is going to have to choose whether it wants to mechanize and standardize agricultural production fully, as the United States has done, nearly wiping out the family farm in the process, or preserve a niche for tenant and subsistence farmers, as economically inefficient as that may be. That is obviously a political decision, and while Lula, as a man of the left who himself comes from a peasant background, made it clear he prefers the second option, future governments may not feel the same way. But then Brazil will have to find some other way to incorporate that idled labor force into other parts of the economy and make them productive members of society.

With both industry and agriculture booming, the past decade has seen a remarkable expansion of Brazil's trade with the rest of the world. Accompanying that upsurge has been a notable improvement in the country's balance of trade compared to recent decades, when a flood of imported equipment and machinery needed in the industrialization process often led to deficits. In 1999, total exports and imports were almost perfectly balanced and fell just short of a total of $100 billion, a relatively small amount for a country of Brazil's size. But by the time those figures were tallied at the end of 2008, just as the financial crisis in the United States was detonating, Brazil's trade had nearly quadrupled to $371 billion, and exports exceeded imports by $24.7 billion. Overall, trade that year amounted to the equivalent of nearly 20 percent of GDP. That was a record for Brazil in modern times, though still below the performance of smaller Latin American countries such as Chile or even Mexico, where trade routinely exceeds 50 percent of GDP.

Trade surpluses are common in countries at Brazil's stage of development, and even larger surpluses had been registered in the middle of the decade, when for three years in a row Brazil's exports exceeded its imports by more than $40 billion. Those surpluses pale, of course, when compared to China's and are largely the result of high demand for commodities ranging from iron ore to soybeans rather than manufactured products, the main source of China's surplus. But, in contrast to China's case, they are not the result of a manipulated exchange rate or policies deliberately meant to restrict imports. In Brazil's case, imports have grown by more than 40 percent in some recent years, in part because the real has strengthened against the dollar, making imports cheaper.

Of equal or perhaps even greater significance is the way Brazil has managed to diversify its trading partners over the past decade or so. Historically, the United States has been Brazil's biggest customer and supplier, a pattern that dates back nearly a century. At times during that period, the United States has accounted for more than two-thirds of all of Brazil's trade with the outside world. But in the 1990s, government planners began pursuing a policy that aimed to reconfigure Brazil's trade patterns so that international commerce would be divided as close as possible into quarters, with Latin America, North America, Europe, and Asia having equal shares. That goal has largely been achieved: In April 2009, in fact, China replaced the United States as Brazil's largest single trading partner, thanks mostly to a surge in demand for iron ore. Overall, Brazil's trade today is broken down this way: 25 percent with the European Union, 25 percent with Latin America, 25 percent with Asia, 14 percent with the United States, and 11 percent with others, including Africa, the Middle East, Eastern Europe, and Canada.

That shift helped cushion Brazil from the full impact of the economic crisis that began in the United States in 2008. Brazil's situation stands in sharp contrast to Mexico, whose economic fortunes remain dependent on its relationship with its northern neighbor, as well as with many other Latin American and Caribbean nations. That is one more reason that Brazil seems especially well positioned to benefit from the uptick in world trade that is expected when the Great Recession finally ends. Thanks to its seemingly unquenchable thirst for natural resources such as iron ore, other metals, and wood pulp, China seems likely to remain Brazil's most important trade partner. What seems to have developed over the past decade or so is a triangular relationship in which Brazil exports raw materials to China, where they are transformed into consumer goods and other finished products that are then sold to the United States. As a result, some institutional investors now regard a presence in Brazil as an indirect form of investing in China, where legal protections are notoriously scarce and the market is manipulated by the government.

Though that arrangement, combined with soaring sales of soybeans and other foodstuffs, has helped Brazil accumulate big trade surpluses and build its reserves of hard currency, doubt and discontent are starting to arise in some quarters in Brazil, especially among business leaders in São Paulo. In colonial times, Brazil's natural riches maintained the prosperity of the Portuguese empire without benefiting Brazilians, and in the nineteenth century, those resources were essential to Great Britain and the United States in their drives to industrialize. Brazilians are very much aware of that pattern. The last thing they want in the twenty-first century is to again be cast in the role of the supplier to an emerging industrial giant, forced to content themselves with crumbs. As a result, demands that China process some of its products in Brazil, thereby creating added value for both sides, are growing. So are complaints about the Chinese export juggernaut, which threatens to wipe out Brazilian domestic industry in such traditional areas as footwear and textiles.

When the global financial crisis of 2008 first erupted, Brazil's initial reaction was to scoff at the problem. "Crisis? What crisis?" Lula asked shortly after Lehman Brothers collapsed in September that year. "Ask Bush. It's his crisis." But the technocrats at the Central Bank and the ministries of finance and planning knew otherwise. To start with, one-fifth of Brazil's credit markets consisted of money that came from abroad. That meant that the instant those lines dried up because of problems in the United States and elsewhere, Brazilian companies were no longer able to get or renew loans. Nor were Brazilian commercial banks able to pick up the slack, since a good part of their liquidity also depended on maintaining abundant flows of capital from abroad. With consumers no longer able to get automobile loans, for example, activity in the industrial sector quickly began retracting, and it looked as if Brazil might be pulled into the Great Recession.

But because the Brazilian government had been building up budget and trade surpluses and following other fiscally responsible policies for so many years, in sharp contrast to the United States under George W. Bush, the Brazilian Central Bank had accumulated, as mentioned above, more than $200 billion in reserves. Those assets were quickly deployed, increasing the availability of domestic lines of credit in dollars to compensate for the sudden evaporation of overseas flows. In addition, the Central Bank lowered an onerously high reserve requirement for banks, giving them an additional source of funds they could loan. It also lowered interest rates, which had been among the highest in the world. As a result, Brazil did not have to spend a single penny to rescue banks, and even before the end of 2008, credit had begun flowing again.

Indirectly, though, Brazilian exports, especially of raw materials, did suffer. With consumers in the United States cutting back sharply on their purchases, China, the source of many manufactured goods, tamped down production and no longer needed to import as much iron, aluminum, copper, or wood from Brazil. But domestic demand, which had been growing at a 9 percent annual rate, continued to be robust. So in contrast to previous crises, such as the financial crunch of 1997, in which the so-called contagion effect of problems in Southeast Asia, Turkey, and Russia eventually infected perceptions of Brazil, this time around Brazil was cast in the rescuer's role. In September 2009, U.S. Secretary of the Treasury Timothy Geithner went so far as to publicly thank Brazil for helping to lead the world out of recession. His remarks drew little attention in the United States, but in Brazil they generated front-page headlines and expressions of astonished pride at the country's new status.

It is also worth noting that Brazil never fell into the trap of believing the mantra repeated in the United States during the Bush years: that an all-knowing market always makes the best choices and therefore does not need regulation. All but one of the country's main political parties endorse the notion of a significant state role, and the state has often actively guided economic policy. That role is not as intrusive as in China, or even Japan, or India, but there is a consensus in Brazil that the profit motive does not always guarantee the best outcome for society as a whole and that some supervision is therefore necessary. That belief is sometimes subject to debate, especially when raised by the business groups that maintain Brazil would prosper quicker if the entrepreneurial spirit could only operate untrammeled. But government regulation of the financial and other sectors clearly helped spare Brazil from the worst effects of the crisis of 2008–2009.

For all that Brazil has achieved in the space of barely one generation, however, it continues to face significant structural bottlenecks that prevent its economy from performing at anywhere near maximum levels of efficiency. The most important of these problems is widespread deficiencies in its physical infrastructure. The second most important is the large, inefficient, and often corrupt bureaucracy that administers a baffling system of forms, permits, licenses, and regulations that is the despair of anyone who does business and is known locally as "the Brazil cost."

Brazil's infrastructure problems are obvious, especially in the transport sector, and can be alleviated, if not solved, simply by more investment. Ports are clogged in large part because there are simply not enough docks and warehouses (though featherbedding labor practices are also a factor). Commercial air transportation, essential in a country of continental dimensions, nearly broke down in 2007 because of the safety issues raised by antiquated air traffic control equipment, including failures of radar tracking systems. There are not enough highways, especially interstate, and many of those that do exist are forced to bear too much traffic or were built in a shoddy fashion, which leads to potholes that slow and damage vehicles. And for a country of its size, Brazil, in sharp contrast to India or China, has no real railway network, even in the heavily populated and industrialized southeast. For decades, for example, Brazilians have talked of building a speedy rail link between São Paulo and Rio de Janeiro comparable to the Tokyo-Osaka bullet train or Amtrak service between New York and Washington, D.C. But only now—after decades of hemming and hawing and deadlines that came and went—does construction finally seem about to begin, and that is because of promises that Brazil made to secure the 2016 Olympics for Rio de Janeiro.

Dealing with bureaucratic bottlenecks, on the other hand, may be an even more complex problem that requires not an increase in investment, but changing a mentality that has been in place almost since the Portuguese arrived five hundred years ago. Demands for certificates, credentials, permits, and other official documents pervade all aspects of Brazilian life, leading to long lines and lost time. I can still recall my astonishment when my wife was required to take her grandmother to obtain a sworn statement that the 80-year-old woman was still alive in order to continue receiving her social security benefits at the bank where she personally picked up her check every month. In the late 1980s, a ministry of debureaucratization was even created to combat the problem, but it merely generated a new layer of inspections and requirements before collapsing under public ridicule.

On a regular basis, the press and business groups conduct studies comparing the process of opening a business in Brazil with that in other countries around the world. Inevitably, the results show that Brazil requires more paperwork and is slower to process those authorizations than almost any other country with significant industrial and commercial sectors. According to a World Bank survey from 2009, for example, on average it takes five months to complete all of the paperwork required to set up a business in Brazil. Of the 181 countries measured in the survey, Brazil ranked 125th, far below most of the countries it sees as its rivals or which it aspires to surpass.

This bottleneck has led to a complex system in which veritable armies of so-called *despachantes*, or "dispatchers," are hired to speed things along. As mentioned earlier, it is the dispatcher's job to "agilize" the paperwork process and prevent forms from languishing for months in dusty corners of government offices. That, more often than not, is achieved through bribes to low-level public servants, who come to expect them as a matter of course for allowing a petitioner's request to jump to the head of the line. At a higher level, officials who have the power to award contracts have been known to demand kickbacks or even percentages of the total. The result is a lack of transparency that damages Brazil's reputation and a system in which personal contacts count for more than the law.

In the past, it was misleading and naïve to look at the combination of Brazil's vast, open expanses and its large population and assume that an economic bonanza was in the offing. For one thing, the bulk of the population lived along the coast, leaving much of the interior undeveloped and beyond the reach of transportation links. But even more deceptive were the census figures released every ten years because millions of Brazilians, perhaps even a majority, lived in poverty outside the money economy.

During the 1970s, the Brazilian economist Edmar Bacha coined the term "Belindia" to describe Brazil's economic and social structure. By that characterization, which remains quite popular among Brazilians even today, he meant to suggest that Brazil was really two countries, "a Belgium inside an India." There was a small elite, living mostly in urban areas, that enjoyed a standard of living like that of Europe and had the material means to distance itself from the rest of society, and a miserable majority, comparable to peasants in India, that was condemned to poverty and struggled desperately to survive from one day to the next.

In reality, that characterization, meant to induce shame among policymakers and voters, was imprecise on both counts. Poverty in the Brazilian countryside, bad as it remains in some pockets of the northeast and the Amazon even today, was never as severe as in India or China. And those at the top of the economic pyramid often indulged in a life of luxury and ease that the European upper class envied when they came to Brazil and visited the apartments, estates, and private islands of their local hosts.

Today, Brazil is increasingly a country with a large and flourishing middle class. According to a study published late in 2009 by the Fundação Getúlio Vargas, the country's leading economic and social research institution, more than half of Brazilians now qualify as middle class, which the study defined, rather generously, as any household with a monthly income between $1,000 and $2,750. That means more than a hundred million Brazilians now have enough disposable income to indulge themselves in such badges of middle-class status as owning cellular phones, taking vacations, or buying on credit. Many of them can also aspire to such luxuries as an automobile, home ownership, and perhaps even private schools for their children, many of which have lower fees than their counterparts in the United States. An additional 16 percent of families earn a monthly income of more than $2,750, giving them elite status and even more disposable income.

This new burst of upward mobility threatens the stranglehold that old families, known in Brazilian slang as the four-hundred-year-olds because their wealth and influence date back to the beginning of colonial times, have always enjoyed over the economy. Between 2006 and 2008, for example, the number of millionaires in Brazil increased nearly 70 percent, jumping from 130,000 to 220,000, according to a study conducted by the Boston Consulting Group. According to the same study, only nine countries have more millionaires than Brazil. In addition, 210 of those households have a net worth of $100 million or more, ranking Brazil tenth globally in that category as well. With about one-sixth the population of India, Brazil had more millionaires than India, the study found. The even more select club of Brazilian billionaires is also growing at an unprecedented pace. The Brazilian business magazine *Exame* calculated that in 2007 alone at least 14 Brazilians became billionaires, compared to three in 2006.

In a matter of a few years, Brazil has seen a new surge in entrepreneurs who have built fortunes from activities as diverse as airlines, cosmetics, slaughterhouses, shoes, toys, and computers. Some of that new wealth was generated by a sudden burst of initial public offerings on the stock market between 2005 and 2008, as companies that traditionally were closely held by family groups decided to sell shares there in order to raise the capital needed to expand their activities. This phenomenon, particularly notable in sectors such as agriculture and ranching and oil and mining, was accompanied by a burst of spending on luxury items ranging from jewelry and designer clothing to private airplanes and yachts, as the super rich indulged themselves.

Ground zero for this explosion of conspicuous consumption is São Paulo. The new rich, like their predecessors, may prefer to vacation in Rio de Janeiro, where they pay scalpers extravagant prices for tickets to Carnival and snap up beachfront penthouse apartments as soon as they are put up for sale, driving real estate prices to levels that leave the locals complaining they are being priced out of the market. But the nouveau riche clearly prefer to shop in São Paulo, the home of luxury malls such as Daslu, where shopping was by invitation and appointment only—until the police stepped in, arrested the owners, and shut the place down because so many products had been imported illegally, their value understated on customs declarations in order to avoid paying excise taxes.

But along Rua Oscar Freire, São Paulo's answer to Rodeo Drive in Beverly Hills or Fifth Avenue in New York City, luxury stores bearing some of the world's most famous brand names continue to flourish. Cartier, Luis Vuitton, Gucci, Giorgio Armani, Hermès, Versace, Calvin Klein, Dior, and Montblanc are among those already represented, and new boutiques selling high-end items seem to open every week. According to a study done in 2008 by the Brazilian consulting firm MCF, the luxury goods market in Brazil is growing three times as fast as the economy itself. With the overall economy growing at a clip of 5 percent a year or more, that has pushed sales of luxury goods to more than $5 billion a year.

Of all the examples of Brazil's new rich, perhaps the most emblematic is the thrifty, acquisition-minded Joesley Batista, known in Brazil as "the king of meat." Born into a working-class family in the interior state of Goiás, he went to work even before he was a teenager at the butcher shop his father had founded in 1953. Along with a pair of brothers, he stuck with the business as it weathered one crisis after another, expanding all the while. When the real was drastically devalued in 1999, the Batista family's company, JBS Friboi, saw the crisis not as a threat but as an opportunity to jump into the export market and took loans from Brazil's national development bank to do that. That strategy, supported by the government, proved so successful that, in 2007, after building up additional capital through an IPO, JBS Friboi was able to buy the American meat packers Swift, one of the best-known brands in the world. In 2009, the Batistas, with Joesley at the helm as president of the company, added Bertin, one of their main Brazilian rivals, and Pilgrim's Pride, another American company, to their list of acquisitions and began trading shares on stock markets outside Brazil.

Today, though almost completely unknown outside Brazil, JBS Friboi is the largest meat-packing enterprise in the world, having recently surpassed the much better-known American company Tyson Foods. Within Brazil, one-quarter of the beef is butchered and packaged by JBS Friboi; worldwide, JBS Friboi's share is one-twelfth. Sales in 2009 were an estimated $29.1 billion, up nearly 2,000 percent compared to 2004. Joesley Batista, by now a billionaire, has been quoted in the Brazilian press as saying that overtaking Tyson Foods was "only the first step" of a larger strategy and that JBS Friboi also envisions itself as becoming a power in milk and dairy products, an area in which it has begun focusing its efforts and investments.

Joesley Batista's rise is more than a contemporary Brazilian version of a Horatio Alger story. It also holds a promising message about the dynamic nature of Brazilian capitalism in the early twenty-first century. When Brazil reluctantly opened its economy to outside competition two decades ago, many analysts predicted that the main international agribusiness conglomerates, such as Cargill, Archer Daniels Midland, and Tyson, would swoop into the country and either wipe out or purchase the local leaders. Instead, exactly the opposite has occurred: At the same time JBS Friboi was buying Pilgrim Foods in 2009, for instance, its main rival in Brazil, Marfrig, was buying Seara Foods from Cargill.

As these examples make clear, Brazil is not simply raising animals and cultivating crops for the world's tables. Increasingly, it is also processing meat, fruit, grains, and vegetables for overseas consumption, an industrial activity that is the real source of profit and jobs in the food business. Three of the ten largest global producers of animal protein are now Brazilian-controlled companies. The expectation is that Brazil's role will grow even larger over the decade to come, as its production of beef, chicken, and pork rises. The same goes for products ranging from orange juice to cotton: Instead of exporting the raw materials to the markets that will consume them, Brazil is choosing to do the processing at home, keeping the lion's share of the profit and stimulating domestic production of the equipment needed to do that processing, also a lucrative business.

Brazil's recent burst of growth and prosperity is not confined to a single geographic region. The triangle formed by São Paulo, Rio de Janeiro, and Brasília, historically the country's heartland in both the economic and political realms, dominates national life in every sense of the word. That situation is not likely to change anytime in the foreseeable future. But new regional centers, in the form of bustling commercial and industrial cities of half a million people or more, have also sprung up in recent years and are now gaining importance. Few people outside Brazil have ever heard of places such as Barreiras, Campina Grande, Goiânia, Londrina, Marabá, Ribeirão Preto, or Uberlândia. Some of them barely existed 50 years ago. But all of them are now booming cities with an expanding and vibrant middle class, which has the effect of spreading Brazil's wealth away from its traditional centers and reducing the painful inequality among regions.

This geographic diversity is especially important in the case of the northeast, historically the country's poorest and most backward region. If one of the central challenges in American history since the Civil War has been to bridge the economic gap between North and South, that same problem is even more accentuated in Brazil because the chasm between regions is even wider and deeper. The flow of poor blacks from the Deep South to the factories of the North during the twentieth century in search of opportunity and relief from racism is an essential part of the American national narrative. Brazil has its own equivalent in the migration of millions of impoverished, uneducated peasant sharecropper families from the northeast, often driven from the land by drought and unceasing exploitation, to the factories of São Paulo. Luiz Inácio Lula da Silva himself lived that experience and has always seemed obsessively driven to improve the lot of those who remained behind, some fifty million people. His successor must find ways to continue and deepen that process.

Even before the crisis of 2008 set in, Brazil was beginning to get recognition for the careful stewardship of its economy. In 2007 and 2008, all three of the major international credit rating agencies (Fitch, Moody's, and Standard & Poor's) bestowed Brazil with a coveted investment-grade ranking. In September 2009, Moody's actually raised Brazil another notch, making the country the first to see its credit rating improve since the onset of the global economic crisis a year earlier. That upgrade put Brazil's creditworthiness on a par with that of India and several East European countries—a feat that would have been unimaginable at the start of the decade and was, therefore, widely remarked upon in the Brazilian press.

But obtaining an investment-grade ranking means more than a matter of pride or a symbolic vote of confidence for a country like Brazil. With that official seal of approval, large institutional investors in the United States and elsewhere, such as the pension funds that control trillions of dollars, are authorized to buy shares on the Brazilian stock market and purchase Brazilian bonds. Many of them were eager to do that, since the main Brazilian stock exchange, the Bovespa in São Paulo, has consistently outperformed most of its competitors in recent years, but were held back by the credit rating agencies' skepticism. Now that they have given their stamp of approval to Brazil, we can expect to see increased flows of foreign investment and trading in stock. That should help ease the eternal shortage of capital in Brazil's domestic market.

The modernization of the Brazilian economy has also extended to the Bovespa. For many years, the Bovespa was an unruly place where shares in just a few companies were traded, so it was susceptible to market manipulation. Some of those problems persist despite efforts to curb them. But the Bovespa has become the fourth-largest stock market in the world when measured in terms of market value and the twelfth-largest in terms of the value of the shares of the 432 companies that are now traded there. As a group, those companies are worth more than a trillion dollars, which represents a doubling of value just since 2004. Taken together, those companies have raised more than $100 billion in resources through share offerings during that period.

In the first half of 2009, no stock market anywhere in the world yielded better results for investors. In dollar terms, investors in the Bovespa saw their shares rise 87 percent in value, compared to 79 percent for the stock exchange that came closest (Shanghai's), and 64 percent in Russia and 59 percent in India. That jump came after a sharp retraction in 2008, of 41 percent.

But even with that global bump included, the Bovespa market index, which measures the performance of stocks that account for 80 percent of shares traded, nearly quadrupled in value between the start of the decade and the end of 2009.

As in the United States, Europe, and Japan, many of Brazil's biggest players in the market are domestic pension funds, representing employees at private companies such as the mining giant CVRD or tens of thousands of workers at equally large state-controlled enterprises like Petrobras and Banco do Brasil. Between the start of the decade and the end of 2009, the total value of the assets that Brazilian institutional investors had placed in the market nearly tripled. A recent study conducted by Bank of America Merrill Lynch predicts that by 2013, the amount held by Brazilian institutional investors will have more than doubled again, to $280 billion. But because Brazil has investment-grade status from ratings agencies, foreign investors are also pouring into the Bovespa, sometimes at rates of $3 billion a month or more. Obviously they are attracted by recent high rates of return in a stable currency that has gained value against the dollar in recent years.

At the same time these sweeping transformations of the economy were taking place, Brazil was also quietly making smaller technical adjustments that have proved to be important in stabilizing the country's long-term financial outlook. At the end of the 1990s, for example, most of Brazil's government debt was denominated in dollars or other foreign currencies. But that left the country vulnerable to abrupt fluctuations in exchange rates of the type that battered the Brazilian economy at the end of 1998 and the beginning of 1999, making it more difficult for Brazilian debtors to meet their obligations. In response, the government gradually began shifting to debt denominated in reals rather than dollars, a step that significantly eased the debt burden and made it easier for government and corporate planners to do their task.

Like other developing countries, Brazil has sought to make itself more attractive to businesses by producing a more educated workforce. After years of investment in this and other areas of social infrastructure, beginning with Fernando Henrique Cardoso and accelerating under Lula, Brazil is now poised to reap the benefits of that effort. In 1995, for example, 15 percent of

Brazilian children of school-going age did not attend classes. But the stability brought by the Real Plan encouraged parents to invest in their children's future. Once the dragon of inflation was vanquished, it was no longer thought necessary to put your child to work at an early age just to help the family make ends meet. During Cardoso's first term, high school graduations increased 35 percent, growing more in absolute terms than in the previous 50 years. By 2005, thanks to programs that Lula's administration continued or expanded, only 3 percent of school-age children were not attending classes. Add in improvements in the quality and availability of health care, and the result is that workers entering the labor force are better educated and can also be expected to have a longer working life, which makes them more productive and ultimately more attractive to the companies that hire them.

That said, Brazil's education system remains a problem that hinders the country's economic and social development. According to figures compiled by the Organization for Economic Coordination and Development in 2009, Brazil ranks second in the world in terms of spending on education as a percentage of GDP, indicating that the government has in recent years considerably stepped up its investment in schooling. But specialists at the World Bank and other international organizations have criticized the quality of instruction in Brazil, noting that, among other shortcomings, teachers are inadequately trained, the school curriculum is not sufficiently rigorous, and the university system is both too small to meet the country's needs and includes too many substandard institutions that are not sufficiently supervised. In addition, nearly 10 percent of the population remains functionally illiterate.

The principal challenge for the government that succeeds Lula's will be to continue the process of bringing those who have been excluded from growth into the economy, creating jobs for them that pay decent wages so that they too can become consumers. One-quarter of Brazil's population remains below the poverty line: The minimum wage, by law adjusted only once a year, was $258 a month in 2009, and millions of people subsist on that salary or even less, since it is still commonplace for many workers to be employed off the books. Millions more may officially be above the poverty line, but they, too, struggle to get by, especially since the size of families tends to increase the further one goes down the income scale.

But President Dilma Rousseff, who took office on January 1, 2011, will have much on which to build. The Brazilian economy is more stable, diversified, and resilient than at any time in the country's history. Much of the hard work of adapting Brazil to a globalized economy has already been done and the political cost already paid. Brazil's resource base is strong and its trading partners varied. Its labor force is young, flexible, and eager to learn and take advantage of the opportunities that come its way. And Brazil has more options about which industries to develop, which crops to plant, which metals and minerals to mine, and what energy sources to exploit than all but a handful of nations.

There is always the danger, of course, that a new president with populist leanings could attempt to alter the course the country has been on for the past 16 years. Politicians of that stripe still exist, and they have personal ambitions and reliable, if diminishing, followings. But the vast majority of ordinary Brazilians have already reaped some of the fruits of the discipline and sacrifice they made beginning in the 1990s, and they seem to realize that more benefits will be coming into reach in the next few years if their country can manage to stay the course. Optimism, both about one's personal prospects and the nation's future, has always been a characteristic of the average Brazilian. But today, more than ever, that seems justified.

SEVEN

ENERGY TO BURN

PETROLEUM, ETHANOL, AND HYDROPOWER

"GOD IS BRAZILIAN": Brazilians are fond of citing this proverb when they look at their country and take stock of the vast natural resources with which they have been blessed. That is especially true as regards the abundance of sources of energy, which seem, as the twenty-first century advances, more likely than ever to become one of the main determinants of a nation's power, influence, and prestige on the world stage. Perhaps that is why the government of Luiz Inácio Lula da Silva in 2009 adopted the slogan "Brazil, Fifth World Power," implying that Brazil's extraordinary energy foundation is capable of projecting the country into the same category as the United States, the European Union, China, and India.

Brazil may, in fact, be more singularly blessed and have more options than any country on earth. It is already self-sufficient in oil and gas, and soon it is likely to move into the category of major exporter thanks to gigantic recent discoveries offshore, the most promising since the start of the new century, that are expected to begin coming on stream by the middle of the decade. Early on, in the 1970s, after the first shock in oil prices sent energy costs zooming, the Brazilian government wisely took advantage of the country's long history of growing sugarcane and its huge expanses of untilled land to seize the lead in production of ethanol, its cheapest and most promising source of renewable energy. And three major river systems, including the biggest part of the Amazon basin, which has the largest volume of water in the world, give Brazil more hydropower capacity than any other country, a potential it has barely begun to tap. On top of that, of course, the country also has solar and wind power in virtually unlimited quantities, which have not been developed at all, as well as significant deposits of uranium for nuclear power.

For Brazil, the challenge of the next decade is how to administer this abundance without also producing economic distortions and damaging the environment, especially in the wake of the new skepticism about offshore drilling that prevails as a result of the "Deepwater Horizon" disaster in the Gulf of Mexico in April 2010. The oil and gas deposits lying offshore may amount to as much as eighty billion barrels, but they are difficult and expensive to get at. Nonetheless, some political leaders seem to have fallen victim to the same kind of euphoria that led to populist binge spending in the Middle East, Venezuela, and Indonesia. And in the rush to develop ethanol and hydroelectric power, environmental and social factors have sometimes been overlooked. Coping with an energy bonanza is obviously preferable to grappling with the scarcities that many nations will face in the years to come. But managing that plenty will require discipline and much long-term planning, two qualities that have almost always been in short supply in Brazil.

Compared to other leading energy producers in Latin America, especially Mexico and Venezuela, Brazil was relatively late in discovering and developing deposits of oil and gas. As recently as 20 years ago, when both Mexico and Venezuela were exporting millions of barrels of oil daily and earning huge amounts of hard currency, that seemed a disadvantage that might hinder Brazil's progress and growth and its aspirations to become a world power. In the end, however, being the straggler has turned out to work very much to Brazil's advantage: Now the world's ninth-largest oil producer, Brazil seems poised, thanks to recent offshore discoveries, to leap into the ranks of the five top producers in the next decade or so, just as reserves seem to be diminishing elsewhere and prices are climbing.

At the same time, Venezuela's production has been declining. Petroleos de Venezuela, the state oil company there, has been crippled by political turmoil, which has led to instability in the executive ranks and the flight of engineers and others with needed technical skills. Hugo Chávez's policy of diverting profits to finance his populist social programs, which has reduced the money available for investment and exploration, has been an equally devastating blow.

In January 2010, a new assessment of Venezuela's Orinoco oil belt doubled the estimate of "technically recoverable" reserves there to more than five hundred billion barrels. But extracting oil from those sands will require enormous expertise and investment beyond Venezuela's ability, this at a time when Chávez has alienated the foreign oil companies and banks that have those resources. So if Brazil plays its cards right and Chávez continues on his current antagonistic course, Brazil is likely to replace Venezuela and Mexico as the leading destination for oil and gas investment in Latin America and could even emerge as the region's leading oil power.

The first discoveries of commercially exploitable oil fields in Brazil occurred in Bahia in the late 1930s and early 1940s, when Getúlio Vargas was the country's dictator. Those finds were extremely modest, however, and a decade later, after imposing rationing during World War II, Brazil still imported 93 percent of the oil and related petroleum products that it consumed. Despite that, many Brazilians were convinced that their country, rich in so many other natural resources, must certainly have oil deposits at least as large as those of its neighbors. Nationalists seized on that sentiment to launch a campaign called "The Oil Is Ours," faulting the government for being unable to locate the deposits that, they claimed, were just waiting to be found. In October 1953, Vargas, back in office as a popularly elected president, responded by creating Petrobras, an oil company that was to be owned and run by the state and was granted exclusive rights to drilling for oil and gas in Brazil.

Since then, Brazil's energy policy has been entwined and at times synonymous with Petrobras, which, though little-known outside Brazil, has grown to become a company whose market value today exceeds that of Microsoft. The company's monopoly on oil and gas extraction and distribution was broken, after an intense political debate and struggle, in 1997, shortly after government control was also diluted by a related decision to allow its shares to trade on stock markets abroad. Despite the gloomy predictions of nationalists who feared competition and a loss of sovereignty, Petrobras has continued to prosper. It remains Brazil's largest company and greatest single taxpayer, with seventy-six thousand employees and a market value that exceeds $291 billion. But it also looms increasingly larger on the world stage: As of 2010, it had become the third-largest publicly traded company in the Western Hemisphere, the fourth largest in the world among publicly traded oil companies, and the sixth largest globally when measured by market value.

Yet Petrobras's path to that exalted status and commanding position has been anything but conventional. When the company began operations in 1954, it was pumping barely 2,700 barrels a day, or less than 3 percent of Brazil's energy needs at that time. Over the next two decades, Brazil continued to import large amounts of crude as it struggled, with mostly discouraging results, to find domestic sources of oil and gas. In 1960, Walter Link, an American geologist working for Petrobras, wrote a series of reports, soon leaked to the press, concluding that, with the exception of the upper reaches of the Amazon River, Brazil's prospects for significant discoveries of oil and gas on land were dim. Instead, he recommended that Petrobras shift its focus to offshore exploration and also invest in oil prospecting abroad.

This was an unpopular position at a time when a nationalist, left-wing government was coming to power, and Link was promptly denounced as a C.I.A. plant whose secret objective was to retard Brazil's development. Under political pressure, Petrobras drilled scores of test wells on land, at a cost of tens of millions of dollars and without notable success. In fact, domestic oil and gas production actually declined between 1960 and 1964, increasing Brazil's dependence on imported energy. It was only after the military seized power in a coup in 1964 that Petrobras finally began emphasizing offshore exploration.

In the 1970s, as exploration of the geologically promising waters of the continental shelf accelerated, Brazil's luck began to change. Beginning in 1974, discoveries were made up and down the coastline, and a year later, Petrobras reluctantly took the first step toward relinquishing its monopoly. With the government in need of capital to expand investment, foreign oil companies were allowed to sign "risk contracts" in which they became minority partners of Petrobras in offshore exploration. That led to a surge of activity, and by 1984, Brazil was producing five hundred thousand barrels a day. Most of that oil came from offshore wells, and though it was not enough to meet all of the needs of a country whose industry and cities were growing so rapidly, it represented nearly a threefold increase over the figure Petrobras had been producing a decade earlier.

By 1997, domestic production had risen to a million barrels a day. That same year, Congress approved the controversial law ending Petrobras's 44-

year monopoly. That legislation not only allowed outsiders to compete with Petrobras on bidding for and developing drilling leases but also reduced energy subsidies, instituted mandatory measures to encourage energy efficiency, and created a regulatory agency to supervise the oil and gas sector. Within a few years, more than seventy companies, foreign as well as domestic, were engaged in oil exploration in Brazil, often in partnership with Petrobras, but sometimes on their own.

In 2003, Petrobras took an important step to raise its profile abroad when it acquired Argentina's second-largest oil company, Pérez Companc Energía, which was also active in Bolivia, Peru, and Venezuela, at a bargain price. Today, Petrobras operates in 27 countries, owns refineries and a fleet of oil tankers, and produces petrochemical products vital to industry. Within Brazil, the company also diversified into the production and distribution of both ethanol and electricity, making it a presence in every aspect of energy distribution to Brazil's nearly two hundred million people.

As Brazil stepped up its efforts to explore offshore, Petrobras became increasingly adept at deep-water drilling, eventually becoming the world leader in that specialty. Over the past 30 years, Petrobras has successfully broken records for drilling the deepest wells offshore; as of 2010, the deepest of these extended through more than nine thousand feet of sea water. Brazilian expertise in offshore drilling is so respected that Petrobras exports its deep-water technology to various countries, sending its technicians to advise other nations and companies and training outsiders at the three campuses of Petrobras University.

Because of that know-how, the company has also increasingly ventured into deep-water drilling in other parts of the world, such as the Gulf of Mexico and West Africa. In September 2009, Petrobras announced what it called "a giant discovery" 250 miles southeast of Houston in the Tiber–1 field, in what was described as the deepest oil well ever drilled. The total distance drilled before oil was struck was nearly thirty-five thousand feet—as far below the surface of the sea as airplanes fly above the earth on long-distance flights. But Petrobras's plans for that project may have been clouded by British Petroleum's "Deepwater Horizon" fiasco, which fouled large areas of the Gulf of Mexico and led to a clamor demanding a halt to additional drilling there.

In 2006, Brazil finally achieved energy self-sufficiency. By then, Petrobras alone was producing more than two million barrels of oil daily, and proven reserves stood at about eight billion barrels, second in South America, exceeded only by Venezuela. Opening up the oil and gas sector had clearly proved a success, both for Brazil and Petrobras, whose shares had been publicly traded on the New York Stock Exchange since 2000. Though the Brazilian government continued to own the majority of voting shares, nearly three-quarters of total equity was in the hands of private investors, making Petrobras much more responsive to international standards of accounting and corporate governance.

Then, in 2007, with the price of oil hovering near $100 a barrel, came the stroke of extraordinary good fortune that seemed the most compelling proof of the saying that God is Brazilian. In November of that year, Petrobras announced a gigantic find some twenty thousand feet below the waters of the Santos basin, just off São Paulo state. The discovery was located in part of what is known as the Sub-Salt area, so called because of the thick layer of salt lying between the floor of the sea and the oil itself. According to Petrobras, between five and eight billion barrels of crude oil and natural gas had been detected in a single field called Tupi, constituting the largest single find anywhere in the world in nearly a decade. If estimates are correct, the size of that single discovery is such that it could move Brazil past Mexico and Canada in total oil reserves, putting the country second only to Venezuela as an energy power in Latin America. In one stroke, in other words, Brazil's proven oil reserves had nearly doubled to just over 14 billion barrels.

Since then, two other mega-fields in the Sub-Salt strata, called Iara and Parque das Baleias, have been found, with predictions that they could yield an additional six billion barrels. Preliminary exploration of other deep-sea fields in the same area has also yielded promising results. No one knows exactly how much oil is out there on the continental shelf, and it is important to guard against what Alan Greenspan might call "irrational exuberance." But Brazilian government estimates leaked to the local press talk confidently of between 50 billion and 80 billion barrels, which if true would be spectacular: The higher of those two figures is more than the combined proved reserves of the United States, Canada, and Mexico. But this much is clear: The 149,000-square-kilometer Sub-Salt area, running from the coastal waters of Espirito Santo state southwesterly past São Paulo, is probably now the most promising oil exploration area in the world, and companies from all over the globe are eager to get a piece of the action.

The Tupi field, nearly two hundred miles offshore, is not expected to begin producing significant amounts of oil until 2014, and full development of other promising Sub-Salt areas is at least a decade away. But as soon as the bonanza was announced, in November 2007, it immediately transformed the politics of energy, both in Brazil and elsewhere in Latin America. At a summit meeting of heads of state in Argentina that same month, Hugo Chávez, who stands to lose the most in terms of influence if Brazil emerges as an oil and gas powerhouse, rather nervously referred to his Brazilian colleague Luiz Inácio Lula da Silva as an "oil baron," and Lula immediately set about exercising the authority that comes with that status. He said Brazil would "obviously participate in the Organization of Oil Exporting Countries," whose 1973 "oil shock" first propelled Brazil onto the road to self-sufficiency but vowed to work within the group to reduce oil prices. One week later, Petrobras informed a chastened Chávez that it was withdrawing from an ambitious natural gas project in partnership with Venezuela, citing unspecified "technical and economic reasons."

Within Brazil, the promise of this bonanza has reawakened the old debate about the proper role of the state in developing the country's energy resources. Seeing themselves as the ideological heirs of Getúlio Vargas, Lula and the Workers Party favor increased state participation and have proposed that Petrobras, representing the state, be given a monopoly over the entire Sub-Salt region. Some government officials have even talked about creating an entirely new state company, to be called Petro-Sal, to control all aspects of Sub-Salt development. While they promise that existing contracts in the area will be honored, they also want a system in which bids for drilling in fields yet to be opened will require foreign companies to take a Brazilian partner, and they have suggested that certain especially promising areas should be closed to outsiders entirely. A government slogan that first surfaced toward the end of 2009 explains the position of the ruling Workers Party succinctly: "Sub-Salt: Patrimony of the Union, Wealth of the people, Future of Brazil."

Brazilian officials argue that the shift away from a concession model is justified because drilling in the Sub-Salt area is "like buying a winning lottery ticket" and claim that 87 percent of test wells drilled have produced commercially exploitable amounts of oil and gas. Independent analysts and energy consultants say the success rate is not nearly that high and point to a number of factors unique to the Sub-Salt area that they say are going to make it difficult and costly to operate there.

First of all, even with Petrobras's recognized expertise, extracting oil from the Sub-Salt region is going to be an enormous technical challenge that will require tens of billions of dollars in new investments. New technologies will have to be developed, and tens of thousands of new workers will need to be trained and hired: at least 285,000 by 2014, according to one industry esti-mate. Dozens of high-seas platforms will have to be bought or built and then installed. The wells drilled from those platforms will have to pass first through shifting layers of sand and sediment even before reaching the thick stratum of salt, which could conceivably corrode tubes or even clog the well. The oil it-self will be mixed with gas and other substances and so will have to be sepa-rated before the oil can be sent back to the mainland, which will itself be a huge logistical and environmental challenge.

Skepticism within Brazil has also grown as a result of British Petroleum's April 2010 environmental disaster in the Gulf of Mexico, which kindled fears of what a similar oil spill in the Santos or Campos basins could do to the beaches, coastal life, and economies of Rio de Janeiro and São Paulo. Petro-bras's safety record in this regard, though not nearly as bad as that of some other companies, is not exactly unblemished. The company operated the world's largest oil platform, known as the P–36, in the waters off Rio de Janeiro until an explosion on board on March 15, 2001, led to the sinking of the platform five days later, with the loss of three lives. In addition, several oil spills have occurred in Brazil, including in populated areas such as the Bay of Guanabara, which faces Rio de Janeiro. All of this has led to questions about the methods that will be used to extract oil from the Sub-Salt stratum.

Early in 2009, Petrobras announced an increase of more than 50 percent in its five-year investment plan, from $112 billion to $174 billion, a large chunk of which is destined for the Sub-Salt effort. The company says it may also try to raise capital by issuing more shares, which would be sold on Brazil-ian and foreign stock markets, and in May 2009, it announced an unusual barter deal with China, whose hunger for raw materials makes it an attractive customer for Brazil. In return for $10 billion from the Chinese, Petrobras would supply between 150,000 and 200,000 barrels a day for ten years.

Still, energy analysts in Brazil and abroad question whether those steps are enough to meet both the cost of developing the Sub-Salt stratum and all of the other undertakings to which Petrobras is committed. In their view, the company is already overextended and will become even more stretched if the government shuts out or reduces the role of the private sector. Many of these analysts oppose the idea of a renewed Petrobras monopoly on both ideological and practical grounds. They recommend a larger role for privately held companies, which have access of their own to capital, as a way of reducing the possible strain on Brazil's economy and Petrobras's capacity.

But there are signs that the Brazilian government may have chosen a strategy of deliberately slowing the development of the Sub-Salt strata. This is partly because the country has other attractive energy options, some of which pollute less, but other reasons also enter into the calculation. Slowing the pace of development would allow Brazil to further develop a domestic oil services industry, for instance. The Workers Party has long talked of its desire to have rigs, platforms, tankers, floating vessels, and equipment manufactured in Brazil (rather than in places like Singapore), which would create tens of thousands of new jobs for Brazilians. In the short run, slowing the pace would mean less revenue to be distributed to state and municipal governments. But the assumption seems to be that the political benefits of creating so many new and well-paying jobs would compensate for a smaller royalty stream.

If Petrobras is not going to allow private investment a significant role in development of the Sub-Salt strata, the opposition also favors slowing things down, though for entirely different reasons. Within Brazil, Petrobras is more than a company; it is also a political power that, at many times in the past, has been managed so as to benefit those who are in power. The company makes huge donations to community and social programs around the country and also underwrites production of movies, plays, books, art exhibitions, and television programs, all of which can obviously be manipulated to favor the interests of the party in power. In addition, figures made public by the federal government comptroller's office indicate that just over 80 percent of Petrobras contracts are awarded without competitive bidding or have severe limits on competition. The result is that many contracts go to a handful of companies, which also turn out to be among the biggest donors to the Workers Party and its allies. The opposition wants more transparency and open bidding and is happy to accept slower Sub-Salt development if it will stem the anticipated flow of political donations to the left-leaning coalition in power as of 2010.

With oil prices remaining at high levels, Petrobras has also begun to re-examine its prospects on land, especially as regards production of oil shale, which is essentially oil trapped in solid form inside rock. Brazil has the world's second-largest known deposits of oil shale, exceeded only by Venezuela, and is already the world's second-largest shale oil producer, after Estonia. Petro-bras developed shale oil extraction technology early on, in 1954, and today op-erates the largest surface oil shale extraction device in the world. But when oil shale is liquefied, it produces a very heavy form of crude oil, sometimes ridiculed as sludge and often disparaged as the world's dirtiest fuel. So oil shale is seen as a fuel to be developed only as a last resort, and then more likely for export rather than for domestic use.

Natural gas, on the other hand, has gradually emerged as a seemingly plentiful and ever more attractive energy source, even though it constitutes only a small part of Brazil's overall energy consumption. High oil prices have helped increase demand for natural gas, which traditionally has been used mainly in industrial applications or at power plants, as a substitute for fuel oil. Since domestic natural gas prices within Brazil remain much lower than fuel oil prices, which follow the international market, the price differential has en-couraged consumers to switch to natural gas.

Petrobras's role in the natural gas sector is perhaps even more dominant than in oil, as hard to imagine as that may be. The company is the biggest producer of natural gas and controls about 90 percent of domestic reserves. It is also the largest wholesale supplier of natural gas and operates Brazil's rather cumbersome and limited domestic natural gas transport system, which in the past has been one of the main bottlenecks to increasing the production and consumption of natural gas. That network includes more than fifteen hundred miles of domestic gas pipelines, which were not interconnected as of 2008, though projects are now underway to link them.

Significant amounts of gas have been imported, especially from Bolivia via a two-thousand-mile-long pipeline that feeds São Paulo, but a combination of events in recent years has encouraged Brazilian planners to spur development of domestic production. In 2006, Bolivia's newly elected president, Evo Morales, a left-wing nationalist who objected to the low price that Brazil was paying under a longstanding agreement, nationalized his country's oil and gas industries. That forced Brazil to pay much higher prices for Bolivian gas and led Petrobras, which had been a big investor in Bolivia and was eager to expand its presence there, to suspend its plans. The new arrangement, which Lula and Morales negotiated personally, required Petrobras to absorb significant losses, in the hundreds of millions of dollars, and reduced it to minority partnership status with the new Bolivian state energy company, with rights to only 18 percent of what it produces.

The bitter taste left by that episode was remedied, however, the next year by the prospect of a bonanza in the offshore Sub-Salt layer. The same areas that are most promising for oil production also appear to have significant gas reserves, as often occurs with petroleum and its byproducts. Petrobras estimates that the Tupi field alone could contain as much as seven trillion cubic feet of recoverable natural gas. As is always the case with such forecasts, especially when a company's stock price is involved, caution is advised. But if that figure is indeed confirmed, it would increase Brazil's total natural gas reserves by 50 percent and also encourage both further exploration and development of a better energy infrastructure.

In the past, Brazil has simply flared a lot of natural gas at the point of extraction offshore, a wasteful practice that seemed justified by low demand and the deficiencies in the country's system for transporting gas. Now the potential reserves of gas involved are so large that it would be foolish to continue to do so. As with oil, huge investments, in the tens of billions of dollars, will be required first to separate the gas from oil offshore, then either liquefy it for transfer to ships that will take it to terminals at ports or build new pipelines to get it on shore and then overland to consumers, both industrial and residential. But the demand is there, and so is the supply.

On land, prospects for gas development also are promising, especially in the western Amazon, just as Walter Link predicted 50 years ago. In 1986, Petrobras made a major find at Urucu, in dense jungle just south of the Solimões River, four hundred miles west of Manaus. But the initial plan to develop the area faced a seemingly endless sequence of geographical, logistical, environmental, and political challenges that ended only when Petrobras finally agreed to share some of the material benefits of the project with local people and to build a pipeline to Manaus in such a way that environmental damage would be limited and mitigated. It was a new and more socially conscious way of doing things in the Amazon, and the change of tactics won the reluctant approval even of the most ardent environmentalists.

Using the Urucu model, Petrobras now hopes to develop oil and gas deposits farther west, in dense jungle near the Juruá River, that were first discovered in 1978. "They have really tried to minimize the impact, and the outcome is not as bad as we had feared," Paulo Adario, director of Greenpeace's Amazon campaign, told me in Manaus late in 2006. "Since they are taking oil and gas out of the heart of the Amazon, creating a model for what will be done in the future, that concern is quite understandable and necessary."

Brazil's economy is probably too big and diversified for it to fall victim to the so-called petrostate syndrome that has crippled or distorted development and fostered corruption in places like Indonesia and Venezuela, about which the novelist Arturo Uslar Pietri once said, "Columbus discovered it, Bolívar liberated it, and oil ruined it." But the promise of the Sub-Salt stratum is dazzling, and the temptation to allow oil and gas development to take precedence over other sources of energy can already be felt. To give in to that temptation would be a mistake, because two other sources of renewable energy in Brazil also offer extraordinary promise. Both face problems of their own, it is true, but those may prove cheaper and easier to resolve than the technological and political challenge of extracting oil and gas from recesses of the earth's crust deeper than mankind has penetrated before.

The development of Brazil's ethanol industry, though one of the country's great triumphs, is a story little known elsewhere. That Brazil has become the undisputed world leader in the field is first of all a testament to the persistence and ingenuity of scientists and government officials who ignored mockery and predictions of failure. But it is also one of the delicious ironies of history that sugarcane, the oldest crop grown in the country, in production continuously for nearly five hundred years, should turn out to be the key to the country's ability to develop the technology and gain the experience that has enabled it to become a superpower in renewable energy in the twenty-first century.

Ethanol, also known as ethyl alcohol, is the product of fermentation, as is beer or wine. It can be produced from a wide variety of organic materials with cellulose fibers, such as corn, beet sugar, wood chips, and switchgrass, all of which the United States, Europe, and China have tried to develop. But of the plants that scientists have examined as potential sources of ethanol, sugarcane is by far the most attractive: For every unit of energy that is expended to produce sugarcane ethanol, the final product generates more than eight units of energy. In contrast, the energy ratio of ethanol made from corn, the favored source in the United States, is less than two to one. In addition, Brazil's lower production costs and cheaper land prices make sugarcane a more economically efficient source of ethanol than competing plants.

Ardent advocates of ethanol tend to describe it as a wonder fuel. It is not a panacea, but it does offer significant advantages over conventional fuels. First of all, it is a renewable energy source, unlike gasoline, and is cheaper to produce, at least in Brazil. Though a car running on gasoline gets more miles per gallon, ethanol has a higher octane rating, which helps compensate for that disadvantage. But most important, ethanol is clearly a more environmentally friendly fuel, especially when used exclusively to power a vehicle instead of being mixed with gasoline. Using pure ethanol instead of gasoline results in a decline of 20 percent or more in emissions of greenhouse gases, particularly carbon dioxide and benzene.

Initially, Brazil's decision to invest in ethanol was a consequence of the Yom Kippur War between Israel and the Arabs in October 1973. The subsequent decision of the Organization of Petroleum Exporting Countries, dominated by Arab and other Muslim states such as Saudi Arabia, Iraq, Iran, and Kuwait, first to suspend production and then to raise prices caught Brazil unprepared. That first "oil shock" also almost immediately brought an end to the so-called Brazilian Miracle, in which the country had enjoyed several years of double-digit economic growth and was being hailed as a model for the developing world.

The generals who ruled Brazil at the time were unnerved by the strategic vulnerability that the first great global energy crisis had exposed and immediately set about trying to find or create alternative sources of energy. They correctly anticipated that similar crises would occur again, and they wanted to reduce—or even eliminate, if they could—Brazil's dependence on external sources of energy. One faction wanted to give top priority to nuclear energy. That group was led by nationalists who were interested in obtaining the atomic bomb but who also rejected sugarcane as an energy source because they saw it as a symbol of Brazil's backwardness. At their prodding, a multi-billion-dollar agreement was signed with West Germany in 1975 to install a series of seven nuclear power plants on the coast near Rio de Janeiro by the year 2000. As of 2010, only two of those units have been completed and are in operation, though various governments have talked of reviving the effort.

But the military government's main focus quickly became the program they named Pro-Álcool, which also was launched in 1975. Through the rest of the 1970s and into the next decade, the government provided generous subsidies to sugar producers, eventually amounting to billions of dollars, to help revive an industry that was becoming moribund as Brazilian agricultural producers expanded into more profitable crops. Similar incentives were granted to big automobile manufacturers, who were hesitant to make cars with engines that ran on ethanol until they were certain the new fuel would be available for the vehicles they produced. It was a chicken-and-egg situation, since sugar producers also didn't want to be stuck with stocks of unsold ethanol that could bankrupt them. By the mid-1980s, though, more than three-quarters of the eight hundred thousand cars then manufactured annually in Brazil ran on ethanol manufactured from sugarcane, grown mostly in the state of São Paulo.

At that point, Brazil seemed well on its way to weaning its motorists from their dependence on costly imported gasoline. But when sugar prices rose sharply in 1989 because of a global surge in demand, owners of sugar mills stopped making their cane available for processing into alcohol and jumped at the chance to profit from the hard currency premium that international markets were willing to pay for sugar. As a result, Brazilian motorists were left in the lurch, as were the automakers that had retooled their production lines to make ethanol-powered cars. Ethanol fell into discredit for reasons that were purely economic, not technical. It continued to be an efficient fuel source, but if a reliable supply could not be guaranteed, consumers preferred to protect themselves by returning to gasoline, supplies of which were never interrupted.

That situation persisted throughout the 1990s. Even after sugar prices returned to their historically low levels, motorists were wary of being tricked again, and sales of ethanol-fueled cars continued to lag. What changed the equation, beginning in 2003, was a technological advance: the development of what came to be known as the "flex fuel" engine, which runs on gasoline or ethanol or any combination of the two. Flex fuel motors give consumers the autonomy to buy the cheapest fuel available, thereby freeing them from both potential shortages in the supply of ethanol or any sharp increase in the price of gasoline. And since ethanol-only engines can be slow to start in colder weather, the flex fuel engine also offered a practical advantage.

Volkswagen was the first automobile manufacturer to introduce the flex fuel engine, but competitive pressures soon forced all of the others, including Brazilian affiliates of the American Big Three, to follow suit. Within three years, three-quarters of the automobiles sold in Brazil were models with flex fuel engines, generally sold without a price increase that would have forced consumers to absorb the cost for the new technology. Today, virtually all of the more than three million passenger vehicles manufactured annually in Brazil, some of which are destined for export to Latin America and Asia, are equipped with flex fuel engines. As a result, sales of ethanol in Brazil now exceed those of gasoline. In fact, even the gasoline sold in Brazil contains a 25 percent admixture of ethanol, a practice that has accelerated Brazil's shift away from costly imported petroleum.

"The rate at which this technology has been adopted is remarkable, the fastest I have ever seen in the motor sector, faster even than the airbag, automatic transmission, or electric windows," Barry Engle, then the president of Ford do Brasil, told me in 2006, when I toured his company's plant in the industrial suburbs of São Paulo. "From the consumer standpoint, it's wonderful, because you get flexibility and you don't have to pay extra for it."

Thanks in large part to the success of the flex fuel engine, the Brazilian auto industry has grown substantially over the past decade, attracting new investments from many of the world's main carmakers. Even with the downturn in production elsewhere, double-digit leaps in the output of cars in Brazil have not been uncommon: Preliminary figures from 2008, the most recent year available, indicate that Brazil has passed France and is now the world's fifth-largest producer of cars and trucks.

Despite these and other advantages conferred by ethanol, however, other nations have for the most part been reluctant to follow Brazil's lead and commit as fully to the use of ethanol or other renewable biofuels. There are several reasons for this, which range from simple economics and the politics underlying trade policy, especially protectionism in industrialized countries like the United States, to environmental and strategic concerns.

If international markets were truly free and the concept of competitive advantage was allowed to operate unchecked, there would be no reason for a country like the United States, much less the members of the European Union, to try to compete with Brazil in the production of ethanol. But farmers are a powerful constituency in both the United States and Europe, and the result is a two-pronged policy that is politically astute but costly in economic terms: subsidies designed to sustain farmers in the Northern Hemisphere who would otherwise be unable to compete and tariffs intended to keep more-efficient Brazilian producers of ethanol out of those markets.

The United States, for example, imposes a tax of 54 cents a gallon on all imports of Brazilian ethanol, a measure meant in large part to help Midwestern farmers who are interested in producing ethanol from corn. The money collected, in fact, is distributed to American agricultural producers as a subsidy for their own crops. Brazil argues that both the tariff and the American subsidy violate the rules of the World Trade Organization. But the Brazilian government has hesitated to file a complaint with that body, and so both the subsidies and the tariff, which many American economists also believe is illegal, continue unchecked. Thanks to Senator Chuck Grassley of Iowa and other senators from Corn Belt states, the current farm bill ensures that both practices will continue at least through 2013.

Brazil would like to expand its ethanol industry at a faster rate, but, like other developing countries, it suffers from a shortage of domestic investment capital. Normally, it would turn to international markets for that money. But because Brazilian ethanol exports to the largest world markets remain blocked, foreign investors have hesitated to commit fully to the construction of new mills and the purchase of equipment and land that producers in Brazil are seeking. The four international giants that control much of the world's agribusiness—Archer Daniels Midland, Bunge and Born, Cargill, and Louis Dreyfus—have shown interest, largely because of the potential the huge Brazilian market offers. But while big investment banks and other institutional and individual investors continue to visit Brazil and make modest bets, Brazil is still thirsting for the capital required to expand the ethanol industry.

Japan, as a developed nation committed to reducing greenhouse gas emissions under the Kyoto agreement, and China, with a booming economy hungry for energy and under pressure to reduce pollution from its large consumption of coal, would seem to be logical markets for Brazilian ethanol. Indeed, both countries, along with South Korea, have shown interest. But Japan, the most promising customer, in particular worries about Brazil's ability to fulfill commitments in any formal export agreement. At the moment, Brazil produces enough ethanol to meet domestic demand and still have plenty left over for exports. But what happens if demand in Brazil continues to grow and the infrastructure doesn't keep up? That is a very real possibility, in view of the shortage of capital. Given a choice between honoring export contracts and facing the wrath of Brazilian voters, what would the government do? Even to pose that question makes government policymakers and business leaders in East Asia uneasy.

Brazil's dominant role in the production of alcohol fuel and its commanding lead in ethanol technology have also emerged as issues braking growth in the use of ethanol internationally. After decades of being forced to rely on oil imported from politically repressive and volatile parts of the globe, such as the Middle East and Venezuela, the last thing most governments want is to trade one form of energy dependence for another. Nor do they particularly relish the notion of paying royalties for the use of cutting-edge ethanol technology developed in Brazil or having to worry that access to that technology might somehow be cut off in a global crisis. Those concerns exist even though Brazil's image around the world is that of a good neighbor and it has sought to assure potential customers of its good intentions.

"We are not interested in becoming the Saudi Arabia of ethanol," Eduardo Carvalho, the director of the National Sugarcane Agro-Industry Union, the main group for ethanol producers in Brazil, told me in São Paulo in 2006.

"It's not our strategy because it doesn't produce results. As a large producer and user, I need to have other big buyers and sellers in the international market if ethanol is to become a global commodity, which is our real goal."

During a visit to Brazil in March 2007, George W. Bush signed a memorandum of understanding in São Paulo, capital of the ethanol industry, with Lula that called for the United States and Brazil, which together produce 70 percent of the world's ethanol, to promote the production and use of ethanol as a fuel. The idea was to jointly help other sugar-producing countries, especially those in the Caribbean and Central America, replicate Brazil's experience in producing ethanol. That would provide Brazil with new markets for its technology and equipment while giving the United States a reliable source of renewable energy in its own backyard. As a byproduct, it would also weaken the power and finances of Venezuela's ruling strongman, Hugo Chávez.

In Brazil, the accord was seen as a potential game-changer, a mechanism for the country to project itself onto the world stage as a big-time player and energy exporter. "This is more than a document, it's a point of convergence in the relationship that is denser and more intense than anything we've seen in the last twenty or thirty years," Antônio Simões, the director of the energy division of the foreign ministry of Brazil, told me. "Brazil will profit, the United States will profit, and so will third countries. It's a win-win situation for everyone involved."

Simões made it clear that Brazil hoped to use the agreement to spur ethanol production throughout tropical Africa, where Brazil has long made an effort to expand its influence and trade, and in sugar-producing Asian nations like Thailand. "The good thing is that a poor country can reduce what it pays for imported oil and earn money exporting this," he explained. "That way they will have more money to invest in social programs, and the production of energy will be democratized in the world, with a hundred countries producing energy instead of just fifteen or twenty."

Despite the opportunities the accord promised, little was done during the remainder of the Bush presidency to follow up on the initiative, and by the time Barack Obama took office in 2009, U.S. enthusiasm about sugarcane-based ethanol all but evaporated. As a senator from Illinois, Obama represented a corn-producing state with a budding though inefficient ethanol industry of its own. To the extent he was interested in ethanol at all as a source of renewable energy, he wanted it to be produced in America, not abroad, even if there was little economic or scientific justification to do so.

"It does not serve our national and economic security to replace imported oil with Brazilian ethanol," Obama argued at a stop in the Midwest during the 2008 campaign. To do so, he added, would only thwart "our country's drive towards energy independence." As president, true to his word, he has taken no steps to eliminate the tariff on Brazilian ethanol, which was reaffirmed in the most recent farm bill passed by Congress.

Brazil's own priorities also seem to be changing. Before the discovery in the Sub-Salt basin in 2007, the government clearly regarded the ethanol program as the single most important strategic mechanism in its drive to achieve energy self-sufficiency. But the size of the recent oil bonanza is so large and so dazzling that hopes that ethanol will be a magic bullet, admittedly unrealistic, seem to be slipping. Brazil continues to invest in and support the program, but some enthusiasm has now been lost, and with it some momentum. It is not clear, for example, what percentage of oil profits, if any, will be directed to the ethanol program and whether the cost of developing the Sub-Salt strata will divert investment from ethanol programs. Already, Brazil's discourse in international forums has also changed: Once the most ardent proponent of renewable green energy, Brazil now has a vested interest in prolonging consumption of fossil fuels (at increasingly elevated prices, of course) for as long as possible.

Ethanol production today is clearly at a crossroads, with difficult decisions that will have to be made in the next few years. Brazil's initial experience with sugar, in colonial times, generated all kinds of abuse and exploitation, from the enslavement of millions of Indians and Africans to the destruction of the country's original landscape in the regions where the cultivation of sugarcane took hold. Already, international environmental groups are warning that the rapid growth of Brazil's ethanol industry is likely to expand and accelerate the destruction of the Amazon, and unions and human rights groups in some countries have sought to block imports of Brazilian ethanol on the grounds that current labor practices in the industry are nearly as deplorable as in the colonial era.

The latter problem is certain to become less worrisome or relevant as the ethanol industry mechanizes and state governments step up their inspections and enforcement efforts on the farms where sugar is grown. In São Paulo state, which accounts for two-thirds of Brazilian sugarcane production for ethanol, half the harvest is already done by machines, and by 2015, all manual cutting is expected to be phased out. The spread of ethanol production to the Amazon, on the other hand, is a legitimate cause for concern and a real test of Brazil's ability to plan, monitor, and administer, especially given the government's dubious performance during previous commodity booms as recent as the surge in soybean production in the Amazon.

Sugarcane does not grow well in the Amazon heartland, where heavy rains and year-round heat reduce yields significantly. According to one government study, an acre of sugarcane in the Amazon yields about 25 percent less sugarcane than an acre planted in São Paulo, and because Amazon cane is not as sweet, the amount of sugar processed from a ton of raw cane grown in São Paulo is 50 percent higher than the amount from a ton grown in the Amazon. But planting cane has accelerated in the savannah areas on the fringe of the Amazon region, with government credit available. Within the region the government defines as Legal Amazônia, only land that is already classified as "degraded" can be planted with sugarcane. But there is little monitoring of what occurs, and an influx of sugar processing mills, which operators want to run at full capacity, seems to encourage violations of that policy. Brazilian environmental groups and left-wing parties have fought to tighten the law and strengthen enforcement procedures, but so far without success.

Alternatives to encouraging the cultivation of sugarcane in the Amazon do exist. José Goldemberg, a Brazilian physicist who has served as both the country's minister of science and technology and the São Paulo state secretary of the environment, calculates that the state of São Paulo alone has enough fallow pasture land, ten million hectares, to accommodate an increase in production to meet all of Brazil's ethanol needs without having to inflict additional damage on the Amazon. Since São Paulo's sugarcane fields are much closer to ports and cities than the jungle that would have to be razed in the Amazon, there would also be additional benefits and savings in the form of a reduced carbon footprint and lower costs in transporting ethanol stocks.

In recent years, some critics have blamed ethanol for the sharp rise in food prices that was observed in 2008 and led to food riots in some poor countries. If there were a direct, demonstrable link, which is still subject to debate, it would be to the production of corn ethanol in the Northern Hemisphere, not sugarcane ethanol in Brazil. While cropland in the United States and elsewhere was diverted to corn production in order to take advantage of a temporary ethanol boom, Brazil is not trapped in the same kind of zero-sum game. It is one of the few countries in the world with fertile land that is still untilled and, as mentioned above, also has plenty of fallow land that can be used to grow sugarcane without reducing acreage for other crops.

Arguments that ethanol is inherently inefficient and polluting also need to be regarded with skepticism. Again, the distinction between sugarcane and corn mentioned above is crucial: Each unit of energy expended to convert sugarcane into ethanol generates eight new units of energy, compared to less than two for corn. And while some studies have indicated that ethanol may increase ozone levels, the energy yield from sugarcane is such that, as mentioned earlier, it reduces emissions of other greenhouse gases much more than corn does.

Encouraged by the success of the ethanol program in recent years, the Brazilian government has also funneled money into research meant to produce an organic, renewable, biodegradable substitute for diesel fuel, which would be used by trucks, buses, tractors, and generators. The biodiesel program is investigating a variety of plants, including soybeans, palm oil, sunflowers, cotton, and even algae. The bulk of the effort thus far, though, has been devoted to *mamona*, a bush that grows abundantly in the northeast of Brazil and produces large, dark seeds. Known in English as the castor bean, *mamona* has traditionally been used in Brazil as a purgative. But its high viscosity and easy solubility give it an adaptability that the other plants and animal fats being studied do not have. Another plus has been that President Lula, a native of the Northeast, is fascinated by the plant's potential and has pushed strongly for its development, often over the protests of those who favor other sources, including another local plant, the *pinhão manso*. But whether his successor will share that enthusiasm is an unanswered question.

As of 2010, the initial results are limited but encouraging. Fleets of buses in Curitiba, a city of two million people in the south of the country, are already using biodiesel as their fuel, and plans call for biodiesel pumps to be installed at gas stations in nearly five hundred cities around the country by the end of the year. In the early test stages of the program, Brazil plans to blend biodiesel fuel with ordinary diesel, which is notorious as a polluting fuel, in small quantities ranging from 2 to 5 percent by 2013 and eventually to 20 percent. That would not require vehicles to modify the engines they use. But if the results continue to be positive, the next step would be to begin manufacturing vehicles with engines that run on pure biodiesel.

As the global debate about ethanol rages on, Brazil continues to take steps to solidify its dominance in ethanol and improve the efficiency of its production. These include technical improvements that promise to increase yields and cut costs even more. In the past, for example, the residue left when sugarcane stalks are compressed to squeeze out juice was simply discarded. Today, Brazilian sugar mills use that residue to generate the electricity used to process the cane into ethanol and apply other byproducts as fertilizer in the fields where cane is planted. Some mills are now producing so much electricity that they sell their excess to the national grid. By 2015, Goldemberg estimates, the amount they produce could rise to ten million kilowatts, almost the equivalent of the electricity produced by Brazil's largest hydroelectric project, Itaipu.

Even more promising from the Brazilian point of view is the prospect of dramatically increasing yields through the cultivation of genetically modified sugarcane. In the late 1990s, Brazilian scientists, funded by government money, mapped the sugarcane genome and began research into tinkering with genes to make the plant sweeter, which is of interest to both ethanol producers and global manufacturers of soft drinks and candies, such as Coca-Cola and Nestlé. Brazil has the capacity to begin modifying sugarcane genetics immediately but has held back until the global debate on genetically modified organisms is resolved, out of fear of losing markets for its agricultural products.

Another possibility is to develop new varieties of sugarcane or genetically engineer existing varieties so that they are resistant to pesticides and natural pests, and even drought. Brazilian scientists have already raised the energy yield of some varieties of sugarcane from the standard 8.3-to–1 ratio to more than 10 to 1 and talk of reaching the level of 20 to 1 or even higher. "We are convinced there is no ceiling on productivity, at least theoretically," Tadeu Andrade, the director of the Center for Sugarcane Technology in São Paulo state where some of the most advanced research is conducted, told me when I visited there in 2006.

Amid the excitement over Brazil's extraordinary recent oil and gas finds and the pride associated with the creation of a domestic sugarcane ethanol industry, there is a tendency, even among Brazilians, to overlook the country's enormous hydropower capacity, barely a quarter of which has been tapped. This potential is concentrated in but by no means limited to the Amazon, which in terms of the volume of water circulating is the world's largest river basin. But in spite of that promise, hydropower continues to languish in third place in Brazil's hierarchy of energy sources.

In theory, that should not be the case. Water is an abundant and renewable resource that produces clean energy. In that sense, it is like nuclear power, but without any of the life-threatening risk and other negative associations that accompany nuclear reactors, and it also stands in distinct contrast to coal, with all the inevitable pollution that brings. And unlike ethanol or oil extracted from Sub-Salt deposits, hydropower does not require the invention of new and innovative technologies. In addition, the cost per kilowatt hour generated is very low. But because of government mismanagement, particularly the lack of attention paid during the military dictatorship to the social and environmental impact of building dams and the lack of proper planning in the civilian governments that followed, hydroelectric power has developed an image problem in Brazil that it is still struggling to overcome.

Brazil's hydropower potential is so vast that even though the country has barely scratched the surface, only China and Canada generate more power from that source. More than 80 percent of the electricity consumed in Brazil comes from hydropower, which has been the case since the 1980s, when construction of the Itaipu project on the Paraná River in the south, along the border with Paraguay, concluded. When Itaipu, gigantic in size and, at $19.6 billion, with a price tag to match, began operating in 1984, it was the largest hydropower project in the world. It has since been surpassed by China's Three Gorges dam, on the Yangtze River, but today, with all twenty of its turbines finally in place and operating, it has a generating capacity of fourteen thousand megawatts. That makes Itaipu one of the five largest sources of electricity in the world and enables it to provide nearly 20 percent of the electricity Brazil consumes. Over the past quarter century, other large projects have followed, including Sobradinho, Paulo Afonso, and Xingó along the São Francisco River in the northeast, and Ilha Solteira and Furnas in the southeastern states of São Paulo and Minas Gerais, respectively.

All of the dams just mentioned, along with others, were built in or near the country's industrial heartland, the São Paulo–Rio de Janeiro–Belo Horizonte triangle, and are meant to serve factories and consumers in that region. But as the Brazilian economy has grown, its appetite for energy has also boomed, and planners have been forced to look much farther afield. The massive Tucuruí project, on the Araguaia River in the Amazon state of Pará and with an installed capacity of 8,300 megawatts, was the first project to be constructed far from population centers, having been built in the early 1980s, when the military dictatorship then in power was still able to stifle the protests of environmental and indigenous groups.

Since the return of democratic rule in 1985, the approval process for dam construction has become more and more complicated. Tucuruí has in many ways served as an example of how not to proceed. In their haste to build the project, which cost $8 billion, Brazil's military rulers didn't bother to remove trees from the eleven-hundred-square-mile artificial lake that built up behind the dam. As a result, over the years the decomposing vegetation has generated millions of tons of carbon dioxide and methane, making Tucuruí a bigger source of greenhouse gases than the São Paulo metropolitan area.

In addition, mosquito infestations have been so intense that some settlements have been forced to relocate, and scientists worry that the increasing acidity of water in the reservoir could corrode the dam's turbines. On top of that, no provision was made to provide permanent housing or employment for the thousands of workers who were brought to the Amazon from the Northeast to build the dam. As a result, once the project was finished, sprawling squatter slum settlements, renowned for their violence, bars, and bordellos and full of desperately poor families, sprang up around the town of Tucuruí.

Originally, Brazil's electricity sector was meant to mimic the Petrobras model. In 1962, the left-leaning government then in office created a state monopoly named, predictably, Eletrobras. Even after the right-wing military coup of 1964, Eletrobras and its many subsidiaries continued to be run according to a statist philosophy, seemingly more interested in achieving the government's strategic and political objectives than adhering to free-market principles. From 1974 to 1992, for example, the price of electricity was fixed at the same level all over Brazil, with no adjustments permitted from one region to another to account for differences in demand or transmission distances. Also, electricity tariffs were at times used as an instrument to control inflation, though without much success. Revenue came mainly from the government budget and a specific tax on consumption, or, when those proved insufficient, from loans overseas, which added to Brazil's growing foreign debt burden.

With the return of democracy in the mid-1980s, two important changes occurred. First, the new Brazilian constitution, ratified in 1988, abolished the electricity consumption tax, depriving Eletrobras of an important source of equity. At the same time, international development agencies were becoming more reluctant to provide low-interest loans for hydroelectric projects, at least in part because of the growing clamor of environmentalists worried about the impact of such undertakings on the environment and the indigenous people who lived near Brazil's most promising dam sites. The result, during the first half of the 1990s, was insufficient investment in electricity generation and transmission. On average, capacity expanded by only 1,250 megawatts annually, far below the increase in demand associated with a booming industrial sector and a growing middle class.

In response, the government decided in 1995 to end the Eletrobras monopoly and open up electricity distribution to private investment. A year later, it created an independent regulatory agency for electricity and followed that in 1998 by allowing private capital to participate in electricity generation, too. The private sector responded enthusiastically to those and other initiatives: Less than a decade later, private investors accounted for nearly two-thirds of electricity distribution in Brazil and more than one-quarter of electricity generation. Today, the government's stake in Eletrobras, which continues to be Latin America's largest power utility company, is barely 50 percent, and the company registers healthy profits.

Once the Eletrobras monopoly ended, investment in new hydroelectric plants and transmission lines boomed immediately. But because such projects require a long lead time before they can begin to operate, the growing demand for electricity continued to outstrip the sluggish increase in supply, and as the new millennium arrived, Brazil's energy matrix became increasingly strained. By 2000, the consumption of electricity was 58 percent higher than it had been in 1990. Installed power generation capacity, on the other hand, grew only 32 percent during the same period.

That led to a full-fledged crisis in 2001, when a severe drought, the worst in 70 years in some parts of the country, proved too much for the system to handle. In many places, water levels in reservoirs fell to considerably less than half their normal levels, crippling the ability of existing dams to generate power. The government of Fernando Henrique Cardoso responded at midyear by imposing electricity rationing, requiring cuts in consumption of between 15 and 25 percent, with industry and commerce forced to bear more of the burden than residential customers.

Those restrictions, which included fines and even suspension of service for failing to reduce consumption, continued into early 2002, which was a presidential election year, and severely hobbled the economy, especially industrial production. Economic growth, which had been 4.4 percent in 2000, slipped to barely 1.5 percent in 2001, and some full-time factory workers were laid off or had their jobs reduced to part time. While the energy crisis was not the decisive factor in the victory of Lula and the Workers Party in the 2002 election, it proved to be an encumbrance for Cardoso's chosen successor, José Serra, and exposed him to criticism that the entire crisis could have been avoided had the government used better management practices and taken a more active role itself.

In the first years after the debacle of Tucuruí, government planners seemed chastened and began giving higher priority to smaller, more modest projects, dozens of which have been constructed. Dams at Balbina and Samuel, both in the Amazon, were subsequently built and operated on that principle. But they too roused the ire of environmentalists, especially because of the large area that Balbina inundated in relation to its very modest output, proportionally even worse than Tucuruí, and its high output of greenhouse gases. But the energy crisis of 2001 emboldened Brazil's powerful electricity lobby to again think big and to warn that the impact of another blackout would be even more damaging economically than the last one had been. Once Lula, a president clearly more sympathetic to a bigger role for the state in economic development, took office in 2002, Eletrobras and its boosters have been pushing aggressively for the construction of megaprojects on a scale similar to Tucuruí.

The two most important of these projects are Belo Monte, at a bend on the pristine Xingu River in the eastern Amazon, projected at 11,100 megawatts, and Santo Antônio-Jirau, on the Madeira River in the western Amazon, which is to have an installed capacity of 6,400 megawatts. An earlier version of Belo Monte appeared to have been shelved at the start of the decade, only to be revived in 2007 in spite of the considerable financial and environmental challenges it presents. As now planned, Belo Monte would be the third-largest hydroelectric power plant in the world, would cost up to $15 billion, and would flood 2,355 square miles of tropical forest, more than double the figure of Tucuruí. Santo Antônio, which consists of two separate dams, one of which would be only a hundred miles from the Bolivian border, would be the world's sixth largest, is expected to cost at least $9 billion, and would flood 210 square miles of jungle.

Both of these hydropower projects have become battlegrounds between the government and construction companies on one side and environmental and indigenous groups on the other. Proponents of the dam projects argue that construction procedures now in place are much more environmentally friendly and less intrusive than they were in the days of Itaipu and Tucuruí. Opponents, on the other hand, say not enough is being done to mitigate damage to the environment and to protect indigenous residents of the affected area, and they also maintain that the efficiency of many of the measures the government has promised is questionable. In the case of Santo Antônio, it is also argued that the project violates a treaty Brazil signed with Bolivia, and Bolivian president Evo Morales has threatened to take the case to international courts.

An additional problem with both projects is that they would require thousands of miles of transmission lines from the dam sites to the national power grid in the south of the country, where the bulk of Brazil's population and industry are located. That would, for starters, be costly and, as currently envisioned, environmentally destructive, because vast expanses of tropical forest in the Amazon would have to be felled. Because electricity tends to dissipate over long distances, a large amount of power, perhaps 30 percent of the total, would be lost in transmission, which raises questions about the economic viability of the projects.

One alternative to those long transmission lines that has been mentioned is the construction of up to five plants in the eastern Amazon to process industrial metals, which would be powered by Belo Monte. But the main beneficiary of that plan would seem to be China, which owns the companies that have expressed a willingness to come into the region to mine and transform aluminum, steel, copper, and nickel. The finished products would be exported back to China rather than used to spur local development or sent south for use in Brazil's existing industrial centers. So the plan, in addition to being environmentally suspect, is also highly unpopular politically.

"Everything in the Amazon that is electricity-intensive has a big Chinese component and is getting strong official support, even though the main beneficiary will clearly be China rather than Brazil," said Lucio Flavio Pinto, the author of *Hydroelectric Projects in the Amazon* and editor of *Amazon Agenda*, the leading newsletter covering the region. "Not only are the Chinese going to be investing a minimal amount themselves, but they will also be shifting the resulting pollution problems to the Amazon."

In the face of such criticisms, Eletrobras and government planners are seeking to adapt the less environmentally intrusive model that Petrobras has developed for its gas pipelines in the Amazon, mentioned above. The government is now proposing construction of a five-dam complex on the Rio Tapajós, the region seen as the next energy frontier in the Amazon, with a total capacity of 10,700 megawatts. Rather than build roads to the dam site and construct huge dormitories for thousands of workers, the ministry of energy and mines proposes to install platforms on the river itself. Instead of living onsite for the duration of the project, workers would be flown in for shifts of two or more weeks at a time and would be housed on the platforms. This system would not only reduce deforestation in the area but also impede the arrival of the illegal loggers and ranchers who usually find their entry into the jungle eased by such projects.

One unforeseen benefit of the 2001 energy crisis was that it made ordinary Brazilians even more parsimonious in the use of energy than they had been previously. Today, Brazil's energy consumption per capita is about one-tenth that of the average American and only one-fifth that of the average citizen living in an advanced industrial nation belonging to the Organization for Economic Cooperation and Development. Brazilians have also been attentive to the importance of diversifying their sources of energy so as not to be caught short again in the event of a crisis. They also seem to be aware of the need for private investment, attractive power generation prices, and a stable regulatory regime. So while neighboring countries such as Argentina and Chile worry about power shortages and blackouts each year when the Southern Hemisphere winter rolls around, Brazil has thus far been exempt from such concerns.

But there are some warning signs on the horizon. Brazil's power consumption is now the ninth largest in the world and is likely to surge even higher as the demands of a booming economy and vibrant middle class continue to expand: In 1970, barely a third of Brazilian homes had electricity compared to 99 percent today. In addition, when Eletrobras was privatized in the mid-1990s, many of the investors who came into Brazil were given 20-year concessions, meaning that those will begin expiring in the middle of this decade. It is not clear whether the government intends to renew those or put them up for new bids, but that decision will have to be made by President Dilma Rousseff, herself a former Minister of Energy. The resulting uncertainty has contributed, not surprisingly, to a gap between demand and installations of new capacity that is reminiscent of the early 1990s. In fact, Luiz Pinguelli Rosa, the same scientist who warned the government then of the shortages to come and was the president of Eletrobras during Lula's first two years in office, is once again warning of an energy crisis early in this decade.

Overall, Brazil's energy system today is one of the least carbon-intensive in the world, with nearly half of total consumption provided by less-polluting renewable fuels. That is a situation that many other countries aspire to achieve but cannot, and it has allowed Brazil to adopt a stance in world climate change negotiations, at Copenhagen and elsewhere, that is more flexible than in the past. But to fill the gap between the supply of and demand for electricity,

Brazil has over the past decade turned to thermal-powered plants, using polluting fuels such as coal, as a temporary solution until new hydropower plants come on line.

That tendency, which could be exacerbated by the uncertain situation that may prevail in the electricity sector after 2015, is an unhealthy one. Combined with the enormous potential and lure of the Sub-Salt strata and the temptation to push sugarcane production into the Amazon, such a trend creates a real risk that Brazil could regress from a situation that is the envy of nations all over the world, just when other countries are finally making an effort to move toward the balanced energy equation Brazil has long enjoyed. That kind of retreat would be a mistake, one that Brazil should resist, both for its own well-being and that of others, especially because its behavior and policies in the Amazon have already inflicted so much damage on the environment.

EIGHT

THE AMAZON

NATIONALISM AND PARANOIA
IN THE JUNGLE

ON THE MORNING OF Saturday, February 12, 2005, a pair of hired guns working for local landowners fired six bullets into the American-born nun, Dorothy Stang, killing her as she walked down a jungle path a few miles north of the Trans-Amazon Highway, on her way to a meeting with peasant leaders, Bible in hand. When I visited a few months later, a simple wooden cross with her name marked the exact spot where she had fallen—and gunmen were still roaming the area, threatening the settlers whose cause Sister Dorothy had made her own, destroying their crops and knocking down their flimsy cabins.

The conflict that took the life of Sister Dorothy had begun a couple of years earlier, when the Brazilian government declared its intention to pave the rutted Trans-Amazon Highway in the region where she had worked since the 1970s. With that announcement, the value of land rose sharply, and loggers, ranchers, and speculators from other parts of Brazil began to flood the area, chopping down trees, setting the forest ablaze, opening sawmills, fouling rivers, killing wildlife, bringing in herds of cattle, and using violence to try to force peasant families that had been there for years off the land.

"The Amazon is ours." That slogan is drilled into the minds of Brazilians from the time they enter kindergarten, repeated throughout their lives with such frequency that it has become a sort of nationalist mantra. Some interpret this principle as meaning "We can do whatever we want with the land, and it's nobody else's business," even if abuses like slavery persist. The Amazon is larger than all of Europe, and during the past 40 years, one-fifth of it has been burned, cut, chopped, or razed. As Brazil makes way for cattle ranches, soybean plantations, highways, lumber and steel mills, hydroelectric projects, railroads, mines, gas and oil fields, and settlements for displaced peasants, it is worth asking whether this really advances the country's economic development or is simply gratuitous devastation of a unique natural resource.

To say that the Amazon is the world's largest rainforest does not even begin to convey the sense of majesty and mystery that the region imprints indelibly on any visitor. Once, while I was visiting Indian villages on the upper Rio Negro, the motorboat I was traveling in ran out of gas. "What now?" I asked the pilot, who wordlessly handed me a canoe paddle. For the next three hours, until we reached the closest settlement and were able to buy some fuel, we paddled amid an almost sepulchral silence, the stillness broken only by the occasional caw of a multicolored toucan, the screech of a monkey, or the rustling of some unknown creature in the bush. All around us, trees, some as tall as two hundred feet and dotted with insect hives and bird nests, stretched to the cloudless blue sky. No longer scared away by the noise of our motor, anteaters and buck-toothed capybaras—at four feet long, the world's largest rodent—emerged from the jungle to peer at us. Swarms of butterflies in brilliant pastel hues fluttered along the riverbank, feeding on the salt in the soil. In the river, curious dolphins and otters splashed around us, and fish leaped from the water and pirouetted in the air, their scales glistening in the sunlight.

But the jungle is not always so idyllic. I've accidentally walked into mud bogs that acted like quicksand and threatened to pull me under. I've been made feverish by the bites of fire ants and the stings of wasps and driven to distraction by swarms of mosquitoes at dusk or flies attracted by the rivers of sweat that any exertion in the relentless heat and humidity produces. The most dreaded animal, however, is not the fearsome jaguar or the infamous piranha, but the candiru, a tiny needle-like fish that purportedly has the ability to worm its way into human orifices: At river beaches in the region, I've seen signs warning menstruating women and people needing to urinate or defecate to stay out of the water, which is infested with candiru.

Although barely 10 percent of the country's population lives in the Amazon, the region accounts for 60 percent of Brazil's territory and contains many of its most prized natural resources. For the bulk of the population, living in cities along the coast in the south, the Amazon has always seemed distant and strange. It is a hostile and unfamiliar place that relatively few Brazilians have actually visited, but it has a mythic aura akin in some ways to that which the Wild West has always had for Americans.

For the rest of us, because of the threat of climate change, the Amazon, source of one quarter of the world's fresh water and home to the largest concentration of fish, plant, and bird species on the planet, is about to become a battleground. Scientists can't predict when greenhouse gases will reach levels so high that the region will cease to be a functioning, viable ecological system, able to pull immense quantities of carbon dioxide from the air and convert them into oxygen. But they agree that because Brazilians are devastating the forest at such a rapid pace, the world moves closer every year to the so-called tipping point, after which climate change is irreversible, and may even reach it in a decade or two unless deforestation is sharply reduced. So the policy of Brazilians toward their national treasure will have crucial importance not just for them but also for the rest of the world.

The rainforest was opened to development on a large scale less than 50 years ago, and since then, government authorities and the business interests that have profited from that advance have reassured us that "only" 20 percent of the forest has been razed and there is nothing to worry about. But the scientific evidence clearly contradicts them. Every July, at the start of the dry season during which most of the destruction occurs, the National Institute for Space Research, outside São Paulo, announces that another area the size of the state of New Jersey (or Israel or the island of Sardinia) has been stripped of its forest cover. Government leaders express their concern and their intention to be more rigorous in enforcing the law, but for the remainder of the dry season, the smoke from the burning jungle being cleared to make new farmland or cattle pasture is so thick that pilots cannot fly over some areas.

Ironically, the country's technology is advanced enough to identify from outer space what its government cannot control on the ground. Though Brazil theoretically has the means to name and punish those who want to exploit the jungle irresponsibly, long-term planning is not part of the country's tradition, and laws often go unenforced. Yet Brazil vowed at the December 2009 Copenhagen summit on climate change to cut its emissions of greenhouse gases by 40 percent, half of which is to come from reduced deforestation. Fulfilling that pledge will be Brazil's biggest environmental challenge in the near future.

As a result of current policies that emphasize exploitation over sustained development, Brazil is now the world's fourth-largest producer of key greenhouse gases. Only China, the United States, and Indonesia spew more carbon dioxide into the atmosphere than Brazil, and if present trends continue, Brazil could soon surpass Indonesia. In contrast to the United States and China, though, Brazil's emissions are neither a product of the wasteful lifestyle of its people nor attributable mainly to a rapidly expanding industrial base that is excessively dependent on fossil fuels. More than three-quarters of Brazil's greenhouse gas emissions stem from cutting down the Amazon rainforest, hence the importance of the promises Brazil made at Copenhagen.

I first journeyed to the Amazon in 1978, at the height of the military dictatorship's effort to open the region by providing "land without men for men without land," as the slogan of the day put it. My first stop was the frontier state of Rondônia, in the western Amazon on the border with Bolivia, where poor peasants from the south of Brazil, some two thousand miles away, were being encouraged to occupy plots of land in the jungle where they would build huts for their families, clear the thicket of trees around them, and begin to farm their rudimentary homesteads. These *colonos*, or homesteaders, had formed settlements with optimistic names like New Hope or Progress, but their utopias lacked support. No secondary roads had been built to enable the peasant farmers to ship their crops of yucca, beans, and pineapple to nearby towns, let alone to the hungry cities in the south, so much of their produce simply rotted or was fed to their animals. Speculators illegally claimed title to the land, and gunmen known as *jagunços* evicted tenants. Because a police presence was almost nonexistent, everything seemed chaotic in the extreme. This was the world in which Sister Dorothy, like other defenders of the forest who have also been killed, such as Chico Mendes, was forced to operate.

Today the government still does not exercise effective sovereignty over large swaths of the territory. Partly because of that, the world's preoccupation with the health of the Amazon's ecosystems, expressed through statements of government leaders and scientists, international campaigns by environmental and indigenous rights groups, and highly publicized visits to the region by celebrities such as James Cameron, the director of *Avatar*, inspires suspicion. Brazilians proclaim that "the Amazon is ours," but they also know that they do not have the means to enforce their dominion there and cannot even deliver basic services to many of the region's inhabitants. The result is a kind of national paranoia, a conviction that outsiders, especially the United States, with its checkered history in Latin America, envy Brazil's ownership of the Amazon and would like nothing better than to seize control of it.

"Everything indicates that the environmental and indigenous problems are merely pretexts" for such a coordinated international onslaught, according to a Brazilian military intelligence report that I obtained in 2007 from a former government official who was concerned about the views it expressed. The report went on to argue that groups such as Greenpeace, Conservation International, the Rainforest Action Network, and the World Wildlife Fund are tools that "hegemonic powers" like the United States manipulate "in order to maintain and augment their domination."

It is hard to convince Brazilians that this conspiracy does not exist, especially since any international show of interest or investment in the Amazon is taken as proof of it. From the 1920s onward, Henry Ford tried to grow rubber on a large scale in plantations along the Tapajós River, about a thousand miles from the mouth of the Amazon, and in the 1970s, the billionaire shipping magnate Daniel Ludwig sunk a large chunk of his fortune into the Jari Project, which was meant to produce paper and aluminum at a plant he had built in Japan and then shipped halfway around the world to a site almost on the equator. But both those undertakings eventually failed, in part because both Ford and Ludwig misread the political climate and miscalculated the practical difficulties of operating on an industrial scale in the jungle. Those same factors have also discouraged other foreign investors and have contributed to the Amazon's economic backwardness.

Sometimes the evidence introduced to support the idea of a takeover plot can be downright silly. In the 1990s, a map said to have been pulled from an American middle-school geography text showed the Amazon under the control of an international consortium. It was accompanied by a text, written in fractured, ungrammatical English by someone who was obviously not a native speaker, which argues that because Brazilians are an "unintelligent and primitive" people incapable of administering the Amazon, the region should be taken from them and made into a global reserve.

For years, both the Brazilian government and the American Embassy have tried to rebut this crude fabrication without success. Instead, other equally improbable fables have proliferated: A Harvard University publication recommends the dismemberment of Brazil, starting with the Amazon. An American general announced to Congress that the United States should invade the Amazon if Brazil's policies there are irresponsible. And there is a 1817 naval memorandum advocating the "destabilization" of Brazil so that the Amazon and the northeast could be carved off and turned into independent republics beholden to the United States. Even Al Gore has fallen victim to a similar campaign. When he won the Nobel Peace Prize in 2007, the Brazilian press quoted him as saying that "contrary to what Brazilians think, the Amazon is not their property, it belongs to all of us." But Gore never made that statement. Those words were in reality uttered by a Republican senator, Robert Kasten, in 1989 at a memorial service in Washington for the Brazilian environmentalist Chico Mendes, and immediately repudiated by Gore.

Although it is difficult to trace propaganda found on the Internet back to its origins, in the case of Amazon paranoia, the trail almost always leads to the site of some obscure nationalist group led by retired officers from the military or the National Intelligence Service, the spy agency that was shut down after the dictatorship fell in 1985. Inevitably, these nationalists are also advocates of accelerated economic development and a greater role for the military, whose reputation and budget have shrunk since then. A few such sites are also operated by groups on the far left, such as Communists and other extremist allies of the governing Workers Party. But they are largely echoing the language and arguments of their former enemies and persecutors on the right, the crackpots nostalgic for the good old days of military rule.

But another group, even more powerful and influential in recent years, also seeks to propagate the myth of foreigners coveting the Amazon. These are the business interests responsible for the bulk of the destruction inflicted on the Amazon over the past generation: ranchers, loggers, miners, construction companies, and rice growers, most of whom have immigrated from the south. They present themselves to Brazilians as the modern-day equivalents of the *bandeirantes*, the pioneers who opened up the interior in colonial times, and claim they are working to build a strong and prosperous Brazil. In reality, however, many are manipulating patriotic sentiment to line their own pockets, and some even resort to enslavement to get the workforce they need. Like similar groups in the United States, they also attempt to discredit the scientists and environmental groups who get in their way by disputing the notion of climate change or denying that their own activities in any way damage the Amazon.

Over the years, I have attended numerous public hearings in places as far flung as Altamira, on the Xingu River in the east, and Porto Velho, on the Madeira River in Brazil's far west, that have been called to discuss projects such as dams. There is always someone there distributing flyers or pamphlets claiming that the United States or the Trilateral Commission or Prince Bernhard of the Netherlands (who founded the World Wildlife Fund) has designs on the Amazon. The only way to stop that foreign conspiracy, the argument proceeds, is by strengthening the Brazilian presence in the region, which is of course best achieved by allowing untrammeled economic development.

This is a clever strategy, which appeals to both the local population's patriotism and its hunger for jobs. Brazil does have an active environmental movement of its own, and environmentalists have sometimes occupied important positions in the government. When Fernando Collor de Mello, for instance, became president in 1990, he appointed José Lutzemberger, an ecologist renowned for his combativeness, as his environment minister, and named José Goldemberg, a leading physicist who had opposed the military's nuclear program at great personal risk, as his minister of science and technology. Environmental groups thus had great hopes for a shift in policy. But Collor was soon mired in a major corruption scandal and resigned while facing impeachment in 1992, and another decade passed before a leading environmentalist would occupy the post again.

While the Brazilian affiliates of international environmental groups such as Greenpeace and the World Wildlife Fund try to promote sustainable development, the land speculators, timber merchants, ranchers, and miners razing the Amazon play the nationalism card to question the environmentalists' credibility and patriotism. This is an old and familiar pattern that goes back to the construction of the Trans-Amazon Highway more than 40 years ago.

At nearly three thousand miles long and largely unpaved, the Trans-Amazon is the backbone of an entire network of roads meant to reach all the way to Brazil's borders and extend the government's reach and authority. With its starting point in the impoverished northeast, it was also supposed to attract millions of peasant sharecroppers to the region and settle them on homesteads of their own. The Trans-Amazon has to some extent done that, but it has also become the principal route by which thousands of peasants from the impoverished states of the northeast, especially Piauí, Maranhão, and Ceará, have been drawn into wage slavery with false promises of good-paying jobs and opportunities to better themselves.

The military regime in power during the 1970s envisioned the resettlement program not only spearheading economic development but helping to keep peasants from the northeast away from Marxist-Leninist agitators. But the traditional political bosses of the Amazon, who are known by the same word that's used for Indian chiefs, *caciques*, saw the Trans-Amazon and the wave of settlers it brought mainly as an opportunity to expand their own power and wealth. I can remember campaigning by boat up and down tributaries of the Amazon in 1980 with the most notorious and durable of these bosses: Gilberto Mestrinho, a longtime governor of the state of Amazonas who at that time was running for the Senate, attempting a comeback after having his political rights suspended for a decade because of corruption.

Mestrinho, who was born in 1929 and remained influential until his death in 2009, well into his eighties, was so smooth a talker that he had been nicknamed the Dolphin, in reference to an Amazon legend about a dolphin with the ability to turn itself into a man and cajole young girls into bed. At every stop we made along the river, he lived up to that billing, speaking of the rainforest as an impediment to his state's progress and growth. The biggest cheers came when he promised that if elected he would supply chainsaws to all who wanted them. Brazilian law at that time prohibited trading in logs and animal skins, and he also vowed to have those restrictions lifted and replaced with new legislation that would allow peasant farmers to cultivate forest lands that were off limits. His aim, he said, was to create a "New Amazonas" in which peasants "will no longer be suffocated by the forest."

Such promises appealed to the traditional inhabitants of the Amazon, known either as *caboclos*, a rather pejorative term that corresponds to "hillbilly," or more respectfully as *ribeirinhos*, or "river-dwellers." Governments had always neglected them, and the sophisticated residents in the south of the country regarded them as inarticulate yokels. Their lives had always been difficult and remain so today. Many of them live outside the money economy, eking out a livelihood from a mixture of fishing, hunting, farming, and trapping. They suffer from tropical maladies ranging from malaria and dengue to leishmaniasis and Chagas disease and often die at a young age. Only a handful of people like Sister Dorothy, who I first met in the 1970s, have taken up their cause.

"It's tough to make a go of it out here, but this is the only world we know," Sebastião Batista Pereira told me in 2005 when I visited his thatched hut on a bluff above the Solimões River, a few miles downstream from Tefé. He complained about government regulations that prevented him from hunting the alligators that ate his pigs and chickens and menaced his children. "No stores, no schools, no medical clinics, no electricity, no police station, no church. We live pretty much as our ancestors always have, which is to say very humbly."

To spur growth and provide settlers the infrastructure they lacked, the military dictatorship in 1966 created an agency called the Superintendency for the Development of the Amazon, or SUDAM. But over the years, this turned out to be more of a godsend for *caciques* such as Mestrinho and Jader Barbalho, in the neighboring state of Pará, than for the river-dwellers who were supposed to benefit. So many contracts were funneled to friends and allies of the bosses for corrupt projects that were of little practical use or actually damaged the environment that in 2001 the federal government decided to extinguish the agency altogether.

The year before, in the process of researching an article about the difficulties of taking the census in the Amazon, I encountered what seemed to me to be a perfect example of development gone awry, Amazon-style. One of the census takers I accompanied as they roamed the Solimões River delta was a

26-year-old woman, France Maria de Souza, who had taken the job only because she could not find work as a teacher. Traveling by boat, we visited a small island with nearly a hundred children, none of whom were going to class for the simple reason that construction of a rural school there had been abandoned after the funds allotted ran out. "I'd give anything to be able to be the teacher here," France said to me wistfully as we moved from house to house. "But the money never gets to where it's supposed to go. It always ends up in the pockets of the politicians and their friends."

Paranoia about what they think are outsiders' intentions to seize control of the Amazon has also led many Brazilians to regard their own Indian population with deep suspicion, as a sort of fifth column. Nationalists have long complained about the unwillingness of tribal groups to embrace the country's dominant language and culture, which over Brazil's five-hundred-year history has often been forcibly imposed, obliterating the culture and identity of those indigenous peoples. But the problem is especially acute in the Amazon, where the traditional homelands of tribal groups like the Yanomami and the Wai Wai straddle uncontrolled borders.

Feeling besieged by the economic and social forces the Brazilian government has unleashed in the Amazon since the construction of the Trans-Amazon Highway, Indian peoples have tried to protect themselves and their culture by forging alliances with sympathetic domestic and foreign organizations and individuals. These range from the Roman Catholic Church's Indigenous Missionary Council to quasi-environmental entities such as Survival International to pop stars like Sting. But the military and its nationalist sympathizers tend to regard the Indians' self-defense efforts with great distrust. To them, the Indians, whose legal status in Brazil for many years was the same as that of a child's, are the pawns of unscrupulous foreigners who, according to this line of reasoning, are looking for an opening to establish a physical presence in the Amazon and undermine the Brazilian state.

In 2002, I visited a reservation of the Yanomami, who have lived for thousands of years on both sides of what today is the Brazil-Venezuela border. The Brazilian armed forces had recently installed bases on the reservation, called Surucucu, against the wishes of tribal leaders, who invited me to hear their complaints. Soldiers had impregnated at least 18 Yanomami girls and transmitted venereal disease to others, they said, and were trying to recruit Yanomami youths into the army. When I wrote a story detailing such abuses, the Brazilian army and ministry of defense accused me of being part of a "systematic and reiterated campaign" to "play the Yanomami card" in order to strip Brazil of its sovereignty in the Amazon.

This problem has been exacerbated by the remarkable demographic resurgence of Brazil's indigenous peoples over the past 40 years. No one knows how many Indians lived in the Amazon when the first Spanish and Portuguese explorers arrived in the sixteenth century, but the estimates range as high as six million people, and contemporary reports talked of large and flourishing communities lining the banks of the main rivers. By 1970, however, Brazil's indigenous population had dropped to just over two hundred thousand people, and some advocates of the indigenous cause forecast the complete disappearance of tribal groups. Yet by the time of the 2000 census, that figure had tripled, to more than six hundred thousand, and in the 2010 census, the number swelled further, to more than 750,000 people.

Many of these tribal groups are nomadic, living in relatively small groups of just a few dozen people. To maintain the traditional way of life they do not want to relinquish, they need large spaces in which to circulate. As their numbers grow, new settlements have been created to accommodate newly formed communities and family groups. This has created some competition for the best land within the areas designated as reservations, which in turn has led some tribes to petition the government to expand the borders of their reservations and cede more land.

Such a demand only enrages the groups most interested in stepping up development of the Amazon. It ends up pitting the Indians against the ranchers, soy growers, and other commercial interests who want to develop parts of the Amazon that are fertile and rich in resources. Many Brazilians with no personal stake in the dispute seem inclined to agree with developers. About 10 percent of Brazil's territory has now been designated as reservations for indigenous peoples, who even with their increased numbers still constitute less than 1 percent of the population. In the heavily populated south of the country, the Indians' demands are often met with the questions, "How much more do they want?" and "When are their demands going to end?"

About a decade ago the government tried to create a new reservation called Raposa–Serra do Sol. Located in the extreme north of Brazil, on the border with Venezuela and Guyana, this area was the traditional homeland of the Macuxi and Wapixana peoples. But rice growers, diamond and gold miners, loggers, and smugglers gradually encroached on the territory, with one former governor going so far as to build a weekend home for himself on land within the reservation's boundaries. Worried about the porous border, the Brazilian military had also established a presence in the area but had been clumsy, arrogant, and inconsiderate in its dealings with the native peoples there and had as a result stirred much resentment among them, as I discovered when I visited in 2004 and 2007.

By government decree, the Indians are the official proprietors of the land. But white protestors armed with rifles and pistols have blocked highways for days at a time with their cars and trucks, and threats have been made against Indian chiefs and shamans. The federal government has always proved unwilling to punish these violations of the law or to prosecute leaders of such protests. Instead it has negotiated accords that have so stretched out the legal process that, as of this moment, the reservation continues to exist only on paper.

No wonder, then, that some indigenous peoples still resist contact with the outside world. Such tribal groups seem concentrated in the western Amazon, near sections of Brazil's borders with Peru and Bolivia that remain undeveloped. Unlike other such groups contacted in the past, many of them are aware that another, more technologically advanced way of life exists around them. But they fear what will happen if they attempt to integrate with that world beyond the one they know, in which they are the masters of their own fate.

The National Indian Foundation, the government agency charged with dealing with indigenous peoples and known by the Portuguese acronym FUNAI, used to have a corps of agents, known as *sertanistas* and celebrated for their bravery, who specialized in first contacts with such tribal peoples. Going back more than a century, their creed has always been "die if necessary, but never kill." But they are aware that the remaining tribal groups are reluctant to engage the outside world, and so the age of the *sertanista* now appears to be ending. The most famous of these intrepid adventurers, Sydney Possuelo, has said publicly that he regrets the damage that has been inflicted on many of the tribes he contacted and has retired from field work.

Because the Amazon is so vast and the federal government's control of it is so tenuous, social abuses such as wage slavery have also flourished, not just in the past, but also in recent years. This was a major problem during the rubber boom of the late nineteenth and early twentieth centuries, when thousands of poor peasants were sent off to remote plantations in the jungle to work in conditions that today would be characterized as inhumane. The problem subsided only after British companies shifted their rubber production to Southeast Asia. But as the economy of the Amazon has supposedly modernized in recent years with the arrival of export-oriented agriculture, logging, and mining, there appears to have been a resurgence of the problem. A Roman Catholic church group has estimated that in any given year, at least twenty-five thousand workers are forced to work in such industries as slaves, and government-led raids have in recent years freed more than a thousand slaves during each dry season.

Slavery in the Amazon does not follow the classic model in which people are directly bought and sold. Instead, peasants from poor states of the northeast sign labor contracts and are transported to work sites deep in the jungle, often hundreds of miles from roads, settlements, or telephones. Once there, they find that they will not receive the wages they have been promised and in addition will be charged exorbitant prices for food, lodging, and the tools and equipment they need to do their work. Since these items can be bought only at an on-site company-owned store, the workers quickly fall into arrears and are prohibited, often at gunpoint, from leaving until they repay their debts, which, of course, grow larger the longer they remain.

In 2001, I spent more than a month roaming the fast-growing area between the Tocantins and Xingu rivers. Vast stretches where jungle had flourished in the 1970s, when I first visited the region, were now dotted with cattle ranches, brazil-nut plantations, logging operations, sawmills, brickyards, and charcoal producers. I was told by the religious and human rights groups that monitor abuses in the region that slave labor was an essential part of all of these activities, and I soon discovered they were not exaggerating.

One of the liberated former slaves I met was Bernardo Gomes da Silva, who told me he had been held against his will for a dozen years, working on four different cattle ranches. "We were forced to start work at six in the morning and to continue sometimes until eleven at night," he said. "But I was never paid during that entire time because they always claimed I owed them money."

Much of the job involved felling trees at sites out in the jungle, where workers slept in thatch huts that leaked when it rained. Food was scarce, and much of what was served was spoiled, including feed deemed unsuitable for cattle. When workers became ill, which was common due to overwork and epidemics of malaria, their accounts were charged for the medicine they needed. Particularly troublesome workers, especially those who pressed to receive their wages, were simply killed.

"I can't read, so maybe a half-dozen different times I was ordered to burn the identity cards and labor documents of workers who I had last seen walking down the road, supposedly on their way out," he said. "We also found heaps of bones out in the jungle, but none of us ever talked about it."

Six years later, a different government was in power, this one headed by a former labor union leader who claimed to be the protector of the Brazilian working man. But Brazil was in the midst of an export boom, and when I returned to the Amazon states of Pará and Maranhão at the urging of antislavery groups, this time traveling east of the Tocantins River, I found that little had changed. The landscape was dotted with hundreds of clay kilns, easily traceable from the highway because of the plumes of smoke they belched into the sky. Often consuming wood that has been illegally felled, the kilns, using slave labor, produce charcoal, which is then transported to steel mills in Marabá, a dusty, gritty city of 250,000 on the banks of the Tocantins. There the charcoal is used to make pig iron, a basic component of steel, which is then shipped to the United States and Europe, where it is used to make cars and household appliances and fixtures.

"The coal kilns are even worse than the ranches, I can tell you that from my own experience," José Alves de Sousa, a 30-year-old who had fallen into wage slavery when he was still a teenager, told me when I interviewed him in a town called Açailândia. "You work surrounded by armed guards who can kill you, diseases are all over the place, you're fed nothing but rice and beans full of grubs, and they make you work long hours wearing nothing more than Bermuda shorts and sandals, with no protection against the heat or fire."

After nearly a decade in captivity, Sousa and a brother who is a deaf-mute decided to flee. "We had to trek through a hundred kilometers of jungle to get to the highway," said Sousa, whose story had been verified by an antislavery group active in the area. "We just got tired of being deceived and decided we weren't going to take it any more. They lie and lie to you, and you have no way to react, to protest, to get justice."

The Brazilian government's reaction to the presence of wage slavery in the Amazon, so clearly damaging to the country's international image, has been contradictory. To its credit, over the last 15 years it has stepped up efforts to combat the phenomenon, raiding ranches and logging and mining operations where workers are held against their will and forcing offenders to pay back-wages. But it has done so reluctantly and incompletely, in many cases responding to threats of boycotts organized by antislavery and consumer groups abroad. Often the government also takes swipes at its foreign critics and their motives in what is clearly an effort to deflect criticism and rally support at home.

To hear the Brazilian government tell it, just as those worried about the environment are secretly plotting to seize the Amazon, foreign critics of slavery are merely protectionists who are envious of Brazil's growing success in exporting its products to the United States and other industrial countries and are intent on unjustly blocking Brazil's access to those markets. "The more competitive our country becomes, the more the barriers that will be placed in our way," Luiz Furlan, Minister of Commerce and Industry during Lula's first term, said when complaints first arose about the pig-iron industry in the Amazon. "Countries improve and end up inconveniencing sectors that had been comfortable."

This attitude is perhaps understandable in an official whose principal duty is to promote Brazilian exports, no matter what the cost. But at the ministry of labor, whose responsibilities include protection of Brazilian workers, the reaction to complaints about slave labor in the Amazon hasn't been much different. When a subcommittee of the U.S. House of Representatives announced it intended to hold hearings on unfair labor practices in the Brazilian pig-iron industry, Luiz Marinho, then the Minister of Labor, pointedly told Washington to mind its own business. "Let the American Congress worry about the Americans," said Marinho, who had been president of the country's main labor federation before coming into government. "As for the Brazilian worker, we'll handle that."

Except, of course, that the ministry of labor has never shown itself able to deal competently with the plague of slave labor. I have traveled with the ministry's Mobile Inspection Teams in both the states where slave laborers are recruited and those where they end up being held against their will, and I have seen for myself how brave and committed to their mission the inspectors are. But they almost never have adequate money, equipment, or protection, which limits their ability to do their job. Police are often unavailable or unwilling to accompany the inspectors, some of whom have been shot or killed by the hired gunmen working for ranchers and other slave owners. Missions often have to be delayed or suspended because the teams don't have enough gasoline for their vehicles or because a vehicle has broken down and replacement parts can't be found.

This is a problem that also afflicts the field enforcement units of IBAMA, the federal government's environmental protection agency, and FUNAI, the agency that supervises every aspect of Indian policy from health care for tribal peoples to demarcation of Indian lands. That broader problem, in turn, again suggests the fundamental conundrum that afflicts Brazil's stewardship of the Amazon. The government itself, confronted with budgetary restraints common in a developing country, does not have the capacity to do everything that needs to be done to protect the Amazon and the people who live there. But because of Brazil's fears of seeing its sovereignty in the region weakened even further, it is unwilling to let outsiders play an active role or even to accept their financial assistance. This in turn strengthens the hand of powerful domestic economic interests that control the Amazon and their allies in the rural caucus of Congress, some of whom themselves are owners of properties where slave labor is used.

One positive development in the Amazon over the past decade or so, though, has been the emergence of a new generation of more enlightened leaders in some parts of the Amazon. The first encouraging signs came from Acre, the small state in the far west where Chico Mendes, the internationally known environmentalist and rubber tappers leader, had worked and was assassinated in 1988. One of his allies, Jorge Viana, was elected governor there in 1998, four years after another of his associates, Marina Silva, a rubber tapper's daughter who grew up in the jungle, was chosen as senator. Both belonged to the left-leaning Workers Party, in opposition at the time, and were natives of the state, unlike many of the ranchers and loggers who had flocked to the area.

Together they brought a new outlook to the Amazon. Instead of regarding the rainforest as an obstacle to their state's prosperity, they saw it as a source of growth if treated properly. They put in place new policies meant to inhibit the razing of the forest to make way for more cattle ranches, which employ few people. Instead, they have encouraged long-term projects based on the economic sustainability of the forest. These included financial incentives and guaranteed markets to encourage *caboclos* to return to rubber growing. One particularly interesting project I visited, in Xapuri, Chico Mendes's hometown, involved the manufacture of "green condoms," made of rubber grown in environmentally certified plantations. The same cooperative also had a guaranteed contract to supply rubber to the Italian tire maker Pirelli.

As Pirelli's involvement indicated, the Acre government was not afraid to set aside the traditional xenophobia and forge partnerships with foreigners. The first time I met Jorge Viana, in his office in the state capital, Rio Branco, he told me his aim was for "this state to become the Finland of the Amazon," which meant using the resources of the vast forest to expand into services and exports of refined products. To that end, numerous environmental groups and universities from the United States and Europe also pitched in, sending researchers to Acre to help in projects designed to commercialize local plants for use in perfumes, balms, and medicines. Deforestation dropped dramatically, and the income of farmers and rubber workers rose considerably, which sparked interest among peasant groups in other parts of the Amazon.

When Lula became president in 2003, there was hope that this new approach could spread to other areas. Environmentalists had been one of the constituencies that helped found the party, and for his Minister of the Environment Lula chose none other than Marina Silva, which added to that initial burst of optimism. But Lula quickly proved to be an advocate of development first, the environment second. Marina Silva was able to stave off the completion of the paving of Highway BR–163, which runs through the heart of the Amazon and topped the wish list of soybean growers eager to expand their activities deeper into the rainforest. But she lost most of the major battles she fought, with Lula choosing more often than not to side with his agriculture and commerce and industry ministers, who saw the Amazon as both a breadbasket for the world and a source of exports to newly emerging industrial powers in Asia. In 2008, after years of frustration, Marina Silva finally stepped down.

In the meantime, however, other leaders whose outlook was congenial to sustainable development and cooperation with the international environmental movement had already taken the stage. The most important of these was Eduardo Braga, governor of the state of Amazonas, Brazil's biggest state, with a territory larger than France, Germany, Great Britain, and Italy combined. One of the problems that Viana and Silva had faced was that their state is small and always on the margins of things. Amazonas, in contrast, accounts for the largest single piece of the Amazon, and even its name evokes the region. As Braga once explained to me during an interview, "When I go abroad, people think that I am the governor of the entire Amazon."

Braga named a prominent ecologist from São Paulo as his environmental secretary and also launched the Green Free Trade Zone program to underwrite efforts to encourage river-dwellers to cultivate rubber, medicinal plants, and fragrances as alternatives to cutting down the forest or migrating to Manaus, the state capital, which is home to three-quarters of the state's 2.5 million people. Soybean cultivation had already led to rapid deforestation in Mato Grosso, the state immediately to his south, and Braga's aim was to provide an economic alternative that would block its expansion into the southeast corner of Amazonas.

Reelected in 2006, Braga, a businessman who belongs to a party allied with the president, proved to be just as innovative in his second term. Just months after being sworn in, he signed Brazil's very first climate-change statute into law at a ceremony in Manaus, which I attended. That pioneering measure allows a monetary value to be assigned to what is known as "avoided deforestation" and permits river-dwellers and Indian tribes to receive compensation for the "environmental services" they provide to the state and the world by not destroying the forest. In other words, foreign governments and international environmental groups were openly being recruited as financiers, guarantors, and monitors for maintaining the forest. The inhabitants of the Amazon would refrain from cutting it down, and in return, wealthier patrons from the north would pay them for their restraint.

Braga took that bold step of asking foreigners to get involved despite the active opposition of powerful sectors of the national government, especially the foreign ministry. In Brazil, as elsewhere, foreign policy tends to reflect domestic concerns and priorities and the pressures of domestic constituencies. So it is hardly surprising that Brazil's position in international climate-change talks has mirrored its fears, real and imagined, about the Amazon. Over the years, Brazilian governments, regardless of the ideology of the party in power and with the foreign ministry in the lead, had resisted any kind of international agreement that would permit compensation for avoided deforestation.

This resistance was clearly on display throughout the United Nations–sponsored negotiations that began in Rio de Janeiro in 1992, resulted in the Kyoto Protocol of 1997, and continued through the first decade of this century. Though it is one of the world's principal polluters of the environment, Brazil traditionally also fought any measure that would force developing countries to cap their emissions or, for that matter, take any steps at all to control them, often working closely with China to block such efforts.

"Everyone knows that the rich countries are responsible for 60 percent of the gas emissions and for that reason have to assume their responsibilities," President Luiz Inácio Lula da Silva said at a meeting of the G-8 in 2007. "We do not accept the idea that emerging countries have to make sacrifices, because poverty itself is already a sacrifice."

Compared to the blunderbuss approach employed by the administration of George W. Bush, Brazil's strategy was more subtle and therefore more effective. But the result has been nearly as damaging. Rather than openly walk away from the talks and thereby damage its international image, as the Bush administration did, Brazil has remained inside the process, participating in the talks but often blocking progress in a way that has sometimes won it the "Fossil of the Day" award that environmentalist groups monitoring the process also awarded to obstructionists like the United States and Saudi Arabia.

For example, Brazil long attempted to sabotage efforts to reach an international agreement to create any sort of carbon credit mechanism based on market forces, the so-called cap-and-trade legislation that the Republican Party in the United States is also fighting. This is a proposal supported by most developing countries, who would be the main beneficiaries of the resources that industrialized countries would provide, whether in the form of money or technical assistance or trade benefits, as a form of compensation for the greenhouse gases their industries and automobiles produce. But Brazil traditionally favored another system, one in which the world's most prosperous nations would contribute to a fund that the developing countries would administer themselves, for the projects their governments deem most necessary, in places they judge most vulnerable.

Most of the governments and environmental organizations that deal with Brazil on a regular basis have fundamental doubts about this proposal or oppose it outright. But they are aware that there cannot be real, effective progress on climate change unless Brazil is fully engaged and cooperating, so they have tended to express their concerns in muted language. From what they say in private, however, it is clear that the Brazilian proposal cannot work because donors will never agree to it.

The main problem is lack of oversight. Given the history of government-sponsored programs aimed at lifting living standards in the Amazon, foreign donors are not willing to hand over hundreds of millions of dollars with little or no say in how and where the money will be spent. But their insistence on accountability as a sine qua non for any monetary transfer runs smack into the traditional Brazilian argument that any foreign say in what goes on in the Amazon constitutes "interference" that would "injure the sovereignty" of Brazil.

On the theory that the best defense is a strong offense, Brazil has also launched counterattacks against the industrial nations that have complained the most about Brazil's erratic stewardship of the Amazon. As Lula put it in 2008, "What we cannot accept is that those who failed to take care of their own forests, who did not preserve what they had and deforested everything and are responsible for most of the gases poured into the air and for the greenhouse effect, they shouldn't be sticking their noses into Brazil's business and giving their two cents worth." This is a popular position in Brazil and also plays to guilt feelings among green sympathizers in the United States and Europe.

That position gave Brazil some cover and traction so long as George W. Bush was in power in the United States and blocked any effort to move beyond the Kyoto Protocol, which the Bush administration had in any case refused to sign. But once Barack Obama entered the White House, Brazil's obstructionist posture became more difficult to defend or justify. Lula and his government then pointed to a substantial reduction in deforestation as proof that they are acting more vigorously, but those figures must be treated with a certain caution. Traditionally, the numbers announced each July correspond to fluctuations that have more to do with the state of the economy than government policies or actions. When times are good and the economy is expanding, deforestation increases, and when times are lean and the economy contracts, so does deforestation.

For all of these reasons, the shift of attitude that Brazil demonstrated during the Copenhagen summit on climate change in December 2009 is a hopeful sign. A month before the conference began, Brazil signaled a retreat from its previous intransigence by promising to make big cuts in carbon emissions over the next decade. That flexibility was rewarded by Brazil's inclusion, along with China, India, South Africa, and, eventually, the United States, in discussions parallel to the formal conference itself. That resulted in a draft agreement, known as the Copenhagen Accord, that, among other things, formally recognized "the crucial role of reducing emission from deforestation and forest degradation and the need to enhance removals of greenhouse gas emissions by forests" through a mechanism to be financed by developed countries.

Brazilians argue that their change of policy has increased pressure on their allies China and India to follow suit. But as critics have noted, that side agreement, modest in its goals, is not legally binding even on the five countries that signed it, was not adopted by the conference as a whole, and contains no compulsory commitments for reducing emissions of carbon dioxide or other greenhouse gases. In addition, Brazil is only pledging "voluntary reductions" as what it calls a "political gesture" to shame the rich nations of the north into accepting larger cuts in emissions and continues to reject the notion of binding "targets" of any kind for developing countries. Finally, for Brazil to reach the goal it is striving for, deforestation will have to decline 80 percent by 2020, which is a very tall order.

It would be unrealistic, therefore, to expect a dramatic alteration of Brazilian policy now that Lula has left office, such as that which came with the United States' shift from Bush to Obama. Other than Marina Silva, who has no chance of winning, none of those who aspired to be Lula's successor are closely identified with the environmental movement. Besides, no Brazilian president can afford to sacrifice growth and development just to ensure the preservation of the Amazon. No politician has ever won a significant following, outside of a few upper-class enclaves in Rio de Janeiro and São Paulo, by espousing the need for restraint in the Amazon. Brazilians, for the most part, continue to regard the region as a treasure chest rich in resources that should be extracted for the benefit of the nation, and they expect their leaders to feel that way too. What that is likely to mean for the Amazon in the next few years is more of the same: efforts to tinker around the edges of the problem, leading to limited progress but no fundamental solution.

Brazil has pledged sweeping changes in its Amazon policy, to be put into place over the next decade. The government deserves praise for finally demonstrating the courage and willingness to engage the rest of the world on a sensitive topic it has always deemed nobody's business except Brazil's own. Yet in view of the trail of broken promises and failed programs that litter the Amazon's past, it may also be worthwhile to remember the phrase that Ronald Reagan used to cite during a very different set of negotiations that nonetheless also had implications for world security: "Trust, but verify."

NINE

BECOMING A "SERIOUS COUNTRY"

ON OCTOBER 2, 2009, the International Olympic Committee (IOC) awarded the 2016 summer games to Rio de Janeiro, which triumphed over Chicago, Madrid, and Tokyo despite personal appeals by U.S. president Barack Obama and the prime ministers of Spain and Japan. Luiz Inácio Lula da Silva, the president of Brazil, had also gone to Copenhagen to lobby the IOC. When he spoke to Brazilian reporters after the official announcement was made, he was so overcome with emotion that he broke into tears and had to daub his eyes with a handkerchief.

"Today I've felt prouder of being Brazilian than on any other day," he said in comments that were broadcast live back to Brazil. "Today is the day that Brazil gained its international citizenship. Today is the day that we have overcome the last vestiges of prejudice against us. I think this is a day to celebrate, because Brazil has left behind the level of second-class countries and entered the rank of first-class countries. Today we earned respect. The world has finally recognized that this is Brazil's time. We've proven to the world that we are citizens, too."

To understand Lula's emotional reaction, we need to go back to the early 1960s, when Brazil and France found themselves locked in a dispute over fishing rights in coastal waters. In a burst of irritation, Charles de Gaulle, then the president of France, is said to have complained that "Brazil is not a serious country." The truth is that he probably said nothing of the sort and that a Brazilian reporter in Paris misconstrued a diplomat's offhand remark. But the phrase *le Brésil n'est pas un pays sérieux* stung so badly, so deeply wounding Brazil's image of itself and its aspirations to play a larger role on the world stage, that it has passed into Brazilian political folklore as a sort of permanent catchphrase. Even today, any time Brazil experiences what it perceives as a slight at the hand of others with more power or prestige—or, for that matter, whenever someone behaves in a manner so absurd or frivolous that is likely to lead outsiders to view Brazil as a nation of lightweights—the "not a serious country" criticism is revived.

If there is one thing Brazil wants above all else in its relations with the rest of the world, it is to be taken seriously, especially by the countries it views as great powers. Brazilians regard their nation as one destined for greatness, and they crave the respect of others, which they interpret as confirmation of their own belief in Brazil's greatness. The image of Brazil as the land of soccer and samba, of beaches and beauties in bikinis, and only that, both irks and embarrasses them. If an American or a European publication mistakenly writes that Buenos Aires is the capital of Brazil or suggests that Brazilians speak Spanish, the reaction in Brazil is intense. And when a head of state makes a similar gaffe, as Ronald Reagan did in 1982 when he offered a toast at a state dinner in Brasília to "the people of Bolivia," the laments over Brazil's lack of global status—and the outside world's lack of knowledge of and regard for Brazil—can at times become deafening.

As a result, Brazil's underlying objective in its dealings with foreigners is not so much to defend commercial or security interests (though these, too, are important goals) as it is to obtain their respect. Behind the warmth with which Brazilians typically treat visitors—for the notion of "the cordial Brazilian" is also an essential part of national identity—lies a deep-seated insecurity. More than a half century ago, the playwright and novelist Nelson Rodrigues, one of the most astute observers of national character, wrote that Brazilians suffer from what he called *o complexo de vira-lata*, or "the mongrel dog complex." The word *vira-lata* literally means "can-turner," and it evokes the image of a frightened mutt rummaging through garbage cans looking for scraps and leftovers. Rodrigues seized on that analogy because he saw Brazilians as suffering from a feeling of inferiority that cripples their self-esteem and poisons their ability to deal with outsiders on a basis of mutual respect and equality.

That is perhaps to be expected in a nation that sees itself as a latecomer to the club of great powers. Like the United States, Brazil is a young country, but one lacking many of the conventional tools through which power is expressed. For much of its history, it has been a typical developing country, forced to focus on occupying its vast territory and struggling to feed, house, and educate its people. Its military has been weak and ill-supplied, and its diplomacy timid, despite an extraordinarily capable foreign service. Notwithstanding its size and resources, Brazil's behavior on the international stage has historically been that of a much smaller country, hesitant and unsure of itself. As a puzzled American ambassador to Brasília once said to me, using a boxing analogy, Brazil is a country that consistently "punches under its weight."

That craving for the respect of others was nakedly on display throughout the campaign to bring the world's biggest sporting event to South America for the first time. The Brazilian government had lobbied long and hard on behalf of Rio's Olympics bid, and when the decision was announced, on a Friday afternoon, hundreds of thousands of people flocked to Rio's Copacabana Beach to celebrate. They waved the green-and-yellow national flag as well as those of their favorite soccer teams, set off firecrackers, tossed confetti into the air, danced and sang to the beat of samba drums, and kissed and hugged one another as the announcement and Lula's reaction were broadcast on a giant screen.

But it was also clear from their response that many Brazilians were commemorating something that, in their minds, went far beyond the competition to host a sporting event. They also seemed to regard their triumph as the world's validation of their status as a rising power. Some even talked of a "consecration" that would allow Brazil to throw a coming-out party to formalize its new status, just at Japan did with the 1964 Tokyo Olympics and China with the 2008 Olympics in Beijing. "Our moment has finally come," one woman, her cheeks painted in the national colors, jubilantly told the television cameras. "For the other contenders, it would have been just another Olympic Games. But for us, it's an opportunity like we've never had before to show the world what we're capable of, strengthen our self-esteem, and achieve new advances."

That same yearning for the recognition and esteem of outsiders helps explain Brazil's enthusiastic embrace of its classification as a member of the BRIC group, along with Russia, India, and China. The BRIC group is essentially an artificial construct, devised by Goldman Sachs in 2003, more as a Wall Street marketing tool than anything else, and it ignores the significant cultural and political differences among the members. But Brazilians are thrilled, even flattered, to be grouped with Russia, India, and China as the up-and-coming economic powers of the twenty-first century, capable of changing the equilibrium of global trade and commerce, instead of being lumped together, as has usually been the case in the past, with the likes of Argentina, Colombia, and Venezuela. Whether it makes objective sense or not, to the Brazilian ear, the term "BRIC group" has an agreeable ring that "developing nation" or "emerging country," the appellations that were most often applied to Brazil in the past, do not.

But the hunger to be respected as a serious country, a member in good standing of what is somewhat naïvely thought to be a kind of club of the next generation of great powers, has sometimes led Brazil to overreach and make missteps that end up undermining those same ambitions. One example is Brazil's nuclear program, which has created unnecessary and easily avoidable frictions and suspicions in relations with friends and allies; another is the country's space program, which has turned into an outright embarrassment. A decade-long campaign to gain a permanent seat on the United Nations Security Council has fallen short of its goal, and various other diplomatic initiatives have also failed. For Brazil, the road to greatness has often proved to be strewn with initiatives that are ill-conceived or ineptly executed. The most recent of these was the failed joint effort with Turkey in May 2010 to avert a showdown over Iran's nuclear program by brokering an agreement in which Iran would ship nuclear fuel abroad in return for the United States and its allies on the U.N. Security Council agreeing not to impose sanctions on Tehran.

Brazil sees itself as having long been unjustly depreciated or disparaged, and Brazilians sometimes perceive slights where none are intended or take affront where none is meant. Foreigners coming into contact with the country for the first time are often unaware of this hypersensitivity, unable to see beyond the affable, cordial exterior of the Brazilians they meet, and unwittingly blunder or offend. This deeply entrenched insecurity and the accompanying propensity to feel snubbed and affronted can emerge even in the most unexpected of moments and contexts.

As a nation of continental proportions and ambitions, Brazil has traditionally defined and compared itself not to its smaller neighbors but to larger states and regional powers in other parts of the world. This focus on the faraway has led to large gaps in Brazil's understanding of nearby countries and a sense of superiority in relation to many of them, especially Argentina, Bolivia, and Paraguay. For example, I've often heard Brazilians call Argentines gringos and even refer to residents of Latin American countries with population that are predominantly Indian as *cucarachas*, after the Mexican song about cockroaches. Psychologically, it is almost as if Brazil has lived most of its history with its back to the rest of Latin America and its eyes fixed on the more distant centers of culture and might to which it aspired.

Initially, this gaze was focused on Europe—though not so much on the mother country, Portugal, which is often the butt of jokes, as on France. More than any other place, France provided a newly independent Brazil with the template for what it sought to be. French culture, dress, and manners were thought to be the pinnacle of attainment; a French education or trip to France was highly valued, and French words were incorporated into the Portuguese spoken in the Imperial court, itself a branch of the French House of Orleans. The preferred foreign language spoken by educated Brazilians was of course French, and upper-class Brazilian families, including the Emperor's, tried to marry their children into well-off or distinguished French families. Even subsequent waves of immigrants from Italy and Germany did little to alter that fascination with all things French.

In recent years, Brazil's horizons have expanded to take in points as far off as Japan, China, and India. Despite the black origins of the majority of the population, the Brazilian establishment recoils from any comparison to Africa, which is viewed as a failed, inferior continent that is a market for Brazilian goods but offers nothing worth emulating. All three of the modern major Asian powers, on the other hand, inspire curiosity and admiration because they offer different templates for pulling yourself up by your bootstraps out of poverty and underdevelopment and into the community of industrialized nations. In Japan's case, ties are also enhanced by the presence of the largest community of Japanese descent outside Japan, the nearly two million Brazilians who can claim some degree of Japanese ancestry.

Increasingly over the past century, though, the United States has become the main focus of Brazil's attention when it thinks of itself in relation to the outside world. There are many reasons for this, starting with certain superficial similarities between the two most populous nations in the Western Hemisphere. Both Brazil and the United States are countries of continental dimensions, built by adventurous pioneers who braved all kinds of dangers and deprivations to populate the vast interior: The saga of the conquest of the American West resonates so strongly in Brazil even today that the term *faroeste* is used to describe an unruly or violent frontier settlement.

Both countries have also had to struggle to overcome the negative legacy of slavery and the extermination of the native peoples who originally inhabited their territory, and both countries have had their modern character shaped by the millions of immigrants who came there from every corner of the world. In addition, they have carved out identities that stand in apposition to the vast Spanish-speaking mass just beyond their borders. They are also societies whose cornerstone is optimism, built on the notion that almost anything is possible, that the most humble of citizens can rise to the top. In both countries, this has translated into a sense of exceptionalism, a feeling of living in a nation blessed by God, with a unique historical role to play. Manifest destiny is a concept that Brazilians understand and appreciate, though they do not use that term.

But Brazil's focus on the United States, which in certain quarters has curdled into a kind of obsession, stems from other factors as well. Precisely because the two countries appear to share so many characteristics, the United States often seems to be a more valid measuring stick and to offer more grounds for comparison than other places. Yet because the United States has risen to world dominance and Brazil has lagged behind, the success of the United States also stands almost as a rebuke to some Brazilians. They cite it constantly in discussions of their own shortcomings, whether material or moral, to gauge their own accomplishments or justify their failures. If the murder rate by gun in Rio or São Paulo is alarmingly high, for example, any discussion of that problem sooner or later is sure to mention statistics from New York or Los Angeles in an attempt to argue that things could be worse.

This mind-set, of course, complicates relations between the two countries, in ways that most Americans do not realize or even think about—which only compounds the offense as far as some Brazilians are concerned. Millions of Brazilians admire the United States and find its ascent inspiring, on the theory, "If they can do it, why can't we?" But there is another train of thought that sees history as a zero-sum game and argues that America's rise was achieved at Brazil's expense. Some intellectuals, especially on the left, go even further and maintain that the United States has, since its earliest days, been engaged in an ongoing effort to keep Brazil from achieving the greatness that otherwise would be its destiny. This is not a fringe school of thought but one expressed by respected historians such as Luiz Alberto Moniz Bandeira, the author of books such as *The Presence of the United States in Brazil*, which are published by leading editorial houses and taught not only in universities but also in training programs of the Brazilian diplomatic service.

Perhaps the most extreme and, from an American point of view, curious example of this phenomenon is the unending debate over who deserves credit for having made the first heavier-than-air flight. Brazilians contend that the airplane was really invented not by the Wright brothers but by Alberto Santos-Dumont, a millionaire coffee-grower's son who spent much of his life in Paris. In Brazil, the Wright brothers are considered frauds and cheats who, in their desire to become rich, stole credit from Santos-Dumont, who piloted the first public flight of an airplane in 1906, three years after the Wright brothers flew at Kitty Hawk, and made the blueprints for his inventions, including the aileron and the hydroplane, available to all rather than seeking personal profit. The Wright brothers' 1903 flight at Kitty Hawk, on the other hand, is said to have taken place in secret, without verification, and to have been aided by a catapult, and is therefore not valid.

A century later, Santos-Dumont remains both a national hero and a symbol of how the world has wronged Brazil. His image, usually in the Panama hat and high, stiff collar that was his favorite costume, is omnipresent around the country. He and his aircraft, called the 14-Bis, have appeared on banknotes and in the dozens of songs, poems, paintings, and books that celebrate his feats. Rio de Janeiro's main in-town airport is named for him, as are streets, squares, plazas, and schools, where students are taught that the American insistence on honoring the Wright brothers is, in the words of one textbook, "not honest and disrespectful to us." Santos-Dumont eventually committed suicide, and Americans sometimes get the blame for that, too, since he is said to have been heartbroken at seeing his invention used for military purposes and not to have gotten the recognition due him.

Most Americans have never heard of Santos-Dumont and are shocked to learn of the vehemence with which Brazilians defend his achievements or, to cite another example, argue that the United States seeks to undermine their control of the Amazon. This, of course, is part of a much larger pattern of indifference and lack of awareness. If Brazilians tend to be obsessed with the United States, the opposite is true of Americans: For many, Brazil barely registers on their radar screen. For Brazilians, the relationship with the United States is all-important; for Washington, it is merely one of many and only gets concentrated attention from the president in times of crisis, when Brazil's cooperation or help suddenly becomes useful or its perceived obduracy a hindrance, as during the current stand-off on Iran's nuclear program.

After taking office in 2003, Lula and his foreign minister, Celso Amorim, repeatedly stated that "never in history" have relations between Brazil and the United States been better than under their care. This is an exaggeration, as both Brazilian and American diplomats acknowledge when they are talking off the record.

Over the past 50 years, relations were probably at their lowest from 1977 to 1981, when Jimmy Carter was in the White House and a military dictatorship was in power in Brazil. Almost from the day Carter took office, there were clashes about human rights. That led to disputes about weapons purchases and nuclear proliferation, which made Carter's visit to Brazil in March 1978, during which he met with civilian critics and opponents of the military regime, tense from start to finish.

I would argue that relations actually reached a historic peak two decades later, during the overlapping presidencies of Bill Clinton and Fernando Henrique Cardoso in the second half of the 1990s. Not only did the two heads of state genuinely like each other, establishing a friendship that lasted long after both left office, they shared ideological affinities and a common worldview, which translated into warmer state-to-state ties. As a result, when Brazil experienced a fiscal crisis late in 1998 and early in 1999, Washington was willing to intervene on Cardoso's behalf, providing financial support and speaking in support of Brazil at the World Bank and International Monetary Fund and on Wall Street.

Cardoso and Bush, on the other hand, were like oil and water. Bush clearly found Cardoso, a renowned intellectual who was the author of several books on sociology and economics, to be rather pompous and condescending, as if the Brazilian were a university professor and Bush a particularly slow student. Cardoso, on the other hand, was appalled at Bush's ignorance and intellectual laziness. In one notorious incident that took place during a visit to the White House in 2001, Cardoso was talking with his American counterpart about Brazilian blacks when Bush responded with surprise at hearing that Brazil even had a population of African descent. When the story leaked out in Brazil, generating laughter, disdain, and the traditional wringing of hands about foreign ignorance of Brazil, the White House denied it. But Brazilians who were in the room when the conversation took place have confirmed it to me, and I have no reason to doubt them.

Since Lula took office, relations between Brazil and the United States have been cordial and constructive. Despite their ideological differences, Lula and George W. Bush—or "Comrade Bush," as Lula once jokingly called him—seemed to genuinely get along and enjoy each other's company. Perhaps that was because the two men are so similar, in ways that go beyond their fondness for barbecue and their tendency to mangle their own language. Both came to office with little experience of the world outside their country's borders, constrained by a rigid, ideological outlook and a limited understanding of international politics and other peoples and cultures. Both lack intellectual curiosity and have relied mainly on a single advisor to shape their worldview and tutor them on the complexities of foreign affairs: Condoleezza Rice for Bush, and for Lula, Marco Aurélio Garcia, a left-wing university professor from São Paulo and the longtime head of the Workers Party's international affairs division.

At a personal level, Barack Obama is clearly even more to Lula's liking, and after Obama replaced Bush, there were excited predictions in Brazil that relations would become even closer and warmer. "He looks like one of us," Lula remarked to Brazilian reporters after he and Obama chatted at a gathering of Group of 20 in London in April 2009. "This is a unique opportunity for Latin America to establish a new relationship with the United States. If you were to meet Obama in Rio, you'd think he was a *carioca;* if you ran across him in Bahia," the Brazilian state with the highest percentage of population of African descent, "you'd think he was a *baiano.*"

For his part, Obama was just as effusive: "That's my man right here," he said, with television cameras rolling as Lula approached him at the same G-20 summit. "Love this guy. He's the most popular politician on Earth. It's because of his good looks." Since Brazilians often tend to view and evaluate state-to-state relations through the prism of personal relations between heads of government, those casual remarks, virtually ignored in the United States, were quickly seized upon in Brazil as an endorsement of Lula's government and policies and a sign that Brazil might finally be about to get its due from the United States.

Yet in spite of the change of occupancy in the White House and the resulting shift in tone and atmospherics, the substance of the bilateral relationship continues largely the same. It is true that Obama, in rejecting the unilateralism of the Bush years, has made an effort to both consult with Lula on regional issues and work actively with Brazil in trying to resolve regional problems together, such as the coup d'etat in Honduras that overthrew an elected president there in 2009. But the United States and Brazil ended up on opposing sides of that dispute, with the American position eventually prevailing, much to Brazil's irritation. And as regards Iran and the simmering dispute over its nuclear program, Brazil and the Obama Administration have also taken conflicting positions and continue to clash. "When Brazil looks at Iran, it doesn't just see Iran," an aide to Marco Aurélio Garcia told Matias Specktor, the coordinator of Center for the Study of International Relations at the Fundacao Getúlio Vargas, in April 2010. "It also sees Brazil."

On Brazil's side, then, relations with the United States continue to be characterized by a schizophrenic approach in which the Brazilian governor takes positions at odds with Washington but often adopt an anti-American tone in many of their pronouncements and actions even while professing to be friends of the United States. Things have largely remained in that state now that Lula is out of office, replaced by another president from the Workers Party. Like Lula, his designated successor, Dilma Rousseff, took office with virtually no foreign affairs experience and a marked reliance on the same small group of experts that tutored or worked with Lula.

This divergence between rhetoric and action is due in large part to the dynamics of Brazilian domestic politics. Like Obama, Lula was elected on a platform that promised sweeping change. On the domestic front, however, he largely continued the market-friendly economic policies of his predecessor, Cardoso, which has made him a Wall Street favorite. But Lula's embrace of capitalism deeply disillusioned the left wing of his own party and others even further left—so much so that Chico de Oliveira, one of the founders of the Workers Party but now a dissident and critic, took to describing Lula's first year in office as "the ninth year of Fernando Henrique Cardoso's presidency."

In most countries, foreign policy always involves a large component of rhetoric and, except for war or other moments of national crisis, is generally of interest only to a small elite. So it is in Brazil. Lula quickly discovered that foreign policy offered him an easy and painless way to assuage the sense of betrayal and irritation that was felt by the party faithful on the left. By "talking left" on international issues, he could compensate at least in part his decision to "act right" on the economy, as the United States wanted him to do. As a result, his government became an advocate of vague but high-sounding concepts that presume a nonexistent community of shared interests and values among all the countries of what used to be called the Third World. Thus, we get much talk of "South-South solidarity," meant to bring Brazil, China, and South Africa into a single group, and the sponsorship of an Arab–South American summit in Brasília, which foundered when Brazil tried to stress trade and the Arab participants insisted on focusing on Israel.

Despite the warmth with which he speaks of Obama, Lula also sought to maintain the perception of distance and independence from the United States and was not above "tweaking Uncle Sam's beard," in the words of the Brazilian press, when that served his purposes. This is a strategy that made sense when the Bush administration was in power, because since polling began in Latin America, no U.S. president was ever more unpopular in the region than

George W. Bush. It makes less sense now, but Brazil has continued to engage in provocative gestures that have caused bafflement and grumbling in Washington. In 2009, for instance, Brazil invited Iran's president, Mahmoud Ahmadinejad, to make a state visit, ostensibly in the name of boosting trade between the two countries, and then gave him a notably warm and friendly reception. Lula defended Iran's nuclear program while standing at Ahmadinejad's side in Brasília and reiterated that position when he visited Tehran in May 2010 to announce that Iran had accepted a Brazilian proposal to ship its nuclear fuel abroad. He then blamed the Obama administration after that deal quickly fell apart and the Brazilian press began to criticize Lula's initiative, which included giving the Iranian president a jersey of the Brazilian national soccer team.

"Nobody likes to see new actors, but who says the United States should be the sheriff of the Middle East and the world?" he complained. "More actors and a new global governance are needed." Shortly after returning to Brasília, he and Garcia professed puzzlement when Obama, by now exasperated, declined an invitation to visit Brazil before the October 2010 elections, and, in leaks to the Brazilian press, blamed the cold shoulder on Hillary Clinton's supposed resentment of Lula's having negotiated an accord that she could not and her husband's friendship with Fernando Henrique Cardoso.

But this is not the first time that the United States and Brazil have been at odds over the nuclear proliferation issue. Of the four countries that comprise the BRIC group, Brazil is the only one that does not have the atomic bomb. This has sometimes rankled nationalists both on the right and the left, who see possession of a nuclear arsenal as a necessary affirmation of status as a great power. In the past, they responded by pushing for a bomb program, which created confusion and unnecessary problems for Brazil. For example, during the military dictatorship in power from 1964 to 1985, each of the three branches of the armed forces had its own secret nuclear program aimed at acquiring a nuclear capability for Brazil.

However, each of the first four civilian governments to come to power after the collapse of the dictatorship took steps to wind down the nuclear effort under pressure from the United States and its allies. José Sarney signed a nuclear cooperation and information exchange agreement with Argentina, the historic rival whose own military-controlled nuclear program ostensibly justified the

Brazilian effort. Fernando Collor de Mello officially acknowledged what the military had been up to and shoveled the first spadeful of dirt to seal a thousand-foot-deep shaft on an air force base in the Amazon that had been built clandestinely to conduct a nuclear bomb test. In May 1994, Itamar Franco's government ratified the 1967 Treaty of Tlatelolco, which had declared Latin America to be a nuclear-arms-free zone. And under Fernando Henrique Cardoso, Brazil finally signed the global Nuclear Non-Proliferation Treaty in 1998.

That seemed to have answered any and all questions and doubts. But during the 2002 presidential campaign, Lula proceeded to raise them again. In a speech in Rio de Janeiro to a club for retired military officers, he criticized the Non-Proliferation Treaty as unjust and scoffed at the notion that countries like Brazil should renounce nuclear arms. "I imagine this would make sense only if all countries that already have them also gave them up," he said. "It is not fair that developed countries, who have nuclear weapons technology, demand that others not have them or deactivate what they have. All of us developing countries are left holding a slingshot while they have atomic bombs. If someone asks me to disarm and keep a slingshot while he comes at me with a cannon, what good does that do?"

After there was an outcry in Brazil and abroad, Lula issued a "clarification," saying that Brazil did not intend to develop nuclear weapons. But no sooner was he sworn in as president, in January 2003, than his newly appointed minister of science and technology raised the issue again in even more inflammatory terms. In an interview with the BBC, Roberto Amaral said that "mastery of the atomic cycle is important" to Brazil because it needed to create a deterrent to potential external threats. Never mind that Brazil has friendly relations with all of its neighbors and that the biggest challenge to Brazilian sovereignty comes not from a foreign army but from drug traffickers and smugglers.

"Brazil is a country at peace, that has always preserved peace, and is a defender of peace, but we need to be prepared, including technologically," he said. "We can't renounce any form of scientific knowledge, whether the genome, DNA, or nuclear fission." Again there was an international uproar, and again Brazil retreated under the pressure. Responding to reporters' questions at a news briefing in Brasília, Lula's spokesman said that "the government favors research in this area solely and exclusively for peaceful purposes."

Later in Lula's first term, however, tensions with the International Atomic Energy Agency arose because of Brazil's unwillingness to allow a thorough inspection of a uranium enrichment plant near Rio de Janeiro controlled by the Brazilian navy. Officials bragged that the facility operated with centrifuges based on "technology that is one hundred percent Brazilian," and nationalist groups were soon trotting out the familiar argument that the IAEA was acting as part of an international conspiracy to steal a valuable scientific secret from Brazil. The basic technology, in fact, was not Brazilian at all, having been acquired from Germany in much the same way that Pakistan developed a similar technology. But the government was loath to make that admission because to do so would tarnish the image of what had been presented to Brazilians as a triumph of their own domestically developed know-how.

Eventually, a compromise was worked out, and the IAEA was allowed to send some of its inspectors into the plant for a partial inspection. But because an arms deal with France announced in 2009 includes a nuclear-powered attack submarine to be delivered to Brazil sometime in this decade, some of those same issues may very well reappear in the near future. For more than 30 years, the Brazilian navy has been struggling to build a dual-use nuclear reactor suitable for powering a submarine and also for generating electricity for civilians. Brazil's position is that such a reactor would not be subject to the international safeguards regimen, which includes inspections. The IAEA and American officials have indicated that they think otherwise and complain privately that Brazil's recalcitrance only complicates efforts to ensure compliance by rogue states such as Iran and North Korea. In this regard, it is worth noting that Brazil has not signed, and continues to vehemently oppose on principle, the "Additional Protocol" to the Nuclear Non-Proliferation Treaty, which provides IAEA inspectors with greater authority to scrutinize nuclear reactors like the one near Rio and to examine documents related to a country's nuclear program.

The larger question, however, is why Brazil, a country with no enemies, should want a nuclear-powered submarine in the first place. The Brazilian navy has argued that a fleet of submarines is needed to protect Brazil's territorial waters, especially the vast oil and gas deposits off the coasts of Rio de Janeiro and São Paulo. It is true that Brazil has a long coastline, more than five thousand miles in all, that is difficult to patrol. But U.S. navy analysts, assessing the National Defense Strategy that Brazil announced in December 2008, noted that the oil fields argument "does nothing to provide an adequate naval justification of the enormous investment the project will require." Submarines are inappropriate to defend offshore oil-drilling platforms, which leads to the conclusion that Brazil's nuclear submarine effort is largely a vanity project meant to leave Brazilians with an impression of their country's growing strength and project an image abroad of seriousness and might.

Brazil has had an almost equally checkered and far more tragic experience with its attempt to build a space program, which successive governments, military and civilian, have also seen as another badge that confers and confirms status as a world power. The effort was born in the late 1960s as part of the military dictatorship's effort to create a "Brasil Grande" and was meant to capitalize on an unusual advantage Brazil had in comparison to the United States, the Soviet Union, and other perceived rivals: a launching pad almost at the Equator, which allows satellites to be lifted into orbit more easily and on less fuel.

The base was quickly built, at Alcantara, on the eastern edge of the Amazon. But while successive governments have embraced the vision of Brazil in outer space, they have, in contrast to both China and India, failed to match that ambition with money. From the start, Brazil's rocket development program, controlled by the military and cloaked in secrecy, was chronically underfunded, which forced researchers to rely on substandard parts and questionable procedures. Three attempts to launch a satellite on a Brazilian-made rocket failed, and in August 2003, a rocket exploded on its launch pad, instantly incinerating 21 top scientists and technicians who were working at the site.

Brazil's satellite program is run by a civilian agency, which cooperates extensively with its counterparts around the world. Brazil and China, for example, have jointly developed four remote-sensing satellites to circle the earth in a polar orbit, which allows both countries to closely monitor much of the Western Hemisphere. Brazilian officials have told me that their main interest in launching such satellites is commercial: By monitoring harvests and growth and weather patterns of American food crops such as soybeans, they are better equipped to deal with price fluctuations on world markets. But they also acknowledge, albeit reluctantly, that the satellite system will eventually give them and the Chinese a way to monitor deployments of American troops and military equipment.

But because the rocket development effort is controlled by the military, the United States has repeatedly blocked Brazilian efforts to acquire certain technologies and has pressured its allies to follow suit. Based in part on Brazil's long-ago flirtation with Iraq on nuclear issues, American officials have long worried that a Brazilian-made rocket could fall into the hands of terrorists. During the Saddam Hussein era, Brazil exported artillery rockets to Iraq, sold uranium that ended up in Iraq's secret nuclear program, helped the Iraqis prospect for uranium themselves, and designed an underground uranium processing plant. In 1990, General Hugo Piva, the former director of Brazil's Center for Aerospace Technology, was detected in Iraq with a team of Brazilian missile experts just as Saddam Hussein was invading Kuwait. He later admitted that he had also sought rocket parts on the black market in order to accelerate Brazil's own rocket program.

The resulting blockade has led to elaborate end-runs and ruses, including the Brazilian air force's clandestine accommodation with Russian scientists after the collapse of the Soviet Union two decades ago. Russian experts were brought to Brazil to teach at universities or to advise the space program, which is based in São José dos Campos, east of São Paulo. In addition, during the mid-1990s, the air force on several occasions acquired essential rocket components in Russia and clandestinely shipped them to Brazil. In one case, the Russian equipment was hidden in a shipment of night-vision goggles and then secretly flown to São José dos Campos aboard a Brazilian air force plane. The Brazilian air force has never publicly acknowledged the Russian role, preferring to sell the space program to ordinary Brazilians as an example of purely Brazilian technology.

In 1997, Brazil was invited to be 1 of 16 countries participating in construction of the International Space Station. The invitation was extended as the result of lobbying by the United States, specifically the Clinton administration, which wanted to encourage scientific and technical exchanges with Brazil and at the same time enhance the prestige of President Cardoso. As its price of entry, Brazil promised to set aside $120 million to build six parts of the station. In return, it would be allowed to use the ISS for scientific experiments and would also have the right to send an astronaut to join the crew there.

But the money Brazil had promised never materialized. The Cardoso government had been counting on a steady flow of money from renting the Alcantara base to American and other private companies that wanted to save money by launching communications satellites at the equator, but the Workers Party scuttled just such an agreement with the United States, on the predictably paranoid grounds that it would allow the U.S. military a platform to infiltrate the Amazon and would threaten Brazilian sovereignty. As a result, Brazil missed the initial deadline and in 2003, after negotiations with NASA, opted for a much more modest role that would require an expenditure of only $8 million. But that money was never appropriated either. Eventually, Brazil was forced to withdraw from the ISS consortium, its credibility among space explorers in tatters.

Brazil continued to harbor ambitions to have some sort of presence in space, however. In 2006, the same Workers Party government that had sabotaged cooperation with the United States managed to find $10.5 million to pay to Russia so that astronaut Marcos Pontes, who had originally trained with NASA, could spend time as a paying customer on a Soyuz craft that traveled to the space station. Not coincidentally, his voyage coincided with the centennial of the first fixed-wing aircraft flight of the aviation pioneer Santos-Dumont. During Pontes's week aloft, some in the press ridiculed him as a "space tourist" and "sidereal hitchhiker." But Lula's government portrayed the flight as a triumph for Brazil. The president talked to him by telephone, and schoolchildren studied the eight experiments he carried out while at the station. For domestic purposes, at least, it appeared that Brazil was a member in good standing of the world's scientific elite, even though the reality was precisely the opposite.

In September 2009, just before Brazilian Independence Day, on September 7, the president of France, Nicolas Sarkozy, visited Brasília. After a boozy official dinner, during which many caipirinhas and much whiskey were consumed, the two leaders announced a "strategic partnership" between their countries, including a military accord. Part of their joint declaration consisted of symbolic affirmations, but the details they revealed also included an arms deal that may be the largest in Brazilian history: 36 jet fighter attack planes,

50 transport helicopters, tanks, four conventional submarines, and a nuclear-powered submarine, for a total package adding up to more than $12 billion.

Brazil has never thought of itself—or been thought of by others—as a military power. It has fought only one major war in its history, against its much smaller neighbors, Uruguay and then Paraguay, from 1864 to 1870, a conflict that proved so nettlesome and costly that it reinforced the pacifist strain that Brazilians regard as part of their national character. Brazil does have an army, navy, and air force, currently with about 375,000 active duty personnel. But with the country facing no serious external threat, the main function of the armed forces since the empire gave way to a republic nearly 125 years ago has been to guard borders, ensure internal stability, and meddle in domestic politics.

But even those roles have withered since 21 years of harsh military rule ended in 1985. Another blow came with the formalization of an alliance between Brazil and Argentina, traditionally seen as an enemy, when the Mercosul trade group was founded in 1991, and the ratification of another treaty in which the two countries agreed to abandon their nuclear programs and allow mutual inspections. Since then, the government budget has been parsimonious with the armed forces, with predictable effects. By the middle of the last decade, more than half the Brazilian air force's 773 airplanes had to be grounded due to a lack of spare parts, and the army's budget was stretched so thin that draftees, 19-year-olds who typically serve at the base closest to their residence, were often sent home to sleep so as to spare the cost of lodging them in barracks and having to feed them.

The Brazilian military, in other words, has become a force in search of a mission, any mission, to justify its existence. Many of the claims that foreign powers, especially the United States, have designs on the Amazon and want to wrest it away from Brazil can be traced to military officers, both retired and active, who are seeking a bigger slice of the budget pie for their comrades. Others have seized on the threat supposedly offered to the Amazon border by the Revolutionary Armed Forces of Colombia, the left-wing guerrilla and drug-trafficking group that began fighting the Colombian government in the 1960s, reached its zenith in the 1990s, and now appears to be in decline.

In hopes of gaining money and experience, the military has also jumped eagerly at nearly every opportunity to serve on U.N. peacekeeping missions, in 23 places as diverse as the Congo, Cyprus, East Timor, and Haiti. Despite the reservations expressed by some on the general staff who fear being drawn into an unwinnable and corrupting conflict, the army has even on occasion been drawn into urban warfare inside Brazil, aiding police in their battle against drug-trafficking gangs and standing guard on the streets during large international events such as the Pan-American Games.

But the "strategic partnership" concluded with France does many things for Brazil. First of all, it gives the air force and the navy, both of which are underequipped, lots of shiny new toys and a sense of satisfaction and importance. That alone may have been sufficient justification for Lula. As a president who represented a left-wing party and comes from a labor movement that the military regime fought and suspected of being Communist-inspired, he devoted a great deal of energy to reassuring his former adversaries of his benign intentions. But giving the armed forces new weaponry also provides Brazilians with a sense of national pride, which Lula often contends is lacking. Brazil may not be a military power, able to project might beyond its borders, but at least it will have the accoutrements of one, like other rising nations that aspire to be great powers.

Supporters of the arms buildup now underway argue that it is necessary if only as a defensive measure, such as to protect the oil riches that have been discovered off Brazil's coast. That threat, if it exists at all, is of course as much an exaggeration as the notion that the rest of the world covets control of the Amazon, a myth discussed in detail in chapter 8. Military and nationalist groups have in fact taken to referring to the offshore deposits as the "the blue Amazon," playing on Brazilians' traditional insecurities about foreign designs on their territory. There may also be a certain subliminal satisfaction in seeing Sarkozy, the successor to de Gaulle, making the long trip to Brazil to plead his case for a "special relationship" and to try to sell his wares to a Brazil more confident, more powerful, and wealthier than de Gaulle could ever have imagined—the very definition of a serious country, in other words.

But does that then also mean that a Brazil equipped with sophisticated new weaponry suddenly has aggressive designs on its neighbors? That seems equally unlikely. Some Brazilians, including members of Congress, sputtered with rage in 2006 when President Evo Morales of Bolivia nationalized the holdings of Brazil's state oil company Petrobras in his country and would clearly have liked to have some sabers to rattle. But that dispute was eventually resolved amicably, through negotiations in which Brazil got the worse of the deal, as was a more recent disagreement with Paraguay over the price Brazil pays for energy from the Itaipu hydroelectric project on the border between the two countries.

Far more likely is the possibility that Brazil is merely trying to keep up with the Joneses. In this case, that would mean Hugo Chávez, the populist president of Venezuela, just to Brazil's north. Chávez has spent more than $6 billion in recent years on arms purchases from Russia, including tanks, antiaircraft missiles, Sukhoi fighter jets, helicopters, diesel submarines, and a hundred thousand late-version Kalashnikov AK–103 assault rifles. Though he has said repeatedly that those arms are exclusively for defensive purposes, they will also give him an offensive capacity that Venezuela can project deep into the heartland of South America. In view of the military cooperation agreement that Venezuela and Bolivia signed shortly after Evo Morales took power, which calls for Venezuelan troops to train Bolivian troops, share weapons, and even to be stationed at Bolivian border posts, Brazil has good reason to question Chávez's motives.

Chávez is by no means an enemy of Brazil and in fact has always presented himself as a friend of Brazil and of Lula. But he has become a major headache for Brazilian policymakers over the past decade. Brazil has always considered itself to be the natural leader of Latin America, and when Lula took office in 2003, his personal charisma and background as a labor leader were seen as factors that would make it easier for Brazil to assume a more visible role. That is a longstanding Brazilian ambition that transcends the ideology of whoever happens to be president. But that aspiration was particularly pronounced in the case of the Workers Party, which had cultivated close ties with other left-wing parties in Latin America and saw itself in the vanguard of a new leftist resurgence in the region.

Instead, as Brazilian policymakers see it, Chávez has hogged the spotlight and elbowed Brazil aside in his eagerness to speak in the name of all of Latin America and to be perceived on the world stage as the region's principal leader.

Those tensions were visible from the start of Lula's term in office, when Chávez showed up late for their first meeting in Brasília as heads of state, and have only intensified since. In spite of whatever ideological affinities that may have existed between Lula and Chávez, Brazil responded coolly to any number of initiatives that Chávez has proposed, especially when they are seen as projecting Venezuela into what Brazil considers its sphere of interest and influence.

Perhaps the grandest, most costly, and most far-fetched of these ideas was that of a gas pipeline project that would run from Caracas to Buenos Aires and link the energy grids of Brazil, Argentina, Uruguay, and Venezuela. But Chávez also urged the creation of a South Atlantic Treaty Organization, meant to bring together the military of each country under a united command, a South American news agency and television network, and a regional development bank. In each case, Chávez has seen himself as leading the new institution, and Brazil, recognizing that the proposal conflicted with its own objectives, has quietly worked to undermine or even sabotage the proposals, even while professing agreement with Chávez's goal of greater regional unity. In doing so, it has acted in what it perceives as its own interests, which in this case converge with those of the United States and have Washington's tacit support and approval.

In subtle ways, Chávez may also be playing on suspicions of Brazil that have sometimes been latent in South America in the past, due both to Brazil's size and its different culture and language. As a former foreign minister of Paraguay, perhaps the neighbor held in lowest esteem by Brazilians, once said to me, "What the United States is to Mexico, Brazil is to us." During the military dictatorship, there was even a book published in Spanish by a Bolivian diplomat titled *The Process of Brazilian Sub-Imperialism*. Or, as a prominent Uruguayan intellectual once put it to me, "The United States is imperialistic by necessity, but Brazil is imperialistic by vocation." By that he meant that Brazil sometimes has a tendency to lord its power over and to see itself as superior to the smaller Spanish-speaking neighbors often overlooked in its efforts to project itself onto the global stage.

During his first term, Lula's chief foreign policy initiative was his campaign to gain a permanent seat, with veto power, on the United Nations Security Council. Brazil traditionally speaks first at the U.N. General Assembly session each September and has served the most years as an elected member of the Security Council. The Brazilian foreign ministry had always paid lip service to this ambition, which was a popular idea, but had never pursued it seriously or aggressively. As Brazilian diplomats explained it to me, if they push too hard for Brazil to become the first Latin American permanent member of the council, they run the risk of alienating both Mexico, which also desires such a seat, and Argentina, which has floated a proposal for a rotating seat that would alternate between Brazil and Argentina.

But when Lula took office, his campaign to join the United States, France, Great Britain, Russia, and China as a permanent member of the Security Council was so high a priority that it became the principal objective of Brazilian diplomacy. In an attempt to gain the support of African nations, for instance, missions were dispatched with tantalizing trade financing offers and promises to forgive unpaid debts. To persuade the United States and France and show that it was capable of playing a larger role outside its immediate neighborhood, Brazil agreed to lead, along with Chile, the United Nations peacekeeping mission in Haiti. That mission had been a headache for Washington and Paris since 1994, when a U.N. military force led by those two countries restored Jean-Bertrand Aristide to power there. To curry favor with Arab states, Brazil recalibrated its Mideast policy and become more critical of Israel and more pro-Palestinian. To win Beijing's favor, Brazil formally recognized China as a full market economy, a step that eased China's entry into the World Trade Organization and provided some concrete trade benefits.

Though the United States was not won over and remained officially uncommitted, Lula's efforts contributed to France's decision to support Brazil's Security Council bid. But the gestures to the Chinese simply backfired. Certifying China as a market economy made it easier for cheap Chinese-made goods to flood Brazil, to the detriment of locally made products such as shoes and toys, which infuriated the São Paulo business establishment. And when it came time for a decision on the plan to expand the number of permanent seats on the U.N. Security Council, China exercised its veto and voted no, thereby killing the proposal. Brazil had made the mistake of allying itself with India and Japan, both of which also wanted permanent seats on the Security Council. Beijing, wanting to remain the only Asian power with that status and the veto power that goes with it, opposed that effort, and Brazil, by putting itself into a package with China's two biggest regional rivals, saw its bid shot down in the crossfire.

At the same time, Brazil has been unable to extricate itself from Haiti and may be even more enmeshed than ever there as a result of the January 2010 earthquake. When he agreed to lead the mission there in 2004, after President Jean-Bertrand Aristide was deposed, and sent twelve hundred troops to Port-au-Prince, Lula seemed confident that Brazil would succeed where successive American administrations had failed. There was no history of especially close ties between Brazil and Haiti other than a certain sentiment of pan-Africanism among some Brazilian blacks. But the "lighter hand" diplomacy Brazil promised, like the claims that Haitians would work better with Latin Americans than white-skinned North Americans or Europeans, have proven naïve and failed to deliver stability or peace. In addition, the economic aid the international community promised was not delivered, and now even more assistance will be required if the country is to recover from the effects of the earthquake. As a result, Brazil now finds itself in a quagmire. Criticisms of the open-ended commitment have been growing, as have complaints that the money spent on the mission could be much better spent in the poor neighborhoods of Brazil's own cities.

The campaign for the permanent U.N. Security Council seat and the consequences that have flowed from that effort represent a serious miscalculation on Brazil's part and show a triumph of ambition and ideology over common sense. In his desire to raise Brazil's image and stature abroad while building confidence and pride at home, Lula reached too far. But he cannot claim he was not warned, because the Brazilian foreign ministry had long been aware of the pitfalls of such a campaign and had in fact advised previous governments against undertaking it too vigorously. This time, however, the sound advice of the professionals went unheeded, and Brazilian diplomacy suffered a setback.

When Henry Kissinger visited Brazil as the U.S. secretary of state in the 1970s, his Brazilian counterpart, Antônio Azeredo da Silveira, took him on a tour of the Brazilian foreign ministry's headquarters in Brasília, a gleaming, ultramodern structure of glass and marble designed by Oscar Niemeyer. Afterwards, as Silveira recalled years later, he asked Kissinger for his impressions.

"It's a magnificent building, Antônio," came the reply. "Now all you need is a foreign policy to go with it."

Brazil is blessed with an unusually large and skilled professional diplomatic corps, popularly known as Itamaraty, which is the name of the palace where the ministry of foreign relations was housed when Rio de Janeiro was Brazil's capital. Highly trained and multilingual, Brazilian diplomats have in various situations been chosen to lead several United Nations agencies and the Organization of American States and also have served at home in cabinet posts such as defense and science and technology. Some Latin American and African nations have sent their own diplomats to study at the Rio Branco Institute, where Brazil's future ambassadors and attachés are trained, but Itamaraty's renown extends much further than that.

During a trip to Washington while Bill Clinton was still in the White House, I once went to talk with Charlene Barshefsky, who was then the U.S. trade representative in charge of negotiating accords on commerce, industry, and intellectual property rights with America's trading partners. At one point, I asked her which country had the most capable negotiators she had ever encountered, fully expecting her to say China. Instead, she surprised me by immediately replying that it was Brazil. "Itamaraty always sends diplomats who are polished, urbane, warm, sophisticated and skillful," she said. No matter what the degree of disagreement over an issue, differences were always expressed in a charming way, she added, and there was always a desire to find a solution, a compromise acceptable to both sides. Without surrendering their own positions, she concluded, the Brazilians also recognized that everyone has interests they need to defend.

Nevertheless, Kissinger's point, though expressed as a joke, was a valid one and remains so today. Brazil's ambitions have grown over the past 35 years, as has its level of engagement with the outside world. But much of the time, even now, Brazilian foreign policy seems reactive, moved not by an overarching philosophy, design, or set of long-term strategic goals, but tacking with whichever way the wind happens to be blowing in order to achieve short-term objectives.

To the extent that Brazil's foreign relations are guided by fundamental beliefs, the main principle traditionally seems to have been simply minimize conflict and avoid making enemies whenever possible. That can be seen in the way that Brazil has approached its relations in recent years with both the United States and Venezuela. The two countries have become adversaries, but Brazil has worked to remain on good terms with both.

Inevitably, the foreign policy of a nation reflects its internal codes and attitudes, and that is clearly the case with Brazil. As we have seen, in their dealings with each other, Brazilians place a premium on the *jeitinho*, an ingenious way of papering over disagreements and finding compromises and wiggle room. Sometimes that approach, discussed at length in chapter two, involves pretending that differences do not really exist, that everyone is on good terms, and that all parties are seeking the same objective. That is one of the reasons that Brazilian diplomats have proved so adept on the world stage and why Brazil is often sought as a mediator of international disputes.

In practical terms, what this means is that Brazil often tries to be everyone's friend and that often its core beliefs, whatever they might be, are not clearly defined, articulated, or defended. Having suffered itself under authoritarian rule, Brazil professes to be a staunch champion of democracy. To its credit, when coups have threatened democratically elected civilian governments in places like Paraguay or Honduras, Brazil has spoken out in favor of respecting the rule of law. But at the United Nations, Brazil won't vote to condemn human rights violations in places like Cuba, often preferring to abstain. And though Brazil claims the mantle of regional leadership, it has often proven unwilling to bear the cost of actually playing that role and demonstrating decisive leadership, even on issues that hit very close to home. That has led to an expression that is increasingly being used in the rest of Latin America: "Brazil: economic giant, diplomatic dwarf."

It was at Brazil's initiative, for example, that the South American customs union called Mercosul was founded in 1990, with Argentina, Paraguay, and Uruguay as the other full members and Chile and Bolivia as associate members. Since 2006, however, Argentina and Uruguay have been quarreling over Uruguay's construction of a paper plant on the banks of the river that forms their common border. As the dispute escalated, both countries wanted Brazil to step in and mediate. But Brazil has refused to get involved, apparently fearful of having to take sides and offend someone. As a result, efforts to further reduce trade barriers among the member countries and adopt a common currency have lagged. Uruguay is the most unhappy at the turn of events and has even flirted with the idea of signing a bilateral trade agreement with the United States, which has drawn criticism from Brazil, as if Brazil's behavior had nothing to do with that decision.

This desire to be all things to all people and avoid having to take sides is very much a traditional approach. It was also evident, for example, in the years leading up to World War II and colored the perceptions that a generation of American diplomats had of Brazil. Initially, Brazil cultivated a warm relationship with Nazi Germany and Fascist Italy, reflecting the ideological predispositions of Getúlio Vargas, the country's dictator, and his police chief, Filinto Müller, the pro-Nazi son of German immigrants. After Pearl Harbor and the entry of the United States into the war, though, Brazil abandoned neutrality, becoming an American ally and declaring war on the Axis powers. To further curry favor with Washington, Vargas sent an expeditionary force of some twenty-five thousand men to fight alongside the Allies in Italy and revived the cultivation of rubber in the Amazon so as to offer the United States a substitute for supplies from Southeast Asian that had been cut off by the Japanese.

Today, the few aging survivors of the expeditionary force march each September 7 in Brazil's Independence Day parade and are treated as heroes. History textbooks extol their sacrifice in Italy, exaggerating the Brazilian contribution to the Allied war effort and artfully avoid mentioning the earlier flirtation with Nazis and Fascists. Some Brazilians even complain that American and European historians deliberately downplay Brazil's role in the war as part of a deliberate effort to deprive Brazil of the credit it deserves for helping to win the war. Overlooked in those recriminations, of course, is any acknowledgment of Brazil's habit of playing both sides against the middle.

Like it or not, Brazil's next president is going to have to be more engaged with the rest of the world than any of its presidents have been to date. Brazil now has more points of contact with other nations than it did a decade or two ago, and thus the potential for both friction and cooperation rises. Not only has foreign investment soared, raising the country's profile and making its opinions more important, but Brazil trades more than ever and has already played an important role in the separate talks aimed at establishing a Free Trade Area of the Americas and extending the trade liberalization features of the World Trade Organization. Both of those multilateral negotiations ultimately failed, with some officials of the Bush administration and the European Union going so far as to blame Brazil and charge it with obstructionism. Though unfair, those accusations are actually a healthy sign because they indicate that at least in the realm of commercial diplomacy, Brazil may no longer be "punching under its weight" and is finally defining, articulating, and defending a coherent vision of its national interest.

On the political front, however, Brazil is likely to continue to experience growing pains as it struggles to find its place in the world. The Haitian situation has been a sobering experience for Brazil and has taught the country's leaders how difficult it can be to grapple with an international crisis. But Brazil is blessed to occupy a corner of the world that has not been cursed with war or ongoing conflicts based on religious, ethnic, or racial differences. So from its comfortable spectator's perch somewhat on the sidelines of international affairs, it has tended to snipe at those involved in trying to resolve such problems, especially those countries it regards as both allies and rivals, such as the United States and major European nations. For all the lessons being learned from Haiti, that kind of second guessing and carping has not stopped, nor is it likely to.

The blues singer B. B. King once wrote a song called "You've Got to Pay the Cost to Be the Boss." In this case, what applies to personal relationships is no less relevant to international politics. Brazil can continue to chafe at the dominance of the United States in the Western Hemisphere, at the slights, real or imaginary, it feels from nations that it regards as its inferiors, and at seeing the role it envisions for itself among Latin American nations eclipsed by Hugo Chávez. Or it can choose to act with more equanimity in pursuit of its national interest and less anxiety about its image in the mind of outsiders. But until it throws off the inferiority complex that has dogged it for so long, Brazil is likely to remain yoked to a foreign policy that is essentially reactive, and the rest of the world will have to continue to tread lightly if it wants to gain Brazil's cooperation and avoid giving offense.

TEN

POLITICS AFTER
LULA AND FHC

SINCE THE COLLAPSE of a right-wing military dictatorship in 1985, two figures have dominated politics in Brazil above all others: Fernando Henrique Cardoso and Luiz Inácio Lula da Silva. Rule number one of Brazilian politics is that, in many situations, personalities and personal ties and appeal can matter more than formal party affiliations or even ideology. Brazilians usually refer to their politicians, especially those they like the most, by affectionate nicknames. Thus, Getúlio Vargas was fondly called just Getúlio, and Juscelino Kubitschek's tongue twister of a name was often reduced to JK. The same rule holds true for Cardoso, who is habitually identified in print simply as FHC, and da Silva, who is universally known as Lula. It may sound overly informal to a non-Brazilian ear, but it is a sign of familiarity that both men cultivate, to the extent that da Silva legally changed his name to incorporate the "Lula" so he could appear as such on the ballot.

Lula and FHC were initially allies in the struggle to topple the dictatorship, and both suffered as a result of that involvement. FHC spent more than a decade in exile, first in Chile and then in the United States, Great Britain, and France, teaching at universities there. Lula, though never forced to leave Brazil, was long persecuted and briefly jailed during the military dictatorship because of his activities as a labor leader. After the return of democracy, they gradually became adversaries, with FHC advocating European-style social democracy and Lula continuing to flirt with Marxism and rail against capitalism until early in the last decade.

FHC and Lula represent dramatically different facets of Brazil. FHC, a general's son born in Rio de Janeiro in 1931 but raised in São Paulo, is an especially enlightened member of the historic elite and benefited from the best that Brazil has to offer its chosen sons. He has a PhD in sociology, speaks five languages, has written numerous books, and clearly lacks a common touch: He confessed in an autobiography to not being a fan of soccer, an almost unthinkable admission from a Brazilian politician. He also has never showed much enthusiasm for Carnival and always has seemed more comfortable sipping a fine French wine than downing a shot of *cachaça*. The party he has represented and helped found, the Brazilian Social Democratic Party, or PSDB, is a moderately left-of-center grouping, similar to Britain's Labour Party or Germany's Social Democrats.

Lula, in contrast, is what Brazilians call *povão*, of the people. Born in October 1945 into a peasant family in the parched, poverty-stricken northeastern state of Pernambuco, as a child he migrated fifteen hundred miles on the back of a truck to São Paulo, where he ended up selling oranges on the street and working as a lathe operator in factories. He dropped out after the fifth grade, and in public even today he often butchers the Portuguese language so badly that there are websites devoted to his gaffes. He is eclectic about what he drinks, imbibing *cachaça*, whiskey, and beer with equal gusto, and in his off-the-cuff public declarations, he often turns to metaphors from soccer to underline his arguments. He is the founder of the Workers Party, about which there will be more later.

In the 1990s, both men ran for president and both times FHC won decisively. It was only in 2002, when FHC was forced out by term limits, that Lula, on his fourth attempt, succeeded in winning a presidential election—and then only after moderating his orthodox left positions. In October 2006, he was elected to a second four-year term. Together, FHC and Lula are largely responsible for Brazil's dramatic transformation since the mid-1990s. For all their differences, personal and ideological, they should be considered the joint architects and executors of a period of economic growth and continuity and social tranquility uncommon in the country's history.

Admittedly, the first decade of the current democratic phase was hardly auspicious, which makes the achievements since then all the more remarkable. Tancredo Neves was elected president in 1985 in a deal brokered in Congress but died before he could take office. As a result, his vice president, José Sarney, a member of the northeastern oligarchy added to the ticket largely to get his region's conservative leadership to support a democratic transition, took office instead. He proved a skilled political operator, adept at cutting deals and sharing the spoils of power with allies. But he was utterly inept at handling the economy and left office with his credibility clouded by accusations of corruption.

When Brazilians finally got a chance to vote in 1989, they elected Fernando Collor de Mello, a young, vigorous, and telegenic candidate who had first come to prominence projecting a reformer's image by attacking what he called *maharajas*, members of the bureaucracy who earned huge salaries for doing nothing. But as the governor of the tiny state of Alagoas and son of a senator famous for shooting at an opponent on the floor of Congress, Collor de Mello, too, was a member in good standing of the northeastern oligarchy, and barely a year after taking power at the age of 40, he was embroiled in a huge corruption and influence-peddling scandal of his own. Impeached in September 1992, he resigned at the end of the year rather than be formally expelled from office. That left power in the hands of a caretaker president, Itamar Franco, a former senator from Minas Gerais who cultivated a reputation as a ladies' man, had a reputation for being temperamental and erratic, and seemed flummoxed by inflation, which soared to more than 2,000 percent in 1993.

FHC initiated the process of stabilization even before becoming president, when as Itamar Franco's finance minister he implemented the Real Plan in 1994. That quickly brought decades of inflation to an end and led to a spurt of growth that ensured his decisive first-round victory over Lula in the election held that year. After becoming president in January 1995, FHC also initiated reforms of the apparatus of state through laws and constitutional amendments that imposed, among other things, budget controls and limits on the salaries of bureaucrats and on the amount of states' and cities' debt that the federal government would have to cover. With savings from those measures and the money obtained from the privatization of inefficient state companies, he invested heavily not only in physical infrastructure but also, acting on convictions he had acquired as an academic studying race, class, and poverty, in education and long-term social programs.

During FHC's eight years, high school enrollments expanded by more than one-third, the number of students entering college doubled, and the number of children not attending school at all dropped to 3 percent, compared to almost 20 percent at the start of the 1990s. At the same time, infant mortality rates declined by 25 percent, and deaths from AIDS were reduced by two-thirds. In addition, nearly six hundred thousand landless peasant families were resettled on homesteads of their own, more than double the total during the previous three decades. In 2002, the United Nations Development Program named FHC the first winner of a prize for outstanding leadership, saying that his administration had "overseen important human development progress" in the areas of education, health, and agrarian reform.

But FHC's most significant gift to Lula may have been that of political stability. When he placed the presidential sash on his successor, on January 1, 2003, it marked the first time in more than 40 years that one elected civilian president had handed over power to another. FHC failed in his efforts to pass reform legislation that would have regulated campaign donations, limited the power of local bosses, and made it easier to govern without the support of small parties that continue to exercise an outsize influence in Brazilian politics even now. But he encouraged respect for the judiciary and its rulings, treated Congress as an equal to the executive branch, sitting down to negotiate with congressional leaders in a democratic manner, and created conditions for a free and critical press to flourish even when it caused problems for him personally. FHC also managed to bring the military under civilian control, an achievement of some significance in a country where the armed forces had a long history of meddling in politics, and one reason that the presidential transition was probably smoother than any Brazil had previously experienced. Small wonder, then, that in a poll taken as FHC was leaving office, Brazilians named him the best president in their history.

FHC would be a hard act to follow, but Lula has for the most part proven equal to the task. After initially promising a "rupture" with capitalism and attacking the business class as parasites, he had the good judgment, once in office, to continue or even extend some of the market-friendly reforms that FHC had begun. That reassured Wall Street, which had reacted with jitters during the transition, driving the real to a record low exchange rate. Lula also built on and expanded social programs, though he sometimes gave them new names so as not to have to give his predecessor credit. At the close of the Lula era, Brazil has gained new recognition around the world, symbolized by the decision to award the 2016 Olympic Games to Rio de Janeiro after a vigorous campaign that Lula personally led—what he saw as his parting gift to the nation.

Lula's eight years in office have also been called the most corrupt in Brazil's history as a republic, both in terms of the amount of money involved and the number of scandals. Yet poll after poll has shown that while Brazilians view the waves of bribery, fraud, sleaze, dishonesty, malfeasance, and nepotism in Brasília with disgust, they do not blame Lula himself for the wrongdoing, instead focusing their anger on members of Congress and cabinet ministers.

Lula was also prone to authoritarian outbursts, as in 2004, when, offended by an article I had written about his drinking habits, he ordered my expulsion, using the same law from the era of the dictatorship that had once been used to silence him. He rescinded that order only after a Supreme Court justice issued a restraining order sharply criticizing him for exceeding his authority. "In a state under democratic rule of law, liberties cannot be submitted to the convenience or opportunity of the sitting government," the ruling said. "And foreigners, like Brazilians, are assured by the Constitution of fundamental rights and guarantees." There have been other efforts to control and intimidate the press, which the Brazilian Congress, to its credit, has refused to approve.

Overall, though, Lula's administration was a positive one as far as Brazilians are concerned. Like people everywhere, they tend to vote with their pocketbooks, and on that score, Lula excelled. Incomes have grown, distribution of wealth has improved substantially, and two decades of hyperinflation have become a distant memory. Long-term investment in physical infrastructure and human development has also increased significantly, though education is lagging. In addition, Brazil is at peace with its neighbors and has become a major exporter, with a stable currency that has strengthened so much against the dollar in recent years that middle-class Brazilians can now easily afford to vacation in the United States and Europe.

Brazil today is clearly in transition. For the first time since the return of democracy 25 years ago, in 2010 neither of these towering figures was a candidate for the country's highest office. January 1, 2011, ushered in an era of new leadership and Brazil is now being governed by a new president whose principal challenge has been to improve the positive balance of the previous 16 years. It has not been easy, and not just because Brazil's new president, Dilma Rousseff, has not had the advantage of Lula's enormous popularity and charisma. As the country continues to grow and prosper, the many deficiencies built into its complicated, patchwork political system are sure to worsen and corruption is likely to grow. As a result, she and future heads of state will be forced to confront both of those challenges.

One fundamental flaw contributing to both problems is Brazil's unusual system of proportional representation, embedded in the Constitution of 1988, the ninth in the country's history. Instead of a winner-take-all system, like that of the United States, Brazil allots representation in its legislative bodies on a percentage basis corresponding to the overall vote. In congressional elections, there are thus no districts: Parties draw up statewide slates, and candidates from the same party jockey to be placed as high as possible on their party's list to improve their chances of winning a seat. What this means is very little competition between parties during campaigns and a great deal of conflict within parties, with an obvious edge going to those candidates who have access to the most money. This leads not just to a lack of loyalty but also to parties that are chronically weak and undisciplined.

One consequence is that politicians often hop from one party to another, looking for the best deal for themselves and their followers. It is not uncommon for a legislator to be elected as the candidate of one party, shift to another once he arrives in Congress, and conclude his term as the member of a third. In the most notorious case, often cited as an example of why Brazil urgently needs political reform, one congressional deputy changed parties eight times during his legislative career, including three separate but brief stays in the same party.

Opportunities to play the system abound because Brazil has more than 20 different political parties, the newest of which, the Social Democratic Party, or PSD, was founded late in 2011 by the mayor of São Paulo, Gilberto Kassab, and other, mostly right-of-center politicians looking for a new home. Not all the so-called dwarf parties have seats in Congress, but enough of them have representation (and a desire to increase their numbers at any cost) to enable the free-for-all to continue. They have also been instrumental in blocking repeated attempts to streamline elections and to make it more difficult for such parties to organize and participate in the system. I can vividly remember interviewing Fernando Henrique Cardoso in April 1999 in Brasília and listening skeptically as he promised that the crowning achievement of his second term would be a sweeping reform of the political system. More than a decade later, that reform has still not occurred, in large part because of the disproportional power wielded by these small "acronyms for rent," as they are known in Brazilian political slang.

This confusing diffusion of representation makes it difficult, or at times perhaps even impossible, for a president to govern with authority, no matter what the size of his or her own electoral mandate. That was obviously to be expected when Fernando Collor de Mello won by a landslide in 1989, running under the banner of a tiny grouping he joined mainly to fulfill the legal requirement that all candidates have a formal party affiliation. But it proved to be just as true of Lula, who twice won by Ronald Reagan–sized margins as the Workers Party nominee. In fact, since the return of democracy a quarter century ago, no president has ever enjoyed the luxury of having his or her party hold an absolute majority in Congress, except for José Sarney during the convention that wrote the 1988 constitution.

As a result, getting any legislation passed requires constant negotiations to achieve the necessity majority, with shifting, unstable alliances whose composition changes from one bill to the next. Some presidents, thanks to their temperament or experience, have been more adept at this than others. José Sarney, himself a creature of Congress, was perhaps the most skilled at forging these temporary alliances when he held power from 1985 to 1990. FHC, despite being an academic and intellectual who had to learn to hold his nose and play the horse-trading game, also acquitted himself surprisingly well, especially in the 1997 negotiations that led to a constitutional change permitting presidents to run for a second consecutive term. Lula, on the other hand, always showed a distaste for the process, despite his ample experience as a labor leader accustomed to sitting across the table from employers and making compromises to strike a deal.

Obviously this situation lends itself to widespread corruption, which unfortunately has become one of the hallmarks of the Brazilian political system, deforming the legislative process. It's one thing for a president—or his aides and the leaders of his party's congressional delegation—to support the pet project of a legislator from another party in return for his vote on a bill the president wants passed. That kind of horse-trading and pork-barrel politics occurs in every democracy. But in modern-day Brazil, efforts to woo legislators often go far beyond that. They also embrace practices such as guaranteeing a cushy no-show job to a close family member or mistress of a legislator, the de facto auctioning off of ministries and regulatory agencies that supervise money-making activities such as communications and transportation, and even the outright buying of votes.

Indications abound that these methods have been used in every administration since the end of the military dictatorship. But the most notorious and public example is the so-called *mensalão* ("big monthly payoff") scandal, which came to light toward the end of Lula's first term and may have indirectly influenced the presidential succession in 2010 by forcing the resignation of some of the president's closest advisers, who were seen as possible successors. In public testimony in 2005, the leader of a small party allied with the president said Workers Party operatives had offered some members of Congress up to $400,000 each to join allied parties and then paid monthly stipends of $12,500 to those who switched. A formal inquiry was ordered, and it named nearly a score of legislators as having been involved in the scheme. Several of those implicated resigned or were impeached and stripped of their political rights, and others are part of a group of 40 people whom federal prosecutors have accused in a case that as of 2011 was still wending its way through Brazilian courts.

This system of back-scratching, string-pulling, and buying and selling support, whether for money or other considerations, antedates the Constitution adopted in 1988. The practice of what Brazilians call *clientelismo*, which the social scientist Augusto de Franco has defined as "an autocratic mode of regulation" involving "a vertical chain of subordination and favors," is so deeply ingrained in the country's politics that it managed to survive two decades of efforts by the armed forces to extirpate it. Lula's successors are sure to inherit this unwieldy, worm-eaten system and will inevitably find that until it's eliminated, a gargantuan task, the need to make deals constantly will continue to constrain the ability to govern.

So what does all this mean as the era of FHC and Lula recedes? Even if Brazilians are tempted to revert to their fondness for charismatic leaders with whom the electorate can form an emotional bond, that is going to be difficult. The 2010 presidential election proved to be an anomaly, with the two leading parties choosing candidates notoriously lacking in that quality. Both José Serra, who represented the Brazilian Social Democratic Party (PSDB) in that vote and gave a concession speech on the night of his defeat that suggested he may be contemplating another run in 2014, and Dilma Rousseff of the Workers Party began the campaign burdened with reputations for being stiff public speakers unable to generate much personal warmth in contacts with voters, and they did little on the campaign trail to change those impressions. It is too early to tell whether the choice of candidates seen as reserved or even *antipático* signals a fundamental shift in the nature of presidential politics in Brazil or whether the 2010 pairing was just an odd coincidence never to be repeated. But that is the unexpected and uncharacteristic dynamic that distinguishes the current scene.

Serra (who alone among major presidential aspirants in recent years is known by his last name) and Dilma may differ on some issues, but both are cerebral figures, technocrats of the type who often flourish as cabinet ministers but have rarely met with success when running for Brazil's highest office. Serra, in fact, lost overwhelmingly in the 2002 election, finishing 20 million votes and 22 percentage points behind Lula in a runoff. His life story, though, is in its own way quite compelling and, like Lula's, also involves a combination of humble origins, social mobility, and political persecution. But Serra, as is his style, has always been reticent about using his personal experiences, such as growing up in an Italian immigrant family and spending years abroad in exile, to win over voters. Instead, he has preferred to emphasize his intellectual attainments and to present himself to the public as a man with administrative skills and ideas. Since there is broad agreement between Serra and Dilma on some fundamental economic and social questions, he will no doubt hear suggestions from advisors that he work at making himself seem warmer and more personable if, as he has been hinting, he throws his hat in the ring again.

LIKE JOSÉ SERRA, Dilma Rousseff is an economist and the child of an immigrant father. Petar Rousseff came to Brazil in the 1930s from Bulgaria, where relatives say he left behind a struggling textile business, debts, and a pregnant wife. He settled in Minas Gerais and became a prosperous businessman, specializing in construction and real estate management. The second of three children, Dilma, born in Belo Horizonte in December 1947, was raised in middle-class comfort: private school, piano lessons, a French tutor, servants, and weekends at an exclusive social club.

Encouraged by her parents, Dilma also became (and remains) a voracious reader, which led to her developing a strong sense of indignation at the social injustices she saw around her. By the time she finished high school, shortly after the military coup of 1964, she had already been radicalized and plunged deeply into student politics. From there, it was only a short step to involvement in the clandestine Marxist-Leninist movement dedicated to overthrowing the dictatorship, and before she turned 21, Dilma had already joined an outlawed guerrilla group, the National Liberation Command.

A year later, after police and intelligence agents tracked down and arrested members of her organization who had carried out a bank robbery to raise funds for their cause, Dilma was forced to drop her university studies, go underground, and adopt a disguise and a new name. Her organization merged shortly afterward with another called the Revolutionary Armed Vanguard, which moved her from one safe house to another in Rio de Janeiro and São Paulo while she helped obtain and hide arms and money, gave classes in Marxist theory, and helped oversee the organization's finances.

Just how important a role Dilma played in the armed resistance to the dictatorship has always been a subject of some debate, which has only increased as her public profile has grown. Military intelligence and prosecutors' reports from the era she was underground refer to her as "the Joan of Arc of subversion" and say that she "controlled large sums of money" for the group. "She is one of the brains of the revolutionary scheme put into effect by the radical left," one document claimed. "This is a person of considerable intellectual gifts." But former associates whom the Brazilian press has interviewed in recent years scoff at that notion, saying that the secret police and spy apparatus deliberately exaggerated Dilma's importance so they could brag about their expertise when they eventually arrested or killed her.

For those reasons, it is difficult, if not impossible, to determine what role, if any, Dilma played in the planning and execution of one of the most notorious acts of "revolutionary expropriation" during the most repressive era of the dictatorship: the 1969 robbery of a safe, containing nearly $2.5 million, from the home of a mistress of Adhemar de Barros, the notoriously corrupt former governor of São Paulo. Campaigning on the slogan "He steals, but he gets things done," de Barros had accumulated a fortune at the public's expense, and the Revolutionary Armed Vanguard deemed his illicit wealth a target whose confiscation would meet with public sympathy. In interviews, Dilma has repeatedly denied being involved in the robbery. Former military and intelligence officials, however, have accused her of both planning the heist and disposing of the money it yielded, and documents purporting to be official reports of her involvement, which may or may not be fabrications, have also circulated in recent years.

Whatever her role in the guerrilla underground, Dilma was in fact captured in São Paulo in mid-January 1970. In jail she was severely tortured. In judicial complaints she later filed, she complained of being beaten, punched, subjected to electric shock, and tied for hours to poles that were suspended horizontally. Convicted of some charges and absolved of others, she was freed at the end of 1972 and moved to Porto Alegre to be near a boyfriend imprisoned there (who became her husband) and to resume her studies in economics, which she concluded in 1977, the same year her only child, a daughter named Paula, was born.

From this point on, all Dilma's political activities occur within the conventional political party system. Initially, she was affiliated not with Lula and the Workers Party but with the Democratic Labor Party, which regards itself as the heir to Getúlio Vargas and his ideas and opposed Lula in the first round of both the 2002 and 2006 elections. She led the party's think tank, the Foundation for Economics and Statistics, and while the party was in office served as secretary of finance in Porto Alegre and state secretary of energy, mines, and communication. After the Workers Party took back control of the state in 1999, Dilma was invited to return as secretary of energy. She decided to accept the offer and stayed on even after leaders of her own party wanted her to leave, which contributed to her changing loyalties in 2000 and joining the Workers Party.

After that, Dilma's rise was nothing short of phenomenal. She first came to Lula's attention during the 2002 presidential campaign as the member of a committee whose function was to draw up energy policy. The head of that group was widely expected to be named energy minister after the Workers Party won. But Lula surprised analysts when he chose Dilma instead. According to other advisors to Lula, he was impressed by her efficiency and organizational skills, command of issues and numbers, poise under pressure, and ability to argue and defend her positions.

Still, Dilma was an obscure figure when she arrived in Brasília in 2003, and she emerged as Lula's successor, handpicked rather than through primaries or caucuses, almost by default, thanks in no small part to her distance from the cavalcade of corruption scandals that tarnished Lula's rule. When the Workers Party first took power, Lula seemed to be grooming two other cabinet ministers to succeed him. The early favorites, both with strong followings and long records within the party, were Antônio Palocci, a physician and former mayor of the city of Ribeirão Preto whom Lula had chosen as his finance minister, and José Dirceu de Oliveira e Silva, known popularly as José Dirceu, his chief of staff. Dilma, as a relative newcomer to the party, cast in a secondary role, was mentioned by no one.

But both Palocci and Dirceu fell in separate corruption scandals during Lula's first term: Dirceu in mid-2005 as part of the *mensalão* affair, and Palocci early the next year after being accused of meeting secretly with lobbyists in a Brasília mansion rented for that purpose. Dirceu resumed his seat in Congress but was impeached late in 2005 and stripped of his political rights for ten years, which prevents him from holding public office until the middle of this decade and has transformed him into a power broker wielding influence behind the scenes. Palocci also returned to Congress but has kept a low profile in recent years. Both men are said to still harbor ambitions for higher office, but despite the Workers Party's efforts to give their image a scrubbing, the rehabilitation of their reputations has proceeded slowly.

To fill the vacuum left by the fall of José Dirceu, who had functioned as a sort of prime minister, attending to all the routine details of daily governance that Lula found boring or disagreeable, the president turned to Dilma. By mid-2005 she had quickly proved herself to be one of the most capable and disciplined members of Lula's cabinet. Since those qualities were sorely lacking in the presidential palace, she was the logical choice to become Lula's new chief of staff. As she solved one administrative problem after another, Lula's admiration for her grew, and by 2008, despite the ambitions of a handful of governors and members of Congress, there was little doubt that she had become his heir apparent.

As Lula's go-to person and troubleshooter, Dilma met with him almost daily and often traveled with him abroad and within Brazil. Although separated in age by only two years, "they have a father-daughter relationship," Lula's press secretary said in 2009. That is not to say there was no grumbling within the Workers Party, and not just because Dilma's rapid rise trampled the aspirations of others. For all her vaunted administrative experience and capacity, Dilma had never run for public office until Lula anointed her as his successor. Yes, she had managed campaigns and written policy papers for candidates. But she had always operated from the sidelines, never as the one in the spotlight or delivering the speech at the podium, and as her profile rose, so did speculation about what sort of plan B Lula might have up his sleeve if her candidacy failed to take off.

Dilma's lack of experience in the rough-and-tumble arena of a national political campaign is not necessarily a fatal flaw. Michelle Bachelet of Chile was also a political novice when she ran for president of Chile in 2005 after serving as health and then defense minister, and she quickly learned how to combine a certain awkwardness in that new role with an almost maternal warmth and make those attributes work in her favor. Dilma, however, did not display that same talent during the campaign, and had to rely on Lula's personal charisma and enthusiastic support to boost her.

One of Dilma's deficiencies on the campaign trail, in fact, has been that she displays precisely the same personality traits that made her such an asset as Lula's right hand and enforcer. Her speaking style continues to be pedagogic rather than inspiring, and she sometimes has seemed curt, abrupt, harsh, impatient, gruff, and severe, almost authoritarian, in dealing with others. No one ever doubted Dilma's intelligence or competence. But even partisans within the Workers Party have worried about her ability to connect on a personal level with voters, which remains a key to success in Brazilian politics. In 2008, Dilma had plastic surgery, which softened her appearance and made her seem less dour. But then the joke at the time was "When is she going to get a makeover for her personality?"

As a candidate whose first campaign was for her nation's highest office, Dilma has also been subject to intense scrutiny about her past, and not just her guerrilla activities. Her official biography initially claimed she had earned both a master's degree and doctorate in economics at one of Brazil's most prestigious universities. But a magazine investigation conducted in 2009 found both of those claims to be false, and amid a storm of criticism she duly revised her curriculum vitae. Questions have also been raised about her health: In April 2009, Dilma announced that doctors had removed a cancerous tumor from her chest, acknowledged she was also suffering from lymphoma, and began chemotherapy. She appears to have recovered, but memories of Tancredo Neves's 1985 ordeal and the national trauma it caused remain in the minds of millions of voters.

Dilma was not the first woman to run for president of Brazil, but she was the first female candidate to represent a party with a realistic chance of winning an election. Like other powerful women leaders, she has been stuck with nicknames such as "the Iron Lady" and has complained of "the straightjacket" of sexual stereotyping. "I'm criticized not because I am tough but because I am a woman," she said in an interview with a Brazilian magazine in 2009. "I'm a tough woman surrounded by meek cabinet ministers." Overall, though, the novelty of the idea of a woman becoming president has worked in Dilma's favor, creating an aura of excitement and curiosity that would be lacking in the campaign of a male candidate with the same qualifications and background. And despite the country's reputation for machismo attitudes, Brazilian voters have not hesitated to elect women as governors, mayors (including two in São Paulo), and members of Congress.

Dilma's election victory largely put those concerns to rest and shifted the focus back to the economy, her area of expertise. Having benefited from the surge of growth that Brazil has experienced in recent years, both of the country's main parties would appear to be fully invested in the market-friendly economic policies now in place. It might therefore seem unlikely at first glance that a new president from either party would suddenly abandon such an approach completely or alter it substantially. That is not to suggest that politicians who favor a populist approach of the sort that Getúlio Vargas and João Goulart once personified in earlier eras and that Hugo Chávez exemplifies today no longer exist in Brazil. Theirs is clearly a minority position, but it does retain a following: In the 2002 presidential election, for instance, two candidates espousing such a philosophy, Ciro Gomes and Anthony Garotinho, received more than 25 million votes, accounting for 30 percent of the ballots cast in the first round.

Even within the Workers Party, founded in 1980 to provide a more modern and less dogmatic alternative to the two traditional Communist parties that had always sought to speak for the left, there is nostalgia in some quarters for a return to a statist approach. Historically, the party has been composed of factions, ranging from former Trotskyites and other hard-liners, known colloquially as "the Shiites," to advocates of liberation theology, environmentalists, and European-style social democrats. From the start, the party's sole continuous point of unity has been the figure of Lula, who has showed a remarkable talent for herding cats. Whether Dilma, a relative newcomer, will have the authority or the inclination as president to rein in those who never really made peace with Lula's abandonment of socialism and who continue to maintain that the party's embrace of capitalism is only "for now" and required "by current conditions" is an open question.

The closing phase of Lula's time in office was characterized by a kind of triumphalism, even hubris, that suggests Dilma might indeed face pressures to deviate from the path of the previous 16 years. The party's public stance is that all of Brazil's recent advances and achievements are due exclusively to the wisdom of Lula and his policies, a position that ignores both FHC's enormous contributions and the Chinese-led international commodity boom of recent years that has helped fuel Brazil's expansion. The conviction that Lula and the Workers Party have a sort of golden touch and are infallible explain both the failed Iran diplomatic initiative of May 2010 and the growing clamor within the party to bring the Sub-Salt oil and gas bonanza under control of the state, sentiments that can be expected to grow now that the party has won a third term in office. It does not help that Dilma's economic writings can be cloudy when it comes to basic questions relating to the proper roles of the state and private enterprise.

As indicated by the nervousness of markets that flares anytime Dilma gets sick, her tenure will no doubt also be plagued by fears of a recurrence of cancer that would force her to undergo medical treatments or otherwise debilitate her to the point of having to step aside in favor of her vice-presidential running mate, Michel Temer. He has served three different times as the speaker of the lower house of Congress and is a member not of the Workers Party but of an allied group, the Party of the Brazilian Democratic Movement. The PMDB, of course, grew out of the sole entity of political opposition the military permitted during most of its dictatorship, but today it has no real ideology of its own. It exists primarily as a refuge for politicians whose main concern seems to be obtaining and keeping a hold on the spoils of power, regardless of who is president, and the party's large congressional bloc has made it an attractive coalition partner for the governments of both FHC and Lula.

Temer, a São Paulo lawyer born in 1940, is cut from just such pragmatic, nonideological cloth. In many ways, he is reminiscent of José Sarney, the vice president–elect who took office at the death of Tancredo Neves in 1985: an extremely skilled political operator and dealmaker with little knowledge of economics and, at least according to his critics, a shaky sense of ethics. At the time the Workers Party named him as Dilma's running mate, Temer's name had surfaced in a pair of corruption investigations: one into a construction company, in which his name appears as the supposed beneficiary of bribes, and another into *mensalão* payments. Temer denies any connection with illegal practices of any kind and has attributed the "vile and dishonorable" accusations against him to machinations by political rivals. But it has never been clear what bedrock convictions, if any, he has on the important political and economic questions Brazil faces.

And though Lula has now served the two consecutive terms as president permitted him by law, his political career may not be finished. Exactly what course he plans to take is not yet clear, but he is not likely to slip into a quiet retirement. Unlike the U.S. constitution, which limits a president to a total of two terms, Brazil's charter permits a former president to run for a third term, so long as at least one term has elapsed since he left office. Lula's popularity is sure to remain strong, and the same month the 2014 election will be held he will turn 69, almost exactly the same age Getúlio Vargas was when he last took office.

Even with Dilma's victory, Lula is likely to want to continue pulling strings within the party, playing the role of kingmaker rather than elder statesman. Just how far this desire will extend is impossible to predict. Dilma owes her ascension almost exclusively to him, and there has been much speculation that Lula envisions a Dilma presidency as a mere four-year placeholder for him. But it is difficult to imagine a sitting president stepping aside in 2014 to let Lula run again without an ugly internal battle erupting.

At the very least, Lula will want to continue to have a say in policies and appointments should the Workers Party remain in power. The party has almost no choice but to allow that. Lula has been its only leader since its founding in 1980, and neither he nor other party officials have done a particularly good job of grooming a younger generation of new leaders who can replace him. For better or worse, the Workers Party is identified with a single person, and its fortunes still depend largely on the image and presence of a leader whom voters find more popular and credible than the party he represents.

Certainly a cult of personality has been constructed around Lula, as if to pave the way for his eventual return. In January 2010, just as the presidential campaign was about to begin, a hagiographic feature film called *Lula, the Son of Brazil*, the most expensive Brazilian movie ever made, was released and immediately became a box office hit. Made with a budget of about $10 million and based on an authorized biography with the same title, the movie artfully avoids the controversies and corruption scandals of Lula's presidency by choosing to tell the story of his life from his birth in poverty until the death of his mother in 1980, just after the Workers Party was founded. The makers of the movie say that they deliberately did not seek funding from government sources so as to avoid criticism that they were beholden to Lula. But at least three construction companies bidding for government contracts did supply money, and the final product offers a sentimental portrait of Lula that critics described as overly idealized and not faithful to the facts.

The current status of the PSDB, the other large, ideologically based national party, is notably different from that of the Workers Party. It is not burdened by a personality cult and has a greater ideological coherence, but it also does not have a single overwhelmingly popular leader to personify the party, define and deliver its message, and excite voters. From the offices of his foundation in downtown São Paulo, FHC remains involved in internal party politics and, it is true, sometimes tries to play a kingmaker's role. But he is not the party's sole authority, and one of his legacies is that he has not only permitted but even cultivated and encouraged competing centers of power to emerge, aware that such an approach is necessary if the party is to survive him. As a result, FHC's desires are sometimes thwarted, and his voice, though often the loudest, is only one of several speaking in the party's name.

Of the younger leaders who have emerged from this nurturing environment, the one who seems to have the brightest future is Aécio Neves da Cunha, born in 1960. The grandson of former president Tancredo Neves, Aécio initially was schooled in politics when he served as the private secretary to his grandfather, a master of maneuvering and negotiation who was nicknamed the Old Fox. Some of the residual sympathy aroused among Brazilians by Tancredo Neves's tragic, frustrating death on the eve of his inauguration may also have transferred to his grandson. But in addition to having a famous surname, Aécio, divorced and raising a teenage daughter, has other intangibles working in his favor, among them his good looks and personal charm.

Aécio's biggest assets, however, are his highly refined political skills and his strong track record as an administrator. He was elected to Congress in 1986 and, shortly after his fortieth birthday, became speaker of the lower house of Congress. In 2002, he was elected governor of Minas Gerais, Brazil's second most populous state, becoming the youngest person to hold that office. He succeeded former president Itamar Franco, who had left the state's accounts in a shambles, but by the end of his first term, Aécio was able to announce that

Minas Gerais was back to a zero-deficit situation. He was reelected in 2006 but according to law could not seek a third consecutive term. He announced a run for the presidency in 2009 but eventually withdrew and ran for the senate instead, his enormous popularity guaranteeing him that seat.

Unlike many in the PSDB, Aécio forged a cordial working and personal relationship with Lula—so cordial that the president tried during his second term to lure Aécio away from his home in the opposition and into the allied Brazilian Democratic Movement Party (PMDB). Had that effort succeeded, Lula appeared ready to turn to Aécio as his successor in the event that Dilma's candidacy failed to take wing, or at least that was the political gossip one often heard in Brasília in the latter phase of Lula's years in power. But since Aécio has chosen to remain in opposition, he is regarded as the PSDB's likely presidential standard-bearer later in the decade, in 2014 or later, depending on what he decides.

The senate seat should give Aécio not just a comfortable political perch for the next eight years but also guarantees him the national exposure he needs if that next presidential bid is to be successful. Certainly he does not lack other leadership qualities. In 2002, when Howell Raines, at that time the executive editor of *The New York Times*, visited Brazil, I arranged for us to have lunch with Aécio, then the speaker of the lower house of Congress, at the Copacabana Palace Hotel in Rio. Tanned, cordial, and exuding confidence, Aécio easily dominated the conversation, and when we were finished and he had departed, I asked Raines what he thought. "I think I've just had lunch with a future president of Brazil," he replied, an evaluation that many others have made before and since. The only question, barring health issues or some unanticipated personal scandal, would seem to be when Aécio will fulfill that prophecy.

But until the political system itself is thoroughly overhauled, no Brazilian chief of state, regardless of party, can hope to be a truly modern executive. Though the economy has been thrust into the twenty-first century as the result of the changes that have occurred since the end of the military dictatorship, the political system continues to lag behind, the prisoner of antiquated attitudes and practices. That gap may actually have widened in recent years, and vast amounts of new wealth threaten to amplify the disparity even further. Newly minted billionaires and the corporations they control have grown increasingly bold in throwing their weight around and corroding democratic principles and values in order to advance their own narrow interests.

To have any impact, reform would have to include several elements that Brazilian political scientists and good-government civic groups have long advocated. Prohibiting, or at least restricting, elected officials from switching parties would be a good start. Voting by district, rather than forcing candidates for Congress and state legislatures to run on statewide slates, could also have far-reaching effects. So could choosing candidates through primaries instead of the backroom wheeling and dealing that predominates in the selection process now. Reallocating the distribution of seats in Congress on the basis of the principle of one man, one vote would also be helpful, since it would reduce the power of states in the northeast that continue to be dominated by family oligarchies and reward states such as São Paulo, Minas Gerais, Rio de Janeiro, and Rio Grande do Sul where the electorate is larger, more educated, and more likely to demand an end to abuses and backward practices.

But passage and enforcement of a strict campaign finance law would probably result in the most immediate transformative changes. As things now stand, neither candidates nor political parties declare all of the donations they receive, a state of affairs that encourages clandestine contributions and widespread abuses and corruption. All the major parties are believed to operate secret slush funds, known in Brazilian political slang as Box Two, to supplement amounts that candidates publicly acknowledge spending on their campaigns. Much of this money is the result of under-the-table donations from companies that want either government contracts, such as construction firms, or legislation that favors their interests. The money, often given in cash, finds it way to overseas bank accounts and then is recycled back to Brazil, providing the bulk of the financing for campaign expenses and political advertising.

Brazilian politics has changed dramatically, overwhelmingly for the better, since I first landed in the country nearly 40 years ago. What the country's military rulers then dreaded most has ended up happening: A left-wing union leader was elected president, and was succeeded by a former guerrilla. But the instability of the early 1960s that brought down democracy did not recur, a sign of Brazil's political maturity. Elected officials can speak their minds freely without having to worry about being jailed or having their rights stripped from them. The press is vociferous and combative, the judiciary doesn't hesitate to criticize or rein in the executive branch, and civic, religious, professional, and environmental groups have all carved out roles for themselves in the governmental process.

Brazilian democracy may be loud, messy, and imperfect, but overall it has served the Brazilian people well. The challenge now is to muster the courage to take the next step and do away with the vestiges of autocratic practices that are hundreds of years old—or risk losing the support of voters and eroding the progress that has been registered over the past quarter century.

POSTSCRIPT

ON JANUARY 1, 2011, Dilma Rousseff was sworn in as Brazil's first female president after winning 56 percent of the vote in a second-round victory over Jose Serra which saw a record 106.5 million ballots cast. Despite the continued economic crisis in Europe and the United States at the moment she took her oath of office, Brazil was sitting pretty, with the economy having grown 7.5 percent in 2010, the third-highest rate worldwide, and the national currency, the real, strengthening against the dollar and the Euro. Exports were booming and currency reserves were growing, as was Brazil's economic and political stature around the world. At the same time, domestic politics were more stable than ever, as evidenced by the calm response of every important Brazilian institution, including the military, to the arrival of a former guerrilla in the presidency.

During her first year in office, Dilma has shown herself to be a pragmatist at heart. With the economy in danger of overheating and inflationary pressures accumulating, she did not hesitate to take steps to decelerate growth through measures such as limiting a rise in the minimum wage and restricting government spending, even if that displeased some in her own party. In the area of foreign policy, she immediately and quite publicly began to move Brazil away from a relationship with Iran that many Brazilians had seen as all-too-cozy: She criticized discrimination against women and human rights abuses there while also signaling Brazil's continued independent stance in the Middle East by refusing to vote in favor of the U.N. resolution that allowed NATO to intervene in Libya and help topple Muammar el-Qaddafi.

That abstention was announced just as the American president, Barack Obama, was arriving in Brasília on a state visit. During the Bush years, disagreement on such an important foreign policy issue would probably have probably cast a chill over the trip. But Obama, who also made a side excursion to Rio de Janeiro to congratulate the city on winning the 2016 Summer Olympics and to make a pitch for American companies that want to sell Brazil equipment for its booming oil, gas, and telecommunications industries, struck a conciliatory tone in which he explicitly stated that the U.S. no longer regards Brazil as simply a regional power. "Increasingly, Brazil is a global leader, a world leader," he said, "going from a recipient of foreign aid to a donor nation, pointing the way to a world without nuclear weapons and being in the forefront of global efforts to confront climate change."

On the home front, Dilma and her allies have showed energy in tackling some of Brazil's most pressing social issues, most notably that of urban violence, especially in the large squatter settlements that ring Brazil's large cities. That problem, if not brought under control, has the potential to besmirch Brazil's image in the run-up to the 2014 World Cup and the 2016 Summer Olympics. As a result, "Police Pacification Units" have been sent into some of the most notoriously crime-ridden and drug-infested favelas in Rio de Janeiro, cracking down on the heavily armed gangs operating there. The "UPP" program actually began late in 2008, but has gained new strength since Dilma's election and, most importantly, appears to have the support of slum residents who in the past regarded the police as being corrupt and inefficient and as much of a plague as the criminals they supposedly combat. It is far too early to proclaim victory over urban violence, but at least a promising start has been made in addressing the problem.

As part of the same effort, social programs meant to improve the lives of the poor, urban, and rural, have also been strengthened. That, combined with the booming economy, has slowed the migration from the northeast to the big industrial cities of the south and in some cases even reversed it, as workers return home to take jobs in new plants opening in places like Campina Grande, Caruaru, and Petrolina-Juazeiro. For the millions remaining on the outskirts of the big cities, they stand to be among the principal beneficiaries of the government money that is being funneled into improving housing, transportation, health care, and education—such as a plan to expand the school year from 180 days to the 200 days that is required by law that has often been ignored in the past.

Offshore, discoveries of oil and gas continue to be made, while out in the fields, bumper crops continue to be harvested. Brazil's strength in those areas has helped attract foreign capital: According to figures published by the United Nations Conference on Trade and Development in 2011, in less than two years, Brazil has vaulted from 15th to fourth on the list of countries receiving the most direct foreign investment. (For 2011, the Brazilian government estimated the figure at a record $60 billion.) In addition, Brazil's largest and most agile business conglomerates are becoming foreign investors themselves, buying up companies abroad in deals such as the acquisition of the American-based Burger King fast food chain by a São Paulo investment group or the petrochemical producer Braskem's purchase of a division of oil giant Sunoco. By some calculations, acquisitions abroad by Brazilian companies, fueled by the strength of the real versus the dollar and euro, now exceed those of foreign companies seeking a foothold in Brazil.

Since the initial publication of the English-language version of this book in September 2010, the growth evident all over Brazil, whether in the form of new stores and businesses or increased consumption on the part of the populace, has already propelled the country past Italy and Great Britain, to make it the world's sixth-largest economy. What is more, some studies now predict that Brazil will overtake France within a decade, thus fulfilling the government's proclaimed goal that Brazil should become "the fifth power." While there may have been some skepticism early on regarding whether Brazil really deserved to be put in the same category and company as China and India, those doubts seem to be easing, as the strengths Brazil displays and the opportunities it offers become more obvious and attractive.

But some warning signs have also surfaced in Dilma's first year in office, particularly with the reappearance of figures closely associated with the corruption of the Lula years, some of them discredited. For instance, she retained Gilberto Carvalho, who was Lula's personal secretary and has been named as a bagman in various money laundering and bribery schemes said to have been operated by the Workers Party, in his crucial post. And as her chief of staff, Dilma first named Antônio Palocci, who had served as Lula's Minister of Finance until forced to step down in 2006. In the words of the Brazilian press, that automatically made him "Dilma's Dilma," meaning that Palocci, who is

13 years younger than the president, would wield great power out of the spotlight and could perhaps be groomed as her successor in the 2018 elections, assuming she were to be re-elected in 2014.

But in June, Palocci once again had to resign, following press reports that, during the four years between his departure in disgrace from the presidential palace and his triumphant return, he had acquired real estate worth several million dollars with money whose origins he declined to explain. In the months that followed, five other cabinet ministers also resigned, all but one of them because of allegations of corruption while in office. The exception was Minister of Defense Nelson Jobim, who angered Dilma by telling a Brazilian magazine that Gleisi Hoffman, the female senator the president brought in to replace Palocci, was a weak and inappropriate choice because Hoffman "doesn't even know Brasília."

In each of the other cases, however, the cabinet minister in question (Transportation, Agriculture, Tourism, Sports) was a member of a small party allied to the president's Workers Party who was accused of using his office for illicit money-making schemes for himself or his party, such as bribes or kickbacks. There are multiple ways to interpret this wave of forced resignations, which stands in sharp contrast to the administrations of Dilma's two most recent predecessors: In his first year in office, Fernando Henrique Cardoso replaced only two cabinet ministers, and Lula fired none. Dilma has said that she will not tolerate incompetence or corruption in her cabinet, so in that respect she appears to be keeping her word. But another reading is that corruption is more widespread and serious a problem than ever, and perhaps impossible to control, given the huge amounts of money that are now sloshing around the Brazilian economy.

Since neither of these interpretations is mutually exclusive, both could be true. But two things are clear: Small parties continue to not only want to extract a high price for their support of the government in power, but to view control of public agencies primarily as a cash cow for their own private purposes. Yet Dilma, like Lula and FHC before her, cannot govern without their support, and has generally replaced the fired minister with another member of his party rather than punish the entire party for its malfeasance by leaving it outside her cabinet.

The dismissal in late October of the Minister of Sports, a member of the Communist Party of Brazil and a holdover from Lula's cabinet, after allegations that he was demanding a ten-percent kickback on contracts to NGOs is particularly revealing and worrisome. Though the post is not ordinarily an important one, Brazil is, as mentioned earlier, to be the host of both the 2014 World Cup and the 2016 Summer Olympics. This means that many extremely lucrative contracts are being assigned and that rigorous construction schedules must also be adhered to. The international soccer federation is already complaining that Brazil is behind schedule on construction of World Cup infrastructure, so the country can ill afford any other mishaps that would raise questions about its ability to host the two events or might suggest even the appearance of corruption and political favoritism. Dilma has already stripped the sports ministry, which traditionally has enjoyed a cozy relationship with the Brazilian Olympic Committee and the Brazilian Soccer Confederation—themselves organizations that have been accused of corruption, nepotism and lack of transparency—of most of its responsibilities in the two showcase events, but room for further damage unfortunately still exists.

As anticipated, Dilma has also encountered some difficulties in controlling the fractious Workers Party, some of whose factions remain jealous of her rapid rise and still harbor doubts about her ideological reliability. In May 2011, the party replaced its sitting president, an ally of Dilma's, with Rui Falcão, a figure closely associated with two of her rivals, one of them being José Dirceu, who had been seen as Lula's likely successor until he was toppled in the 2005 *mensalão* crisis. Party leaders also saw fit to bring back into the fold Delúbio Soares, who was the party's treasurer during that scandal, which the courts still have not entirely resolved. "In 2010, everything was on behalf of Dilma," Falcão said after being elected. "Now it's everything for the Workers Party."

But on October 29, 2011, all political calculations were called into question when Lula announced that he had cancer of the larynx and would immediately begin a program of chemotherapy. At the urging of his doctors, he will have to remain silent for at least several months, and his ability to travel and campaign on behalf of the Workers Party in the run-up to the 2012 midterm elections may also be limited, depending on the seriousness of his case.

As Brazilian political analysts immediately noted, that deprives Dilma of a valued and trusted ally, at least temporarily, and could contribute to increased fractiousness within the party as it chooses its candidates and tries to make deals with potential coalition partners. Lula, after all, has demonstrated long coattails in previous elections, and is the only Workers Party leader with sufficient prestige and authority to keep members in line.

Relations with the opposition, on the other hand, appear to have improved, especially with the Social Democrats. Lula's almost pathological envy and resentment of FHC, and FHC's pleasure in getting under Lula's skin with public barbs, had made that impossible previously. But Dilma has been gracious and friendly to both FHC and PSDB governors of large states such as São Paulo and Minas Gerais, going so far as to invite FHC to sit at her side at public events, with television cameras rolling, and to dinner at the presidential palace. As a result, the political atmosphere, though polluted by corruption, seems less toxic in partisan terms than during Lula's years in power.

Since the Workers Party and the PSDB are in broad agreement on the economic and social model Brazil should follow, as became clear during the 2010 election campaign, when Dilma and Serra had to resort to peripheral issues like abortion and foreign policy to distinguish themselves from each other, that could pave the way for diminished hostility, and perhaps even greater cooperation, in the future. That, in turn, could lessen Dilma's need to make unsavory deals with the smaller parties that are now essential allies of her government.

More crucial to the country's long-term future, though, is how Dilma and her team handle the bottlenecks that have begun appearing as a result of the country's rapid growth and rising prosperity. Though Dilma's Minister of Finance, Guido Mantega, has proclaimed that these are "nice problems to have," they have the potential to slow Brazil's growth and prevent it from advancing to the next level of economic and social development. Already, labor shortages in key sectors have begun to appear, and the deficiencies of the education, transportation, and communications systems are becoming more obvious by the day.

An annual World Bank study of global competitiveness released late in 2011, for instance, showed Brazil slipping six notches to 126th among the 183 nations surveyed and cited problems in areas such as obtaining electricity, setting up a business and obtaining construction permits. Within Latin America, that was a better performance than Venezuela, but much worse than Chile, Mexico, and even Peru. And a related study by the Conference Board, an American business group, published at the same time, found that the productivity of Brazilian workers was lagging, in part because of deficiencies in education and investment: In 2010, the average Brazilian worker produced only 20 percent of the wealth of an American worker and one-third that of a worker in South Korea. Between 2005 and 2010, the report also determined the productivity of Brazilian workers increased by 2.1 percent per year, far behind the other members of the BRIC group, which was led by China, which showed an average annual gain of 9.8 percent.

Another concern is a related one: Wage increases outstripping productivity gains in recent years contribute to inflationary pressures. The Central Bank admitted that inflation for 2011 would exceed the 6.5 percent ceiling that had been part of the official target, the first time in more than a decade the government had failed to meet its goal, but promised that the figure for 2012 would be below the 4.5 percent ceiling that has been established. But the Brazilian Congress is forecasting 5.5 percent, which seems more realistic in view of the huge investments in roads, airports, ports, and stadiums that are part of the preparations for the World Cup and Olympics.

Brazil also remains vulnerable to outside forces. To cool down the economy in 2010, the government imposed a tax on short-term money coming into the country only to take advantage of Brazil's much higher interest rates. But a double-dip recession in the United States and Europe, or the weakening or collapse of the euro, could lead to a rapid deceleration, which Dilma's government also wants to avoid. Brazil escaped the worst consequences of the Great Recession that began in 2008, in large part because of the prudent policies discussed in chapter 6. But it would be more exposed and at risk the second time around, especially if, as appears possible, the economy of China, Brazil's leading trade partner, also decelerates. Late in 2011, the Brazilian Finance Ministry revised its estimate of growth for 2012 downward to four percent or less, a figure that would be welcome just about anywhere in North America or Europe, but is considered a disappointment for a country at Brazil's stage of economic development.

Nevertheless, Brazilians continue to be optimistic, and not without reason. Of course, there still exists the possibility that Brazil could regress, as Brazilians are well aware. As I do interviews and give lectures across the country, I am often asked what guarantee there is that in a decade I won't be obliged to write another book called *Brazil on the Decline*. My answer to Brazilians is always the same: No such guarantee exists, since the country's future is in your hands and depends largely on the decisions you make as a people. But at the moment, nothing on the horizon suggests such a catastrophic fate; on the contrary, most indicators point to Brazil remaining where it is, as a rising intermediate power, or even reaching the next level, in the rarefied company of true world powers.

ACKNOWLEDGMENTS

THE ORIGINS OF THIS BOOK date to the 1970s, when I would talk with my father-in-law and his brother-in-law every time I returned to Rio de Janeiro from an extended trip to some remote corner of Brazil. Inevitably, they would remark, "You ought to put that in a book." So let me start by thanking David William Amaral and Sinval Paranhos Haefeli for that suggestion. My only regret is that neither of them have lived to see the publication of this book.

I owe a debt of gratitude to other members of my Brazilian family as well. Thanks especially to my mother-in-law, Anna Maria Haefeli Amaral, and my aunts Euclea and Lucie, as well as to my cousins by marriage and their children,: Leonardo, Ana and Raphael, Paula and Vítor; Luciana, Fred and Priscilla; Mônica, João and Lorena; and Teodoro and Magda. They were the ones who first took me to Maracaná stadium and the Feira dos Nordestinos in São Cristóvão and who invited me to join them at Salgueiro's home grounds for Carnival rehearsals, thereby opening vistas that have allowed me to experience Brazil from the inside.

I am also indebted to Leonardo de Melo Haefeli and Ana Parrini for inviting me to stay with them in Rio de Janeiro and Teresópolis during the time I spent in Brazil in 2008 and 2009 researching and writing this book. In a similar vein, Antônio Callado and Débora Matedi were extremely generous in offering me the use of an apartment in Botafogo as a writing studio. More than a quarter of this book was written there, with a panoramic view of Sugarloaf Mountain and Botafogo Bay and the music of Rio's streets to inspire me.

During the nine years I was the Rio de Janeiro bureau chief for *The New York Times*, I received invaluable assistance and guidance from Mery Galanternick, the bureau manager there. She not only provided a much-needed institutional memory, but also knows virtually everyone in Brazil, or so it seems, and is quick to share her knowledge and make useful suggestions. Thanks as well to Luiz Carlos Gomes and Magno Silva for keeping me abreast of the latest slang and explaining the intricacies of fundamental aspects of Brazilian life and popular culture like the *jogo do bicho*, Carnival, samba, futebol, telenovelas, and how to deal with corrupt, imperious, or racist cops.

Over the years, I have also benefited enormously from discussions (and debates) with some of Brazil's most astute sociologists, anthropologists, historians, political analysts, economists, and scientists. They have not always agreed with me, nor I with them, and I imagine that some of what I have written here will spark future debates with them. But my reading of the writings of (and my conversations with) Roberto DaMatta, Gilberto Dupas, David Fleischer, Elio Gaspari, José Goldemberg, Hélio Jaguaribe, Felipe Lampreia, Bolívar Lamounier, the late Darcy Ribeiro, and Rubens Ricupero have been essential in shaping my vision of Brazil.

In my reporting trips around Brazil, I often have been accompanied by dedicated and perceptive photographers who helped me to look at and really see the country and appreciate the beauty of both its geography and its people. My thanks, then, to Lalo de Almeida, John Maier, João Silva, and Adriana Zehbrauskas. I also must mention the late Nicolas Reynard, who was the ideal traveling companion in the Amazon, a talented visual artist and a font of practical and arcane knowledge about the region. His death in a seaplane crash in the Rio Negro north of Manaus on November 11, 2004 deprived me of a cherished friend and the Amazon of one its most effective and passionate champions.

It is impossible to work in the Amazon without relying on the kindness of others, and in 50-odd trips over more than 30 years, I have incurred many debts. I met Lúcio Flávio Pinto in Belém and Márcio Souza in Manaus during my first visit to the region in 1978, and I remain an admirer of both, not only for unselfishly sharing their knowledge with me but also for their personal warmth and humor. On scientific questions, Philip Fearnside at the National Institute for Amazon Research in Manaus and Dan Nepstad of the Amazon Institute of Environmental Research in Belém have been patient and informative tutors. I also am greatly indebted to numerous Roman Catholic priests, nuns, and lay workers who often sheltered and fed me and, through the church's commissions on justice, peace and land tenure, provided story ideas and documentation when I needed them most.

In that regard, I am especially grateful to three members of the clergy. Msgr. James Ryan, a fellow Chicagoan, came to the Amazon in 1942 to be chaplain at Henry Ford's rubber project on the Tapajos River, later served as bishop of Santarem, and was a dear friend until his death in 2002 at the age of 89. Eurico Kräutler, prelate and bishop of the Xingu, and Alano Pena, as bishop of Marabá, also provided hospitality, friendship, and news tips to the wandering Jew who periodically appeared on their doorstep.

One of the singular blessings of my 40-year involvement with Brazil has been the opportunity to immerse myself in its extraordinary culture. As the son of a musician, I have always found my conversations with Gilberto Gil and Caetano Veloso to be especially stimulating and helpful in guiding me to an understanding of the country's remarkable artistic output. Multiple encounters with other notable creative figures, from Jorge Amado, Paulo Coelho, and Moacyr Scliar to J. Borges, Carlinhos Brown, and Joãosinho Trinta also have had a permanent impact on me and fed my consuming curiosity about Brazilian culture.

In the United States, I must start by expressing my gratitude to the editors of *The New York Times*, especially Joseph Lelyveld, for sending me to Brazil and giving me the autonomy and budget to write about a multitude of subjects. The encouragement and sound advice of my agent, Nancy Love, has eased my path and my mind. I am grateful to all at Palgrave Macmillan for offering me the opportunity to write this book and especially to my editor, Luba Ostashevsky, for pertinent questions, helpful suggestions and a sharp sense of focus that helped keep me from getting lost in the Amazon jungle of my own words. And though they did not work directly on this project, my Brazilian editors, Roberto Feith and Bruno Porto, also deserve mention. Their questions and our lively discussions and debates about Brazil during the editing of my previous, Portuguese-language book, *Deu no New York Times*, meant that I came to the writing of this book already in fighting trim.

My greatest debt, however, is to my wife, Clotilde Amaral Rohter. My very first contacts with Brazil and Brazilians were through her and under her guidance. She taught me to speak and write Portuguese and made the initial suggestions about what I should read, see, listen to and eat that started me on the road that led to the writing of this book. Were it not for her, I probably would have become a China scholar and missed out entirely on the grand adventure that is Brazil. Add to that her steadfastness and sacrifice, and it should be obvious that I owe her far more than words can hope to express.

BIBLIOGRAPHY

Abreu, Alzira Alves de. *Dicionário Histórico-Biográfico Brasileiro*. Rio de Janeiro: Fundação Getúlio Vargas, 1999.

Albin, Ricardo Cravo. *Dicionário Houiass Ilustrado da Musica Popular Brasileira*. Rio de Janeiro: Paracatu, 2006.

Almeida, Alberto Carlos. *Por Que Lula?* Rio de Janeiro: Record, 2006.

Almeida, Roberto de. *Relações Internacionais e Política Externa do Brasil*. Porto Alegre: Editora UFRGS, 1998.

Araújo, Joel Zito. *A Negação do Brasil*. São Paulo: Senac, 2000.

Bandeira, Luiz Alberto Moniz. *Presença dos Estado Unidos no Brasil*. Rio de Janeiro: Civiliza-cão Brasileira, 1978.

Bellos, Alex. *Futebol: Soccer, The Brazilian Way*. New York: Bloomsbury USA, 2002.

Bernardes, Roberto. *Embraer: Elos Entre Estado e Mercado*. São Paulo: Hucitec, 2000.

Botelho, Raul. *Proceso del Subimperialismo Brasileño*. Buenos Aires: Eudeba, 1977.

Buarque de Holanda, Sérgio. *Raizes do Brasil*. Rio de Janeiro: José Olympio, 1993.

Bueno, Eduardo. *Coleção Terra Brasilis*. 4 vols. Rio de Janeiro: Objetiva, 1998.

Cabral, Sérgio. *As Escolas de Samba do Rio de Janeiro*. Rio de Janeiro: Lumiar, 1996.

Cardoso, Fernando Henrique. *A Arte da Política: A História Que Vivi*. Rio de Janeiro: Civi-lização Brasileira, 2006.

———and Geraldo Muller. *Amazônia: Expansão do Capitalismo*. São Paulo: Brasiliense, 1977.

Carrasco, Lorenzo. *Ambientalismo Novo Colonialismo*. Rio de Janeiro: CapaxDei, 2005.

Castro, Ruy. *Chega de Saudade: A História e as Histórias da Bossa Nova*. São Paulo: Companhia das Letras, 1990.

Chacon, Vamireh. *História dos Partidos Brasileiros*. Brasília: UnB, 1998.

Conti, Mario Sérgio. *Notícias do Planalto*. São Paulo: Companhia das Letras, 1999.

Costa, Haroldo. *Fala, Crioulo: O Que É Ser Negro no Brasil*. Rio de Janeiro: Record, 2009.

DaMatta, Roberto. *A Casa e a Rua*. Rio de Janeiro: Rocco, 1997.

———. "O Que Faz O Brasil, Brasil." Rio de Janeiro: Rocco, 1984.

———and Elena Soárez. *Águias, Burros e Borboletas: Um Estudo Antropológico do Jogo do Bicho*. Rio de Janeiro: Rocco, 1999.

Del Priore, Mary. *História do Amor no Brasil*. São Paulo: Contexto, 2005.

———. *História das Mulheres no Brasil*. São Paulo: Contexto, 2004.

Diniz, Andre. *Almanaque do Samba*. Rio de Janeiro: Jorge Zahar, 2006.

Farias, Patricia Silveira de. *Pegando uma Corn na Praia: Relações Raciais e Classificação de Cor*. Rio de Janeiro: Biblioteca Carioca, 2006.

Fausto, Boris. *Getúlio Vargas*. São Paulo: Companhia das Letras, 2006.

Freyre, Gilberto. *Ordem e Progresso*. Rio de Janeiro: Record, 2000.

———. *Sobrados e Mucambos*. Rio de Janeiro: Record, 2000.

———. *Casa-Grande e Senzala*. Rio de Janeiro: Record, 1998.

Furtado, Celso. *Formação Econômica do Brasil*. São Paulo: Companhia das Letras, 2007.

————. *A Hegemonia dos Estados Unidos e o Subdesenvolvimento da America Latina*. Rio de Janeiro: Civilização Brasileira, 1978.

Gaspari, Elio. *A Ditadura Encurralada*. São Paulo: Companhia das Letras, 2004.

————. *A Ditadura Derrotada*. São Paulo: Companhia das Letras, 2003.

————. *A Ditadura Envergonhada*. São Paulo: Companhia das Letras, 2002.

————. *A Ditadura Escancarada*. São Paulo: Companhia das Letras, 2002.

Gawora, Dieter. *Urucu: Impactos Sociais, Ecológicos e Econômicos*. Manaus: Valer, 2003.

Goldenberg, Mirian. *Nu & Vestido: Dez Antropólogos Revelam a Cultura do Corpo Carioca*. Rio de Janeiro: Record, 2002.

Guimarães, Samuel Pinheiro. *Desafios Brasileiros na Era dos Gigantes*. Rio de Janeiro: Contraponto, 2006.

Hirst, Monica and Andrew Hurrell. *Brasil-Estados Unidos: Desencontros e Realidades*. Rio de Janeiro: Fundação Getúlio Vargas, 2009.

Ituassu, Arthur and Rodrigo de Almeida. *O Brasil Tem Jeito?* Rio de Janeiro: Jorge Zahar, 2006.

Kamel, Ali. *Não Somos Racistas*. Rio de Janeiro: Nova Fronteira, 2006.

Lafer, Celso. *A Identidade Internacional do Brasil e a Política Externa Brasileira (Passado, Presente e Futuro)*. São Paulo: Perspectiva, 2004.

Lessa, Ricardo. *Brasil e Estados Unidos: O Que Fez a Diferença*. Rio de Janeiro: Civilização Brasileira, 2008.

Margolis, Maxine L. and William E Carter. *Brazil: Anthropological Perspectives*. New York: Columbia University Press, 1979.

Marx, Anthony. *Making Race and Nation: A Comparison of the United States, Brazil and South Africa*. New York: Cambridge University Press, 1998.

Mendes, Candido. *Lula: A Opção Mais Que o Voto*. Rio de Janeiro: Garamond, 2002.

————. *A Presidência Afortunada*. Rio de Janeiro: Record, 1998.

Nascimento, Abdias do. *O Genocídio do Negro Brasileiro: Processo de um Racismo Mascarado*. Rio de Janeiro: Paz e Terra, 1978.

Novais, Fernando. *História da Vida Privada no Brasil: Contrastes da Intimidade Contemporânea*. São Paulo: Companhia das Letras, 1997.

Paraná, Denise. *Lula: o Filho do Brasil*. São Paulo: Fundação Perseu Abramo, 2003.

Parker, Richard G. *Bodies, Pleasures and Passions: Sexual Culture in Contemporary Brazil*. Boston: Beacon Press, 1991.

Pinto, Lucio Flavio. *Hidrelétricas na Amazônia*. Belém: EJP, 2002.

Prado, Caio. *The Colonial Background of Modern Brazil*. Berkeley: University of California Press, 1971.

Prado, Eduardo. *A Ilusão Americana*. São Paulo: Ibrasa, 1980.

Rega, Lourenço Stelio. *Dando um Jeito no Jeitinho*. São Paulo: EMC, 2000.

Ribeiro, Darcy. *O Povo Brasileiro*. São Paulo: Companhia das Letras, 2006.

Rohter, Larry. *Deu no New York Times*. Rio de Janeiro: Objetiva, 2008.

Santos, Roberto. *História Econômica da Amazônia*. São Paulo: T. A. Queiroz, 1980.

Skidmore, Thomas E. *Politics in Brazil 1930–1964*. London: Oxford University Press, 1967.

Souza, Tarik. *Tem Mais Samba: Das Raízes à Eletrônica*. São Paulo: Editora 34, 2003.

Spektor, Matias. *Kissinger e o Brasil*. Rio de Janeiro: Jorge Zahar, 2009.

Staden, Hans. *Duas Viagens ao Brasil*. Porto Alegre: L & PM, 2008.

Varnhagen, Francisco Adolfo de. *História Geral do Brasil*. 3 vols. São Paulo: Melhoramentos, 1978.

Veloso, Caetano. *Verdade Tropical*. São Paulo: Companhia das Letras, 1997.

Wagley, Charles. *An Introduction to Brazil*. New York: Columbia University Press, 1971.

INDEX